T0203439

Practical Charts

The essential guide to creating clear, compelling charts for reports and presentations

Nicholas P. Desbarats

Practical Reporting, Inc.

Published by
Practical Reporting Inc.

P.O. Box 77021, RPO Old Ottawa South
Ottawa, ON K1S 5N2
Canada
www.practicalreporting.com
Email: info@practicalreporting.com

© 2023 by Nicholas P. Desbarats

All rights reserved. Protected under the Berne Convention.

COPY EDITORS: Nan Wishner (who disagrees with my use of "data" as a singular noun 🙂) and Bryan Pierce
COMPOSITION: Wayne Kehoe and Bryan Pierce
COVER DESIGN: Jason Anscombe and Nick Desbarats
PRINTER AND BINDER: C&C Offset Printing Company

Reproduction or translation of any part of this work in any form or by any means, electronic or mechanical, beyond that permitted by Section 107 or 108 of the 1976 United States Copyright Act without the expressed permission of the copyright owner is unlawful. Requests for permission or further information should be addressed to Practical Reporting Inc. at the email address above.

Limit of Liability/Disclaimer of Warranty: While the publisher and author have used their best efforts in preparing this book, they make no representations or warranties with respect to the accuracy or completeness of the contents of this book and specifically disclaim any implied warranties of merchantability or fitness for a particular purpose. No warranty may be created or extended by sales representatives or written sales materials. The advice and strategies contained herein may not be suitable for your situation. You should consult with a professional where appropriate. Neither the publisher nor author shall be liable for any loss of profit or any other commercial damages, including but not limited to special, incidental, consequential, or other damages.

ISBN: 978-1-7388883-0-6

This book was printed on acid-free paper in China.

10 9 8 7 6 5 4 3 2 1

For my kids, Alexandre and Jennifer, and for my wonderful wife, Lizanne, who gave me the support I needed to complete this challenging undertaking, as well as a lot of great ideas that ended up in it.

Acknowledgments

In "acknowledgment" sections of informational books like this one, the author typically acknowledges that the book was only possible because of the work of others that preceded them, that they're standing on the shoulders of giants, blah, blah, blah. This one is no different ☺

If this book contains anything innovative in the field of data visualization education, it's a tiny addition to a huge body of knowledge that has been compiled by smart people over decades and centuries. I can only hope to add some miniscule scraps to the amazing heap that others have built, and will, I hope, continue to build long after I've left the field.

In addition to the thousands of past researchers and practitioners on whose work I rely, there are contemporary luminaries to whom I'm also particularly indebted:

My friend and colleague, Stephen Few, who took a chance on me in 2013 and trained me to teach his foundational courses. I struggle to find words to describe just how invaluable and life-changing that training was, and I'll never be able to repay him for the data visualization, teaching, and general reasoning skills that he so generously shared with me, and for his huge contributions to the field of data visualization that permeate this book. Saying that this book wouldn't have been possible without Steve would be a criminal understatement. Without him, I wouldn't even be in this field.

My friend and colleague, Bryan Pierce, who provided uncountable, crucial suggestions and corrections that made this book infinitely better than it would otherwise have been. His world-class knowledge of data visualization and effective communication are reflected throughout this book and are what allowed me to write it in the first place.

The manuscript reviewers who so generously pulled my foot out of my mouth at many points in the manuscript. Thanks again, Xan Gregg, Nicolas Kruchten, Lisa Muth, Andy Cotgreave, and Steve Wexler.

The data visualization community on social media. Despite all its (many) flaws, social media was absolutely instrumental in the writing of this book. There were plenty of times when I hesitated between recommending one guideline over another, and, each time, I just puked my question onto Twitter or LinkedIn and some of the smartest chart makers on the planet weighed in to help me answer it!!! These pros include Xan Gregg, Ben Jones, Steve Wexler, Andy Cotgreave, Jeff Schaffer, Alberto Cairo, Nicolas Kruchten, Lisa Muth, Enrico Bertini, Dan Zvinca, Stacey Barr, Louise Watson, Chris Weiss, Brent Dykes, Amanda Makulec, Jorge Camoes, Elijah Meeks, Steve Haroz, Cédric Scherer, Frank Elavsky, along with many glaring omissions that I'll realize that I forgot to include five minutes after sending this book to be printed.

Participants in my training workshops. If you find good ideas in this book, know that a lot of them were suggested by smart people who attended my in-person and online training workshops. Guys, at the beginning of each workshop, I warned you that I'd steal any good ideas that you proposed and, well, ta-daa!!! Equally valuable were the workshop participants who were just beginning their dataviz journeys and who had the courage to ask questions and make comments that were instrumental in helping me understand where the gaps in peoples' knowledge tend to be, and what people tend to know already when it comes to making charts.

In many ways, I feel more like the editor of this book than its author. While some of the ideas are my own, many more are from others that I've ~~stolen~~ collected and organized into what, I hope, is an easy-to-consume structure and format.

About the author

As an independent educator and consultant, Nick Desbarats has taught data visualization and information dashboard design to thousands of professionals in over a dozen countries at organizations such as NASA, Bloomberg, Visa, The United Nations, Yale University, Marathon Oil, Shopify, The Internal Revenue Service, The Central Bank of Tanzania, and many others.

He regularly delivers keynote or main-stage talks at major data conferences such as Tableau Conference, TDWI World Conference, SAS Explorers, Data Innovation Summit, and others, and his articles in The Journal of the Data Visualization Society (Nightingale) are among the publication's most widely read.

Nick was the first and only educator to be authorized by Stephen Few to deliver his foundational data visualization and dashboard design courses, which he taught from 2014 until launching his own courses in 2019. Prior to that, Nick held senior executive positions at several software companies and was a cofounder of BitFlash Inc., which raised over $20M in venture financing and was sold to OpenText Corporation. In 2012, Nick was granted a United States patent in the decision-support field.

Contact or follow Nick at:

practicalreporting.com/contact

linkedin.com/in/nickdesbarats/

twitter.com/nickdesb

Table of Contents

Part 2: Choosing a chart type *(cont.)*

Part 2: Choosing a chart type *(cont.)*

Why buy this book? What will you learn?

YOU MAY HAVE heard advice like this before on how to create good charts:

- "Keep it simple."
- "Know your audience."
- "Tell a story."
- "Make it engaging."

This is all good advice, but the unfortunate reality is that, even after hearing it and trying to follow it, many chart creators still routinely make charts that...

- Confuse the audience
- Bore the audience
- Fail to have the impact they were supposed to have (to make the audience aware of something, to help them understand something, to persuade them to do something, etc.)
- Seem like too much work to interpret, so the audience just skips reading them altogether

Because of these and other problems, audiences often complain about the charts that they receive:

- "This chart isn't useful. It's not telling me what I need to know."
- "Why are you showing me this data? What's the point of this chart? What am I supposed to get from this?"
- "I'm not sure what I'm looking at. What does this data represent?"
- "This chart is too complicated/unfamiliar. I don't understand how to read it."
- "This chart isn't well-designed. Make it better."

Worse yet, a surprisingly large number of charts mislead audiences by misrepresenting the underlying data even when the chart creator wasn't *trying* to deceive anyone. In many of these cases, neither the chart creator nor the audience even *realize* that they're not seeing the data accurately, and then can't figure out why the decisions made based on those charts don't work out well.

Why are audiences so often dissatisfied with the charts that they receive, or so often left bored, confused, unconvinced, or misled? Why does this happen even when the chart creator *wants* to provide clear, compelling charts; even when the chart creator has years of experience working with data or is a professional graphic designer; or even when the chart is from a major news media outlet, research organization, government agency, high-tech company, or other organization that, one might reasonably assume, should know how to design good charts?

When I see charts flop with audiences, the reasons are usually disappointingly mundane: poor chart type choices, poor color choices, poorly designed scales, no visual highlighting, insufficient or ambiguous labeling, and the like. These charts are like potentially great pieces of writing that are ruined by basic spelling and vocabulary mistakes.

Data visualization (a.k.a. "dataviz") has its own "spelling and vocabulary," i.e., a set of skills and guidelines that must be learned in order to design charts that communicate clearly and effectively.

These skills and guidelines involve things such as knowing how to choose chart types, color palettes, and scale ranges, along with knowing how to make many other chart design decisions.

If a chart creator hasn't learned the basic "spelling and vocabulary of dataviz," their charts will routinely flop with an audience even if…

- They're really **trying** to make helpful, good charts.
- They **know their audience** inside and out.
- They're a spellbinding **storyteller**.
- They have **super-valuable insights** to share.

Charts with bad dataviz spelling and vocabulary are like documents with bad spelling and word choices. It doesn't matter how great the ideas in the document are or how hard the writer tried to communicate clearly and compellingly; poor spelling and inappropriate word choices will still leave the reader confused, exasperated, bored, or misled. In many cases, they'll just decide to stop reading.

Dataviz spelling and vocabulary are easy to learn (with one exception, which I'll point out when we get to it later in the book), but they're not always intuitive. No one is born being good at chart design, and we're unlikely to figure out these skills and guidelines on our own unless we've read a good book or taken a good course about them. Unfortunately, many chart creators have never done either, which goes a long way to explain why so many charts don't go over well with audiences, fail to have the intended effect on them, or accidentally mislead them.

What do charts with bad dataviz spelling and vocabulary look like? I'm glad I assumed that you asked. The following five chart examples show a few common dataviz spelling and vocabulary problems in action, along with versions of the same charts with those problems solved. Just for fun, hide the "improved" charts in the right-hand column below using a sheet of paper and try to spot problems in the charts on the left. Think about how you might improve them before looking at the "improved" charts on the right:

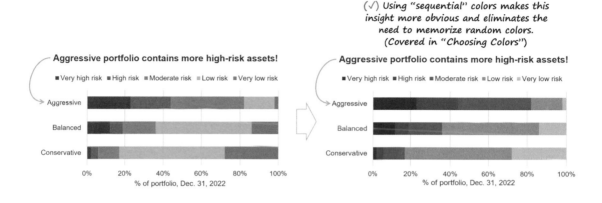

(√) Using "sequential" colors makes this insight more obvious and eliminates the need to memorize random colors. (Covered in "Choosing Colors")

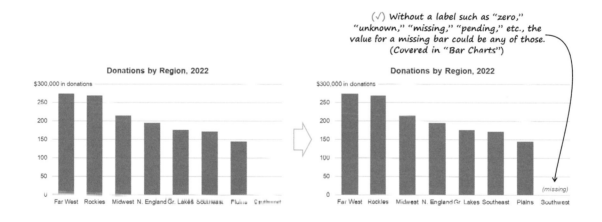

(√) Without a label such as "zero," "unknown," "missing," "pending," etc., the value for a missing bar could be any of those. (Covered in "Bar Charts")

(√) Graphs make patterns and insights (e.g., the cyclical pattern in the East region) more obvious than tables. (Covered in "Tables")

The East experienced a quarterly cycle!

	East	West
Jan	$53,201	$48,271
Feb	$57,276	$46,676
Mar	$47,452	$47,529
Apr	$55,494	$48,591
May	$59,388	$49,109
Jun	$54,184	$47,752
Jul	$60,384	$48,752
Aug	$62,555	$48,499
Sep	$50,611	$41,249
Oct	$60,686	$48,626
Nov	$64,514	$50,094
Dec	$59,523	$50,074

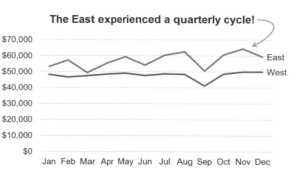

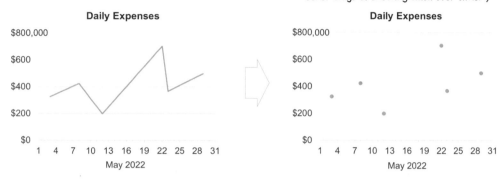

(✓) Expenses for most days are missing so we don't have enough data to know what really happened during this time. Connecting points with lines makes it look like we DO know what happened, though! ☹ A "dot plot" is safer. (Covered in "Line charts and other ways of showing data over time.")

(✓) "Inset charts" allow small values to be seen clearly and compared easily when there are large outliers. (Covered in "Quantitative Scales")

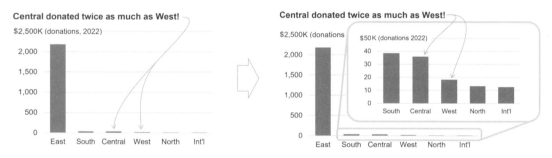

This book will teach you essential dataviz spelling and vocabulary guidelines that will allow you to reliably create charts that make insights obvious, and that are easy to read, compelling, and accurate. This book won't make you a world-class dataviz expert, but it will make you far better at creating everyday charts than the vast majority of the workforce and it might make you the most competent chart creator in your organization. What matters most, of course, is that the audiences for your charts will be far more satisfied and productive.

> **Key takeaways: What you'll learn from this book**
> *There will be many of these "key takeaway" blocks throughout the book.*
>
> - Dataviz has a "spelling and vocabulary," a set of guidelines that need to be learned in order to create clear, compelling, and accurate charts.
> - Charts often flop with audiences because they have basic dataviz spelling and vocabulary problems, leaving audiences bored, confused, unconvinced, or misled.

> • This book will teach you essential dataviz spelling and vocabulary guidelines.

WHO THIS BOOK IS WRITTEN FOR

This book is written for those who create simple, "everyday" charts for presentations and reports. For readers who want to go beyond everyday charts and create beautiful "data art," infographics, live data dashboards, or non-standard or scientific visualizations, please visit practicalreporting. com/pc-resources and click "Recommended books and courses" for a list of resources that cover those more specialized chart types. If you intend to create those specialized chart types, I'd still honestly recommend reading this book first because most of the basic concepts and guidelines that are covered here apply to more specialized types of charts, as well. You can't write beautiful poetry or world-changing research papers if your spelling and vocabulary suck…

> Do I seriously need to read an entire book to learn how to design simple, everyday charts? How much skill does that really require?
>
> *Speech bubbles like this appear throughout the book and are questions or objections that a ~~grumpy~~ constructively critical reader might have.*

As it turns out, creating charts that *look* simple and obvious actually requires a high degree of skill, just as writing documents that are clear and simple to read requires a surprisingly high degree of skill. If creating "simple" everyday charts were easy, you wouldn't constantly see poor chart type choices, poor color palette choices, poor scale formatting choices, poor labeling choices, and many other design problems in charts in reports, presentations, news articles, research studies, etc. Unfortunately, though, after reading this book, you'll see those problems all over the place.

Sorry about that.

Who, exactly, should read this book? I wrote it for the kinds of people who take my *Practical Charts* course, on which this book is based. Participants in my workshops include healthcare professionals, educators, marketers, human resource professionals, investment fund managers, researchers, sales managers, journalists, and accountants, as well as more obviously data-centric roles like business intelligence professionals, data analysts, data scientists, statisticians, and software developers. If you create charts for communicating data to other people, then this book is written for you.

In terms of expertise, participants in my workshops range from novices with relatively little chart-making experience to seasoned pros with decades of data-wrangling experience. People of all experience levels regularly reach out after workshops to tell me that they found the course to be valuable and directly relevant to their work—even the pros with decades of data experience because they've often had little training on how to communicate data effectively to others (more on that later). In terms of industry sectors, workshop participants come from a wide range, from banking, the public sector, manufacturing, media, non-profit, and high finance to insurance, high tech, education, military, healthcare, and more.

No prior dataviz training is needed before reading this book although it's helpful to have at least *some* experience creating simple charts in a software product like Microsoft Excel, Tableau Desktop, Google Sheets, Qlik Sense, JMP, or a similar tool. A basic working knowledge of one or more of those tools is fine; it's not necessary to be an expert user. None of the chart types or techniques in this book require advanced software expertise or specialized software features.

A few of the chart types in this book might be new to some readers, but, once you've learned about them, you'll likely find yourself needing to use them regularly. If you're unsure about how to create anything you see in this book using your software of choice, just Google "how to create [name of chart type or technique] in [name of software product that you're using]" to find tutorial videos or articles. For example, searching for "How to create a stacked bar chart in Excel" will return dozens of decent, free tutorial videos and articles.

> What makes you think that you can teach me these skills?

Well, I've been embarrassingly fortunate to have had the opportunity to teach dataviz to thousands of in-the-trenches professionals just like you, from hundreds of organizations in many different countries. Prior to that, I was a senior executive at several software companies and was on the receiving end of a lot of bad charts. Those experiences taught me many things; the four that are most relevant to this book are:

- What decision-makers really want from charts
- Which specific chart design challenges tend to arise in real-world organizations and which ones don't
- What the most common chart design mistakes are
- Where the gaps in chart creators' knowledge tend to be, and what they tend to know already

Those experiences enable me to:

- Teach you how to create charts that are helpful to—and appreciated by—decision makers
- Teach you how to handle more than 90% of the chart design challenges that come up in the many organizations with which I work
- Teach you how to avoid more than 90% of common chart design mistakes that I see "in the wild"
- Teach you these skills *quickly* by only covering guidelines that are likely to be new to you and skipping ones that you probably knew already

WHAT THIS BOOK *WON'T* TEACH YOU

How to create specialized charts

As I mentioned, this book only covers simple, everyday charts for reports and presentations. There's no discussion of specialized charts for fields like mineral exploration, advanced financial analysis, genomics, etc. However, most of what this book teaches will apply to those more specialized charts, as well.

How to create artistic charts, data art, infographics, etc.

Everyday charts for reports and presentations generally don't need to be artistic (although they shouldn't be *ugly*; more on that later).

Information dashboard design

Information dashboards entail a whole other set of challenges that don't arise when creating individual charts. Please visit practicalreporting.com/pc-resources and click "Recommended books and courses" for recommended books on information dashboard design.

How to use specific dataviz software products

As I mentioned, this book assumes that you have a basic (not expert) working knowledge of at least one dataviz software product and access to an Internet search engine to look up anything that you're not sure how to do in the software product that you use.

Using charts for data analysis rather than communicating data to an audience

While charts are obviously an effective way of communicating data-related insights to others, they're also a powerful way to explore and analyze data on our own. Using charts to explore and analyze data on our own is fundamentally different from using charts to communicate insights to an audience, however. For example:

- When using charts to communicate insights to an audience, we should try to make key insights and takeaways obvious by adding them to charts in callouts and chart titles and using other techniques found in this book. When using charts to analyze data on our own, however, we obviously don't need to worry about that since we're the only ones who will see those charts.

- When creating charts to communicate insights to an audience, we should try to stick to chart types that we know the audience is familiar with. For most audiences, this means sticking with simple, common chart types such as bar charts and line charts. When analyzing data on our own, however, we can use any chart type we like, including less common, more "advanced" chart types such as scatter plots, histograms, and cycle plots because the audience will never see those charts; they'll only see the insights that we discover using those chart types and then report back to the audience using simpler charts or prose (e.g., as bullet points on a slide).

The chart types and design guidelines that we'll use when creating charts for our own analysis can, therefore, be quite different than those that we'll use when creating charts to show to other people. This is a crucial distinction that, perhaps surprisingly, many chart creators don't seem to appreciate. I often hear people talk about "dataviz best practices" without specifying whether they're talking about charts for analyzing data for ourselves or charts for communicating data to an audience. **This book only covers creating charts for communicating data to others.**

Therefore, **this book only covers chart types that most audiences are familiar with,** such as bar charts, stacked bar charts, clustered bar charts, line charts, pie charts, etc., along with a few chart types that are required to communicate data accurately in specific but common situations, such as step charts, dot plots and merged bar charts. If your audience is relatively sophisticated and can grasp "advanced" chart types such as scatter plots, histograms and cycle plots, my book, *More Practical Charts: Additional chart types for data-savvy audiences* covers those chart types and is scheduled to be published in 2024.

This book also doesn't cover how to decide which insights we should communicate to an audience, which questions we should answer for them, etc. Those skills go far beyond dataviz and fall under general business skills, performance management, strategic planning, and other areas. This book "begins" when we have some data and something to say about that data, and covers how to do that effectively.

> **Key takeaways: Who this book is written for**
>
> - This book is written for those who create "everyday charts" for communicating data to others in reports and presentations.
> - This book doesn't cover data art, infographics, information dashboards, scientific charts, charts for data analysis, and other specialized types of charts (although it does provide a foundation for learning how to design those more specialized chart types effectively).

WHAT MAKES THIS BOOK DIFFERENT

Many excellent books have been written on dataviz during the past century or so, so why did I think that the world needed another one? What makes this book different from others? A few things:

Specific guidance

For many chart design choices, the guidance in other books often boils down to "use your judgment" or "it depends on the situation." Although judgment is inevitably required for *some* chart design decisions, "use your judgment" or "it depends on the situation" isn't helpful advice, especially for those who haven't yet accumulated years of chart-making experience.

In this book, I've tried to go as far beyond "it depends on the situation" as possible and define *specifically* what chart design choices depend *on*. I've tried to distill as many design choices as possible into specific guidelines that can quickly guide chart creators of any experience level to expert-level design choices. This guidance is summarized in one-page "cheat sheets" throughout the book such as the example below, which provides specific guidance on how to format tables, a topic we'll cover in more detail later in the book:

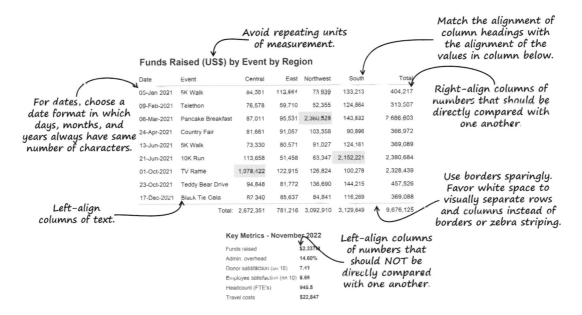

…or the "decision tree" cheat sheet below, which we'll encounter later in the book when we discuss when it makes sense to use a pie chart or another chart type to show the breakdown of a total:

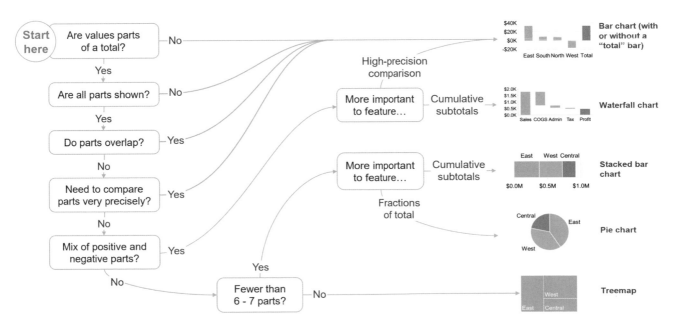

Specific guidelines like these allow us to become competent chart creators quickly, and they instantly reduce the risk of making basic chart design mistakes.

> I've seen "chart chooser" diagrams like the pie chart one before.

Yes, there are many "chart chooser" diagrams and tools floating around online, but all the ones that I've seen are, in my opinion, not specific enough to make reliable chart type recommendations in a wide variety of situations. For example, when recommending whether to use a pie chart or an alternative chart type, other tools that I've seen take two or three factors into account (e.g., whether the values shown in the chart are parts of a total, how many parts there are, etc.). If a chart-chooser tool takes just two or three factors into account, I don't think it can be specific enough to make good chart type recommendations. In the pie chart decision tree above, for example, there are eight decision factors.

Also, most chart-chooser tools don't recommend a *specific* chart type for the situation at hand. Instead, they recommend a *group* of chart types and then advise the chart creator to "use their judgment" to choose from within that group. As I mentioned, though, "use your judgment" isn't helpful advice, especially for less-experienced chart creators.

Now, not *all* chart design choices can be distilled into specific guidelines like the ones above, so I *will* sometimes resort to "use your judgment" or "it depends on the situation." I've bent over backwards to avoid doing so whenever possible, however, and have tried to distill all the design choices that *can* be distilled into specific guidelines.

Some experienced chart creators object to guidelines that are as specific as mine, arguing that there will always be exceptions to those guidelines or that they constrain creativity. I actually *agree* with those objections! I consider the guidelines in this book to be a *starting point* for learners, but a starting point that's a lot more useful than "use your judgment" or "it depends on the situation." Consider the guidelines in this book to be "training wheels" like the ones that help kids learn how to ride a bike: They get learners up and running quickly and prevent them from "falling over," i.e., making basic chart design mistakes. Once you fully understand the guidelines in this book, you may decide to take the training wheels off and start deviating from these guidelines in certain situations, which is fine! The first step in knowing when to "break the rules," though, is knowing what "the rules" are in the first place (though I prefer the softer term "guidelines" that I use throughout the book).

It's also important to be aware that the dataviz field has its fair share of best practice debates, and the guidelines that I offer in this book reflect my own interpretations of dataviz research and my own professional experiences (just like every other dataviz educator). Most of the guidelines in this book are relatively uncontroversial in the dataviz community, but some are the subject of ongoing debates. When we hit a guideline in this book about which many experienced chart creators disagree, I'll let you know. You can then decide for yourself if you want to go with what I recommend or make crappy charts. JK! 🙂

Just what you need to know and nothing you don't

In teaching thousands of workshop participants, I've learned which guidelines most people tend to know already. This has allowed me to cut information from the book that you probably knew already, and my hope is that most of the guidelines in it will be new to you. My work with many different organizations has also allowed me to see what kinds of challenges *don't* tend to arise in practice and to omit those topics from the book.

This book also doesn't discuss how human vision works, the history of dataviz, dataviz research studies, or any other topic that isn't absolutely necessary to know about in order to design good everyday charts. I encourage exploration of those topics and provide pointers to resources for those who are interested, but I don't think that it's essential to know about them in order to design good everyday charts, so I didn't include them in this book.

> If you were able to cut so much from this book, why isn't it shorter than other dataviz books?

Completeness

There are definitely shorter dataviz books out there, but they don't address many questions and challenges that come up all the time in practice, such as how to visualize outliers, or when to include or not include zero in a chart's scale. This means that, for many common design choices and challenges, you're on your own.

This books aims to equip readers with enough knowledge to handle more than 90% of the chart design challenges that I see in practice and to avoid more than 90% of the design mistakes that I see chart creators make, by covering:

- 30 chart types, all of which are needed regularly when making everyday charts, plus about a dozen common chart types that I suggest avoiding when making everyday charts

- Dozens of common challenges with solutions, such as how to show missing values, or how to show values that occur at irregular intervals of time.

- Dozens of common design mistakes, such as failing to label zero-length bars in bar charts, or using a non-sequential color palette for sequential categories.

Even though this book covers more topics than other dataviz books that I've read, I expect that you'll be able to read it fairly quickly because, well, there are lots of pictures (once you get past this introductory part, anyway). There's another reason why I think you'll be able to read this book quickly, which has to do with…

Friendliness

With some notable exceptions, dataviz books tend to be written in a formal or academic style. In writing this book, I've aimed for a basic reading level and avoided jargony terms like "encoding," "graphical objects," and "preattentive attributes of visual perception" for several reasons:

- It makes the dataviz field more approachable for beginners.
- It makes this book more accessible to those for whom English is a second language.
- Simpler language makes concepts easier to absorb for readers of any reading level by allowing them to focus on understanding concepts, not vocabulary.
- I don't think chart creators need to know jargon in to order to design good everyday charts.

I also tend to keep things informal. You'll see lots of "IMHOs" and "TBHs," and maybe even a few spicy "WTHs," as well as things that I inexplicably consider to be jokes. Or not. Sheesh. Tough room.

> **Key takeaway: What makes this book different**
>
> - This book offers guidance that's as specific, complete, streamlined, and approachable as possible.

WHAT THIS BOOK WILL *REALLY* TEACH YOU

> Whatnow? It's going to teach me how to make good everyday charts, right?

Yes, but, in my interactions with thousands of chart creators and readers, I've noticed that different people often have very different definitions of what a "good chart" is. If we're going to be learning how to make "good charts," then we'd better sort that out first.

Depending on who you ask, you might hear definitions of a "good chart" such as:

- **Precise** (allows precise estimation and comparisons of values)
- **Fast to visually process** (suggesting that a chart is easy to read)
- **Slow to visually process** (suggesting that a chart is engaging)
- **Creative/beautiful** (represents data in novel, original, or artistic ways)

- **Simple/familiar** (uses simple, familiar chart types and techniques that are *not* novel, original or artistic)
- **Versatile** (allows the audience to answer a wide variety of different questions about the underlying data, or makes a wide variety of insights about the data obvious)
- **Memorable** (allows the audience to recall a lot of the information in a chart after seeing it)
- **Obvious** (explicitly states key insights and takeaways in chart titles or callouts)
- **Objective/neutral** (*doesn't* explicitly state insights or interpretations from the chart creator)
- **Inspiring/evocative** (provokes an emotional response from readers, such as sympathy, curiosity, or outrage)

Although all of these qualities can affect how good an everyday chart is, I don't think that any of them *ultimately* determines how good it is.

> So, what do **you** consider to be a "good everyday chart"?

When it comes to everyday charts for communicating data to an audience, I consider that…

> **A good chart is one that does the job that it was created to do, quickly, comfortably, and safely.**

> What's "the job" of a chart?

Well, there are *many* different jobs that people use charts to accomplish:

- To make an audience **aware** of something (a problem, an opportunity, a strange trend, etc.)
- To **persuade** an audience to take a specific action (greenlight a project, get vaccinated, etc.)
- To **answer** a question that the audience is wondering about
- To allow an audience to **filter or look up** values

Those are just a few examples; there are many others. In fact, there's an almost infinite number of different "jobs" that a chart can have. In other words, "the job" of everyday charts is different from one chart to the next. Qualities like precision, speed of interpretation, creativity, and memorability still matter, but only because they tend to improve the odds that a chart will successfully do the specific job that it was created to do, whatever that job might be.

> What does "...quickly, comfortably, and safely" mean?

- **"...quickly..."** means the chart can be read and understood in as little time as possible. Sometimes, the information that a chart needs to communicate is fundamentally complex, so "as little time as possible" could be several minutes, but a good chart requires as little time as *possible* to read.

- **"...comfortably..."** means the chart demands as little cognitive effort as possible to read. In practice, this means trying to avoid forcing the audience to learn new chart types, read vertical or diagonal text, do calculations in their head, etc. Again, sometimes, the information that a chart needs to communicate is fundamentally complex, so "as little cognitive effort as possible" could still be quite a bit, but a good chart requires as little cognitive effort as possible to understand.

- **"...safely..."** means the chart has a low risk of causing the audience to misinterpret the data. We've already seen one or two examples of how easy it is to accidentally misrepresent data in charts, and we'll see plenty more throughout the book to help us learn how to avoid the most common "accidental misrepresentation" mistakes and ensure that our charts show data "safely."

Key takeaways: What I'm going to consider to be a "good everyday chart" in this book

- A "good everyday chart" does its job (answers a specific question, explains a specific concept, persuades the audience to take a specific course of action, etc.) as quickly, comfortably, and safely as possible.
- Charts can do many different jobs, so the specific definition of a "good chart" differs from one chart to the next.

If there's a central idea in this book, it's that charts are "graphics for doing a job." This is different from the way that most people think about charts, though. Most people think of charts as "visual representations of data," but I don't think that that's a useful way to think about them: **All charts (including really bad ones) are "visual representations of data," but only *good* charts "do their job."**

> Why does a chart have to have a job? Why not make charts that "just show the data" without trying to explain/answer/persuade/etc.?

We'll talk more about this question in "Part 5: Making charts obvious," but the short answer is that I don't think it's even theoretically possible to make charts that "just show the data" without saying something *about* the data (unfortunately).

For most chart creators, moving away from thinking of charts as "visual representations of data" and toward thinking of them as "answers to questions," "explanations," "sales pitches," etc., will entail profound changes to the way that they go about making charts.

For example, when sitting down to design a new chart, chart creators typically ask, "What's the best way to visualize this data?" After reading this book, though, the first question we'll (hopefully) ask ourselves will instead be, "Do I know _why_ I'm making this chart?"

- Is there a question that I'm trying to answer for the audience? If so, what is it?
- Is there a problem that I'm trying to make the audience aware of? If so, what is that problem?
- Am I trying to persuade the audience to do something? If so, what do I want them to do?"
- Etc.

If we don't know specifically what job our chart is supposed to do—which happens surprisingly often—then we'll know that we need to step away from our software and find out. Perhaps we'll need to do some exploratory analysis or speak with our target audience. One way or another, though, we need to figure out what, specifically, our chart is supposed to _do_ in order design it effectively.

We'll also know that, once we've figured what our chart's job is, **that job will be at the center of most of our design decisions** (choosing a chart type, deciding how wide or narrow to make the scale(s), choosing colors, and so on). This is quite different from the way that most chart creators tend to make (or, at least, try to make) design decisions, which is usually based mostly on the nature of the data (Is the data a time series? Parts of a total? Does it have many/few values? etc.). Yes, the nature of the data is _a_ consideration in many design choices, but the chart's job is the _main_ consideration. That's why most of the guidelines in this book depend on the specific job of the chart.

> **Key takeaways: What everyday charts are for**
>
> - Rather than thinking of everyday charts as "visual representations of data," a more useful approach is to think of them as "graphics for doing a job."
> - The main consideration in most chart design decisions is the specific job that the chart is designed to do. The nature of the data to be visualized is also a consideration but it's not the main consideration.

OK, but what, **exactly**, will I be learning?

MAJOR TOPICS IN THIS BOOK AND HOW THEY'RE ORGANIZED

This book is organized into seven parts:

Part 1: General chart formatting guidelines

In Part 1, we'll learn formatting guidelines that apply to all chart types (the "spelling" of dataviz), as well has how to avoid common chart formatting mistakes:

- Formatting gridlines, tick marks, axis lines, borders, and other "non-data" elements
- Formatting scales (categorical, quantitative, time)
- Choosing colors
- Formatting legends/keys
- Formatting text, numbers, and dates

Part 2: Choosing a chart type

Part 2 is the longest part of this book, containing detailed information on 30 important chart types that are commonly needed when making everyday charts (the "vocabulary" of dataviz) and when to use each, organized into seven groups:

- Line charts and other ways to show data over time
- Pie charts and other ways to show the breakdown of a total
- Maps
- Bar charts
- Tables
- Combo charts
- Chart types to use cautiously or avoid

Part 3: Showing data with a more complex structure ("small multiples")

Part 3 discusses how to handle common, challenging situations when the data to be visualized has a more complex structure.

Part 4: Interactive filters and chart animations

Part 4 discusses the unobvious but significant challenges that interactive filters and animation can create for audiences and provides suggestions for how to avoid using these features.

Part 5: Making charts obvious

Part 5 covers techniques for making key messages and takeaways obvious, such as visually highlighting the most important part(s) of a chart, explicitly stating insights and recommendations in chart callouts and titles, and adding comparison/reference values.

Part 6: Making charts less boring

Part 6 summarizes techniques from other chapters that make charts interesting and engaging, and includes a list of other ways that chart creators often try to "spice up" charts but that end up making charts harder to read, less obvious, or more prone to misinterpretation.

Part 7: What now?

Part 7 provides suggestions on how to continue learning and improving, as well as my take on some emerging technologies that might (or might not) change dataviz in the future.

Although the sections of this book are organized for easy reference, I recommend reading it once from beginning to end because a number of foundational ideas are built up throughout the book.

Enough with the fluffy theoretical stuff. Let's get into the meat and potatoes, beginning with…

PART 1

General chart formatting guidelines

In this part of the book, we'll cover formatting guidelines that apply to all chart types (bar charts, line charts, maps, etc.). These guidelines are the "spelling" of dataviz. Later, in "Part 2: Choosing a chart type," we'll see some additional formatting guidelines that only apply to specific chart types.

In this part of the book, we'll cover...

- *Formatting gridlines, tick marks, borders, and other "non-data" chart elements*
- *Formatting chart scales (categorical, quantitative, time)*
- *Choosing color palettes (categorical, sequential, diverging, "special" colors)*
- *Formatting legends (a.k.a. "keys")*
- *Formatting text, numbers, and dates*

These design choices might seem purely cosmetic, however, they're anything but. Yes, poor formatting choices will reliably produce fugly charts, but, as we'll see, they also make it hard for charts to do their job or—worse—cause audiences to fundamentally misinterpret the data in a chart.

Let's start with...

Chapter 1

Gridlines, tick marks, borders, and other "non-data" elements

MOST CHARTS CONTAIN "non-data" elements like gridlines, tick marks, axis lines, and borders. In other words, the elements that would remain if we were to delete the source data from a chart:

Original chart

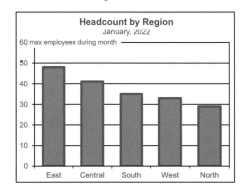

Non-data elements of chart

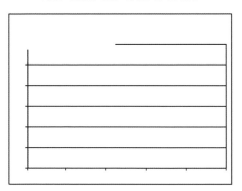

Because non-data elements are obviously less important than data elements such as bars, lines, and numbers, non-data elements shouldn't "visually compete" with data elements. However, many charts contain non-data elements that are very dark, thick, or otherwise formatted in a way that calls attention to them and distracts readers from the data elements. Many charts also contain non-data elements that serve no purpose other than adding a bit of unnecessary clutter.

When it comes to everyday charts, then, **it's generally a good idea to get rid of as many non-data elements as we can and to "tone down" whatever non-data elements remain** (make them lighter, thinner, etc.) so that they don't visually compete with the bars, lines, or other data elements in the chart.

Let's have another look at the chart above on the left to see which non-data elements we can tone down or get rid of altogether, starting with…

BORDERS

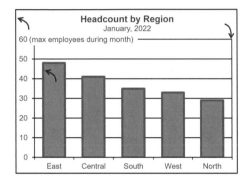

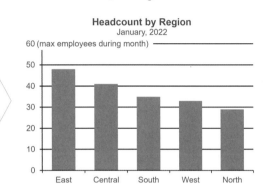

Even if this chart were to appear on a page, dashboard, or presentation slide that contained several other charts, it would still be obvious where this chart ends and others begin, so the borders weren't actually doing anything.

TICK MARKS

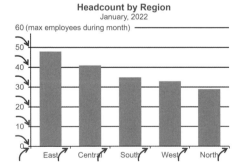

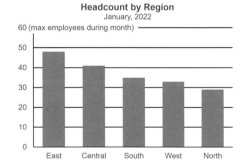

As with borders, in most cases, tick marks aren't necessary. If we're not sure whether they can be removed, we can try removing them and see whether the chart is harder to read without them. In most cases, it won't be.

Axis lines

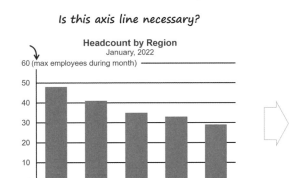

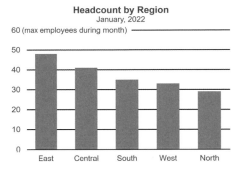

It's not a big deal to keep axis lines in quantitative scales (e.g., scales of employee headcounts), but I generally remove them because, as we can see in the example above, they're usually not necessary. Why not also remove the horizontal axis line (i.e., the line for the "Regions" scale)? I left it in because that line is also acting as a gridline (specifically, the gridline for "0"), speaking of which…

Gridlines

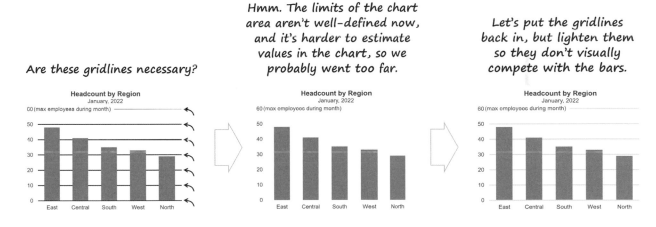

I almost always keep gridlines in everyday charts for three reasons:

1. They make it clear what the chart area is (the area that can contain bars, lines, dots, etc.).

2. They make it easier to estimate and compare values.

3. They make the "quantitative direction" of the chart instantly obvious: Horizontal gridlines mean that shapes that are higher up in the chart represent larger quantities, while vertical gridlines mean that shapes that are further to the right represent larger quantities (e.g., in a horizontal bar chart).

Although the chart that we started with was certainly *usable*, removing or toning down its non-data elements makes it easier to read, cleaner, and more professional-looking:

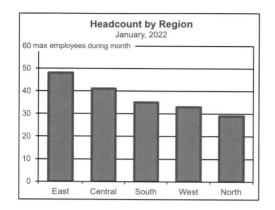
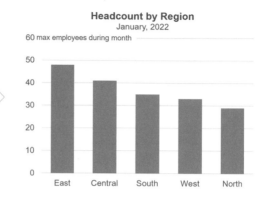

BTW, these same guidelines also apply to tables:

(!) Heavy non-data elements

(✓) Lightened/deleted non-data elements

Units Produced by Region | Jan-Apr 2022

Region	Jan	Feb	Mar	Apr
East	41,427	35,936	36,949	39,016
Central	37,284	39,005	37,185	40,915
North	22,371	17,983	17,505	15,076
West	20,134	25,130	25,598	30,776
Total:	121,215	118,055	117,237	125,783

Units Produced by Region | Jan-Apr 2022

	Jan	Feb	Mar	Apr
East	41,427	35,936	36,949	39,016
Central	37,284	39,005	37,185	40,915
North	22,371	17,983	17,505	15,076
West	20,134	25,130	25,598	30,776
	121,215	118,055	117,237	125,783

We'll talk more about formatting tables later, in the "Tables" chapter.

Key takeaways: Gridlines, borders, tick marks, axis lines, and other non-data elements

- In everyday charts, remove "non-data" elements except when doing so makes the chart harder to read or ambiguous.
- Tone down (lighten, thin, etc.) whatever non-data elements remain.

Pretty straightforward, I hope. The next topic is considerably more involved, however, and that is…

Chapter 2

Scales

THERE ARE THREE major types of scales that we'll need for everyday charts:

East	Central	Northwest	Southwest	North	*Categorical scales*
		Region			

0	100	200	300	400	500	600	*Quantitative (linear) scales*
			Transactions per day				

27	28	29	31	1	2	3	4	5	6	*Time scales*
	October					November				

> Why do we need to talk about formatting scales? Don't dataviz software products generate chart scales automatically?

Yes, but, as we'll see, the scales that software products generate can be deeply problematic and often need to be fixed before a chart is published. In fact, problems with scales are among the most common reasons why charts end up confusing or misleading audiences, and I see a wide variety of scale formatting problems all the time in charts in the wild. Most chart creators don't put much thought into scale formatting, but they definitely should because there are many ways to mess them up.

How should we format each of the three major types of scales? Let's start with…

CATEGORICAL SCALES

Most charts contain one (or, occasionally, more than one) *categorical* scale:

Categorical scales tell the audience what the values in a chart represent (what region, what department, etc.) and come in two flavors:

1. ***Sequential* categorical scales** (also called "ordinal" categorical scales) have a built-in sequence; i.e., they should almost always be listed in a certain order, for example:

   • Schooling level (Primary, Secondary, Undergraduate, Post-Graduate)

   • Satisfaction level (Very Dissatisfied, Somewhat Dissatisfied, Neutral, Somewhat Satisfied, Very Satisfied)

   • Army rank (Private, Corporal, Sergeant, Lieutenant, Captain, Major, Colonel, General)

2. ***Non-sequential* categorical scales** (also called "nominal" categorical scales) *don't* have a built-in sequence; i.e., they can be listed in any order, for example:

   • Department (Marketing, Sales, Operations, Finance, Research & Development)

   • Region (East, Central, North, South)

   • Type of animal (Mammal, Fish, Bird, Reptile, Amphibian)

Formatting categorical scales is pretty straightforward although I see poorly formatted ones fairly often. There are really only three guidelines that might not be obvious to most chart creators:

1. If the categories are non-sequential, consider sorting them by value:

(✓) Sorting <u>non-sequential</u> categories by value usually makes charts easier to read.

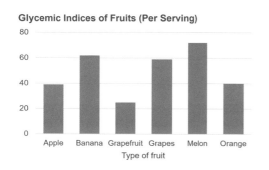

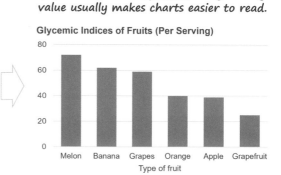

When non-sequential categories are sorted by value, the "shape" of the data is clearer, the audience can quickly spot the highest and lowest values, and similar values end up close to one another, making them easier to compare. **Sorting non-sequential categories is a simple improvement that chart creators often forget.** It usually makes sense to sort from largest value to smallest; however, in some cases, smaller values are of greater interest than larger ones. In those cases, it makes sense to sort from smallest value to largest.

If the categories *are* sequential (e.g., education levels), however, it's usually best to show them in their "built-in" order (i.e., *not* sorted by value).

> **Key takeaways: Sorting categories in a categorical scale**
>
> - If the categories in a categorical scale are non-sequential, consider sorting them by value.
> - If the categories in a categorical scale are sequential, consider sorting them by their "built-in" sort order (not by value).

2. If the nature of the categories is obvious, consider removing the axis label:

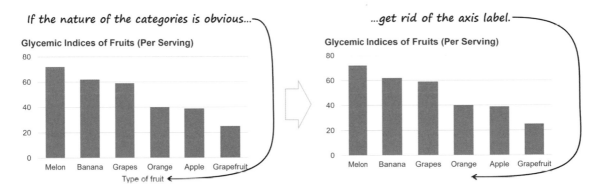

If the nature of the categories *isn't* obvious, though, add an axis label to clarify. For example, if the categories are "Low," "Medium," and "High," we'd need to label the axis with something like "Threat Level."

> **Key takeaway: Axis labels for categorical scales**
>
> - If the nature of the categories in a categorical scale is obvious, consider removing the axis label.

3. If the categories have long names, consider rotating the chart 90°:

(Yes, these are real place names. I made up the weirdness scores, though 😊)

Rotating the chart 90° might seem like an obvious way to avoid having vertical or diagonal category names in a chart, but I have to include this guideline in the book because I see charts all the time with diagonal or vertical text that could be easily avoided by simply rotating the chart.

> **Key takeaway: Handling long category names**
>
> • If the categories in a categorical scale have long names, consider rotating the chart 90°.

As we can see, categorical scales are pretty simple to format effectively. The next type of scale that we'll see is considerably more involved, though, so let's dig into…

QUANTITATIVE SCALES

In addition to categorical scales, most charts also have a *quantitative* scale (or, occasionally, more than one quantitative scale):

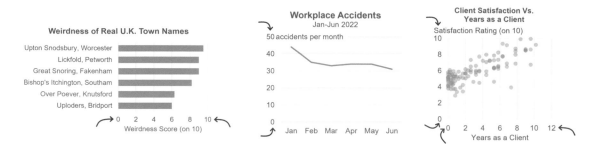

The most common type of quantitative scale is called a "linear" quantitative scale, such as those in the three chart examples above. A linear quantitative scale is simply one where the "jump" (a.k.a. the "interval") between each label on the scale is the same (all intervals of 10, all intervals of 500, etc.). There are other types of quantitative scales, such as logarithmic scales, but we're not going to spend much time on those because they're generally not needed when making everyday charts (they're mostly needed in charts for doing advanced mathematical, scientific, or financial analysis).

Simple, right? How many ways could there be to screw up a quantitative scale? Well, as it turns out, a lot. This chapter on quantitative scales is surprisingly long for several reasons:

1. Problems with quantitative scales are among the most common reasons why charts confuse or mislead audiences, perhaps second only to making a poor chart type choice.

2. Manipulating quantitative scales is probably the single most common way that dishonest chart creators deliberately try to mislead audiences.

3. There are at least a dozen common mistakes that chart creators make all the time when formatting quantitative scales.

In this chapter, we're also going to tackle several of the most common questions that come up in my training workshops, such as how to handle outliers and whether dual-axis charts are a good idea, because these questions all relate to quantitative scales.

Because there's a lot to talk about when it comes quantitative scales, I've cut this section into bite-sized sub-sections to help it go down easier:

1. Quantitative scale formatting basics

2. Six common mistakes with quantitative scales (with solutions, obvy)

3. Four common questions that people often ask about quantitative scales, such as if or when it's necessary to extend a quantitative scale to include zero

We'll summarize all of the key takeaways from all three sections in a one-page cheat sheet at the end. For now, though, let's begin with some…

Quantitative scale formatting basics

Have a look at the quantitative scale in the following chart. I can spot three ways in which it could be improved; some are obvious, others less so. Take a minute or two and try to spot all three before moving on to the list of improvements that follows:

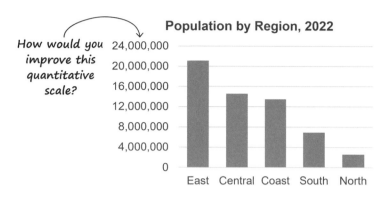

1. Hide the zeros and label the "order of magnitude."

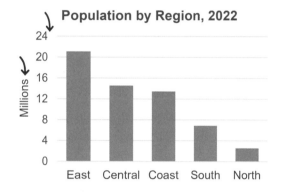

When a quantitative scale contains very large numbers, hiding the zeros cuts down on visual clutter, and labeling the order of magnitude (thousands, millions, billions, etc.) makes it easier for the audience to quickly know what they're looking at without having to count zeros.

The conventions for labeling different orders of magnitude vary by audience and region (e.g., "000s" versus "K" versus "M"), so we should use whatever is most familiar to our audience. To avoid any risk of confusion, I'll often write names of orders of magnitude out in full, rather than using abbreviations, e.g., "millions" rather than "M," which could mean either thousands ("mille") or millions to different audiences.

The same guidelines apply when showing very small numbers, e.g., millionths, billionths, etc.

> **Key takeaway: Scales with very large or very small value labels**
>
> • When a quantitative scale contains very large or very small values, consider hiding the zeros and labeling the order of magnitude.

2. Relocate the quantitative scale label (a.k.a. the unit of measurement), and make it more specific.

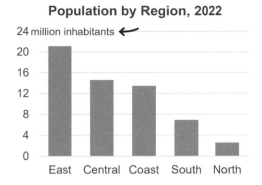

I usually locate the unit of measurement label as shown in the chart above for three reasons:

1. Horizontal text is easier to read than vertical text.

2. There's lots of room for highly descriptive units of measurement, which, as we'll see in a moment, is really important.

3. The unit of measurement is visually associated with the part of the chart to which it relates (the quantitative scale), which is a little more intuitive than putting the unit of measurement in the chart title, e.g., "Population (Millions of Inhabitants) by Region, 2022."

Unfortunately, many software products don't support this type of axis labeling "natively," so we might need to add the axis label as a floating text box on top of our chart.

> **Key takeaways: Axis/unit of measurement labels**
>
> - Try to locate the unit of measurement label as close as possible to the quantitative scale to which it refers.
> - Avoid vertical scale labels (and vertical text in general; more on that later).

3. Choose an interval based on 1, 2, or 5.

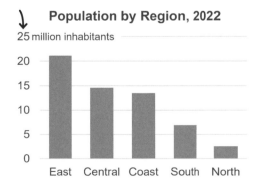

The scale in our original chart had an interval based on 4 (0, 4, 8, 12, etc.). Audiences generally find it a little easier to use scales with intervals based on 1, 2, or 5, however. Why? When the audience is trying to estimate the value of, say, the bar for the East region in the chart above, they actually have to do a bit of mental math, i.e., "The bar for the East is about a fifth of the way from 20 to 25, so it's about 21." Because we all grew up with the decimal system (base 10), we find it a little easier to do that math based on intervals that are naturally divisible into 10, which are 1, 2, and 5 (not 3, 4, 6, 7, 8 or 9).

Some chart creators think that intervals based on 2.5 are also intuitive. I personally find that they're a little less intuitive, but it's probably not a big deal to use them (e.g., 0, 250, 500, 750, etc.).

Occasionally, the audience may think of certain types of units as occurring in intervals of other sizes, such as eggs (dozens) or degrees of rotation (45, 90), in which case the interval should be based on those interval sizes, even if they're not 1, 2, or 5.

> **Key takeaway: Choosing an interval size**
>
> - Consider choosing intervals for quantitative scales that are based on 1, 2, or 5 unless the audience thinks of units as occurring in intervals of another size.

Now that we have some basic guidelines for formatting quantitative scales under our belts, let's move on to…

Six common quantitative scale problems

Unfortunately, I see these six quantitative scale problems all the time in charts in the wild:

1. Unequal scale intervals
2. Ambiguous units of measurement (vague axis titles)
3. Different units of measurement on same scale
4. Dual-axis charts
5. Broken scales
6. Inconsistent numbers of digits after the decimal point

Let's have a closer look at each of these, starting with the simple problems then moving on to ones that are a little more involved.

PROBLEM 1: UNEQUAL SCALE INTERVALS

Occasionally, I'll come across a chart like this:

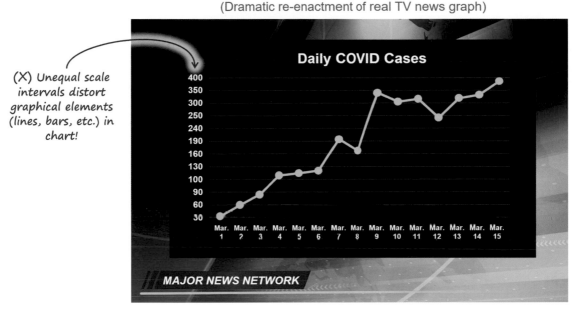

(Dramatic re-enactment of real TV news graph)

(X) Unequal scale intervals distort graphical elements (lines, bars, etc.) in chart!

If you look closely at the value labels on the quantitative scale in this chart, you'll see that some of the intervals are 30, while others are 10, and yet others are 50 even though their spacing on the axis is equal. What does this do to the shape of the line in this chart? Completely distorts it.

> **Key takeaway: Equal intervals**
>
> • In linear quantitative scales, ensure that all intervals are the same size.

PROBLEM 2: AMBIGUOUS UNITS OF MEASUREMENT (VAGUE AXIS TITLES)

At first, this chart might look fine:

But what, exactly, does "transactions" mean in this chart?

- Number of transactions per month?
- Average daily transactions for each month?
- Cumulative total transactions since January?
- Attempted transactions, successful ones, or both?
- Something else?

Obviously, these are very different types of units. Simply by looking at the chart, though, the audience has no way to know which type of unit is being shown, or, worse, might assume they're looking at units that *aren't* what the chart is actually showing.

Also, does this chart represent January to June of the *current* year? What if this chart were on a printout that was printed *last* year, and it ended up showing up in a meeting *this* year, and everyone assumed that it was showing data for the current year? That could do some damage.

Charts with ambiguous labeling are very common so it's crucial to make sure that chart titles, unit names, and other labels are very specific, leaving no room for misinterpretation:

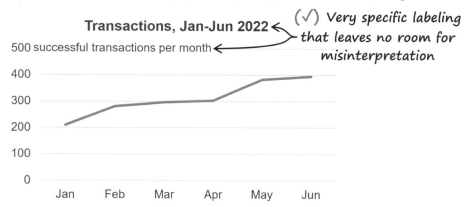

Even if it takes four, five, or even more words to precisely describe the unit of measurement in a chart, do it. Many of the charts that I make have unit-of-measurement labels that are five or six words long. Better that than the audience not understanding what the values in a chart actually *are*.

One of the advantages of orienting the quantitative scale label horizontally and locating it beside the quantitative scale, as we discussed earlier, is that, in most charts, this allows for descriptive, specific (i.e., long) unit of measurement names, like "successful transactions per month."

Key takeaway: Unambiguous chart labeling

- Be very specific and descriptive in chart labeling. Ensure that there's only one possible interpretation of the name of the unit of measurement.

PROBLEM 3: DIFFERENT UNITS OF MEASUREMENT ON SAME SCALE

The chart below shows some data from four call centers; specifically, caller satisfaction ratings and wait times on hold. However, these two different units are shown on the *same quantitative scale*:

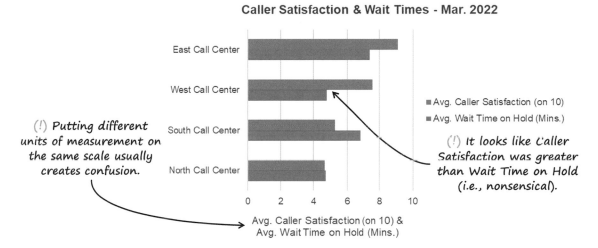

When we're showing two or more different types of units and all values happen to fall in the same numerical range (0 to 10, in the above example), it can be tempting to show the values for different units on the same quantitative scale to save space. As my purple callouts in the chart above point out, though, showing different units on the same scale can encourage the audience to make nonsensical comparisons.

It's almost always clearer to show each unit of measurement on its own, separate scale. In these situations, "merged" charts are often useful:

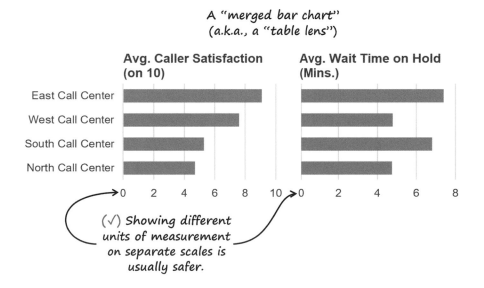

In this chart, the audience is only encouraged to directly compare caller satisfaction ratings with other caller satisfaction ratings (which they should do), and not with wait times on hold (which they shouldn't do).

> **Key takeaways: Different units of measurement on the same scale**
>
> · Avoid showing different units of measurement on the same quantitative scale.
> · Instead, split charts so that each unit of measurement has its own scale (using a "merged" chart if appropriate).

PROBLEM 4: DUAL-AXIS CHARTS

You've probably seen charts that have two quantitative scales for two different variables in the same chart:

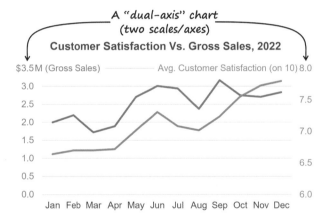

Although this might seem like a good way to compare two completely different variables in the same chart, most of the experienced chart creators that I know avoid dual-axis charts because of the risk that audiences will come to some pretty wonky conclusions about the data:

Are there less problematic ways to compare two completely different variables? Yes. The two that I use most often are:

1. Merged charts

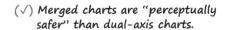

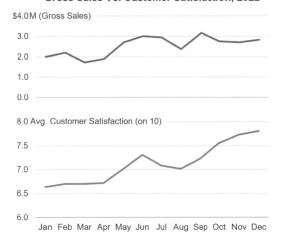

Yes, it's harder to directly compare the lines when they're separated like this, but that's the point! These two lines shouldn't be directly compared with one another! By separating the lines into different charts, we reduce the risk that the audience will, for example, perceive one line as representing more or less quantity than the other. The audience can, however, still compare patterns of change (spikes, dips, etc.), as long as the horizontal scale (usually, time) is the same for both charts, as it is in the chart above.

If the main point of a chart is to compare the patterns of change of the two variables, though, it might be better to use the other dual-axis alternative that I often reach for, i.e.,…

2. Index charts

If you do a bit of math, you could convert (or "index") the two variables to a common variable like "percentage more/less than January":

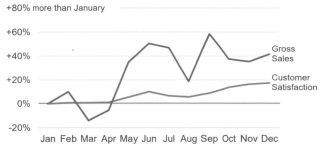

Our chart is no longer a dual-axis chart because there's only one variable, which is "% more/less than January," and the patterns of change can now be perceived and compared accurately. For example, in the previous chart, it looks like Gross Sales was more volatile than Customer Satisfaction and that it increased more rapidly, and that's exactly what happened in reality (but is not what the original dual-axis version of this chart showed). The downside of index charts is that they don't show the actual values, e.g., Gross Sales in dollars. We'll learn more about index charts in "Part 5: Making charts obvious."

When should we use a merged chart versus an index chart? As usual, it depends on the specific job of the chart. If its job involves comparing patterns of change, use an index chart. If it's more about the actual values (dollars, satisfaction ratings, etc.), use a merged chart.

Now, there *is* a rare exception to the "avoid using dual-axis charts" guideline: dual-axis charts can be used to show two units of measurement that are *directly equivalent* (or, in more jargony terms, that are "mathematical transformations of one another"):

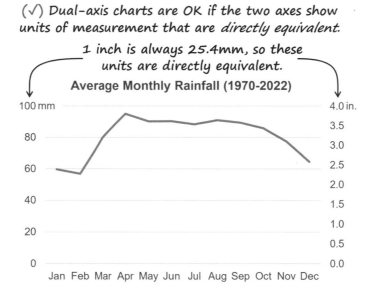

We need to be careful that the two units of measurement have the same equivalence for all of the values in the chart, though, since this is often not the case, as in the following example:

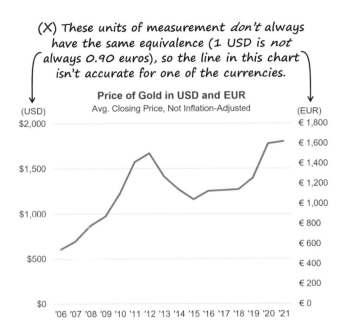

(X) These units of measurement *don't* always have the same equivalence (1 USD is *not* always 0.90 euros), so the line in this chart isn't accurate for one of the currencies.

Price of Gold in USD and EUR
Avg. Closing Price, Not Inflation-Adjusted

Key takeaways: Dual-axis charts

- Avoid dual-axis charts. Consider using merged charts or index charts instead.
- Dual axis charts can be used to show two units of measurement that are directly equivalent for all values in the chart (which is relatively rare).

PROBLEM 5: BROKEN SCALES

Charts with "broken" quantitative scales have a break or gap in the quantitative scale, like this:

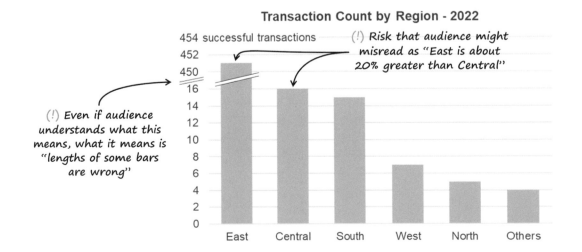

Transaction Count by Region - 2022

454 successful transactions

(!) Risk that audience might misread as "East is about 20% greater than Central"

(!) Even if audience understands what this means, what it means is "lengths of some bars are wrong"

As you can see from my purple callouts, I think that breaking quantitative scales is a bad idea for several reasons:

1. The audience might not notice that the scale is broken and then come to some pretty inaccurate conclusions about the data, such as thinking that the East region is only about 20% greater than the Central region (it's actually more like 28 times greater).

2. Even if the audience notices that the scale is broken, they might not understand what the scale break *means*. Again, this is likely to lead to some very wrong interpretations of the data in the chart.

3. Even if the audience both notices and understands the break in the scale, all the break means is, essentially, "Some of these bar lengths are wrong. Don't compare their lengths with the other bars." Umm… Thanks? What's the point of a bar chart if the audience shouldn't compare the lengths of the bars?

If breaking the quantitative scale is so problematic, why do chart creators sometimes do it? It's almost always to deal with *outliers*, i.e., values that are much greater or smaller than the other values in the chart. For example, if we "unbreak" the scale in the chart above, we can see just how much of an outlier the East region really is, and how hard it would be to compare the smaller values with one another on an "unbroken" scale:

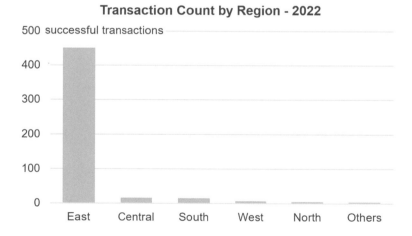

Now, if the insight that we need to communicate is, "The East region is much greater than the others," then this chart is fine and doesn't need to be "fixed." If, however, we need to say something about how the smaller values compare with one another, this chart clearly wouldn't cut it, but I don't think that breaking the scale is a good idea. Is there a better way to deal with outliers? I think so, but this is a bit of a tangent, so let's tackle it in a…

Sidebar: Dealing with outliers

In workshops, when I show charts with outliers like the previous one, participants sometimes suggest switching the quantitative scale from a linear scale to a *logarithmic* scale, like this:

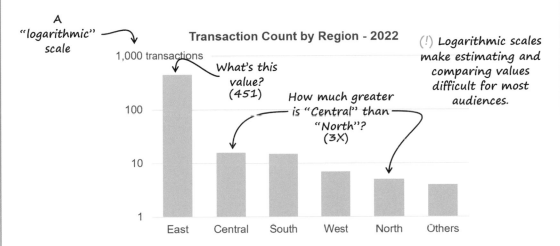

A "logarithmic" scale

Transaction Count by Region - 2022

What's this value? (451)

How much greater is "Central" than "North"? (3X)

(!) Logarithmic scales make estimating and comparing values difficult for most audiences.

Unlike a linear scale, the intervals on a logarithmic scale are all *different*. Specifically, the intervals increase *exponentially*, for example, "1, 10, 100, 1,000, 10,000, etc." The logarithmic scale in the chart above has a base of 10 (10^0, 10^1, 10^2, etc.), but logarithmic scales can be have bases of 2, 16, or any other number.

One of the effects of switching the scale in the chart above from a linear scale to a logarithmic scale is that it makes bars that represent smaller values "taller." In theory, this solves our outlier problem because the shorter bars are now tall enough to be compared with one another easily.

In practice, however, most audiences struggle to read logarithmic scales even remotely accurately, assuming they understand how to read them at all. Without the purple callouts in the chart above, how accurately would you have estimated the value for the East region? Or how the Central region compares with the North region?

I'm not saying that logarithmic scales should never be used, though. They can be very useful when doing certain types of advanced analysis. But for everyday charts, I avoid them because most audiences aren't able to read them with a useful degree of accuracy.

Key takeaways: Logarithmic scales

- Most audiences won't be able to estimate or compare values even remotely accurately in charts based on logarithmic scales.
- Avoid using logarithmic scales for everyday charts unless the audience is very data savvy.

Is there another solution to deal with outliers? Yes, we could use one of my favorite dataviz tricks, "inset charts":

(✓) An "inset chart"

An inset chart allows the audience to see the "big picture," i.e., that the East region has a much greater value than the other regions, but it *also* allows the audience to compare the smaller values easily and precisely. The risk that the audience will misinterpret the data in this chart is very low, and it requires little, if any, explanation.

Inset charts can be used to handle outliers in almost any chart type, not just bar charts:

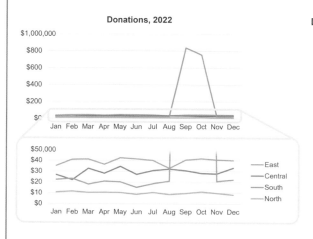

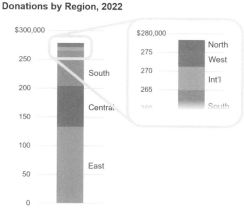

A downside of inset charts is that dataviz software products generally don't offer them as a built-in feature, so we have to do some copying and pasting and "manually" draw lines and rounded rectangles to create them. This also means that inset charts are hard to generate dynamically, which would be a problem on, for example, a dashboard of live data.

Key takeaway: Using inset charts to show data with outliers

- When the data contains outliers and it's important for the audience to be able to compare small values precisely, consider using an inset chart.

PROBLEM 6: INCONSISTENT NUMBER OF DIGITS AFTER THE DECIMAL POINT

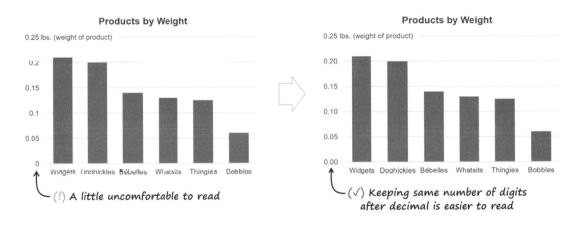

'nuff said.

Key takeaway: Digits after decimal point

- When showing digits after the decimal point in quantitative scale labels, show the same number of digits in all scale labels.

That's it for the common problems that I see with quantitative scales in everyday charts, but we're not done with quantitative scales yet. There are still a few common questions that participants in my workshops ask about that we haven't addressed, so let's tackle those in a...

Quantitative scale FAQ

What are the common quantitative scale questions that we haven't addressed yet? They are:

- "Does my quantitative scale need to start at zero?"
- "What range should my quantitative scale span?"
- "Can I just label all the values in a chart directly and then remove the quantitative scale altogether?"
- "How many intervals should my quantitative scale have?"

These are important questions that come up all the time in practice, so let's tackle them each in turn, beginning with…

DOES MY QUANTITATIVE SCALE NEED TO START AT ZERO?

This is actually a surprisingly complicated question. Googling "does my chart's scale need to start at zero?" returns plenty of articles and videos that say that chart scales always need to extend to zero, and plenty that say that extending the quantitative scale to zero is always optional. Neither of these guidelines holds up to even casual reality-checking; it's easy to come up with scenarios in which the scale clearly *must* be extended to include zero, and just as easy to come up with scenarios in which it's clearly *not* necessary to extend the scale to zero.

The not-so-simple truth is that there are situations in which we must extend the scale to include zero and other situations in which it's not necessary, and determining which situation we're in with a given chart can be tricky. This is a very important design decision, however, and I regularly come across charts that fail to do their job or that misrepresent the underlying data because the chart designer didn't extend the scale to zero when they should have, or vice versa. So, let's dig into it.

For the majority of charts, it will be pretty obvious that the scale should extend to zero because the chart would look weird or potentially deceptive otherwise:

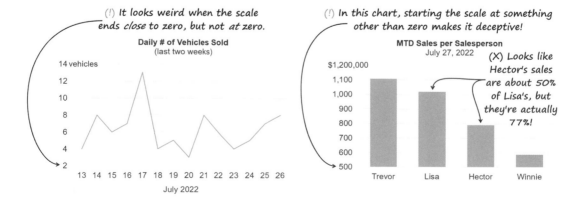

Some situations are less obvious, though. Specifically, if all the values in a chart fall within a narrow range that's far from zero, it can be tempting to "truncate" the scale (start it at something other than zero) to make it easier to see small differences among the values:

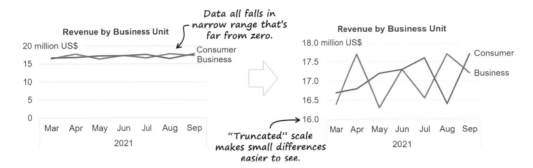

If we're thinking of truncating the scale in a chart, we should first ask ourselves (as usual) what, exactly, the chart needs to say about the data. If the job of the chart in the above scenario is, for example, to communicate that these values are very stable over time, the chart above on the left does that perfectly and doesn't need to be "fixed."

If, however, we need to say something about the small patterns of change in the values, the chart on the left won't cut it because the changes are too small to see clearly. Going with the "truncated scale" chart on the right makes those small patterns of change a lot easier to see, but truncating the scale might cause the audience to misperceive the data. For example, the chart on the right makes it look like the values in this chart were very volatile (bounced around a lot over time), but they weren't volatile at all, as can be seen in the original "starts at zero" chart on the left. So, should we truncate the scale or extend it to zero in this situation?

Simple guidelines that work in something like 95% of situations:

1. By default, extend the quantitative scale to include zero.

2. If the values all fall in a narrow range that's far from zero *and* small differences among the values need to be featured, add an inset chart, similar to what we saw in the "How to handle outliers" sidebar (like I said, inset charts are one of my favorite tricks):

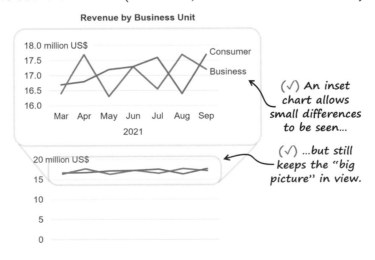

With an inset chart, we can show small differences among the values without worrying about perceptual problems like making those small differences look bigger than they really are because the "big picture" (e.g., that these values are very stable over time) is being shown along with the "truncated" view. As we saw earlier, inset charts can be used with most chart types, and this is the case in situations when all values fall within a narrow range:

(✓) Inset charts can be used to handle data that falls within a narrow range in almost any chart type:

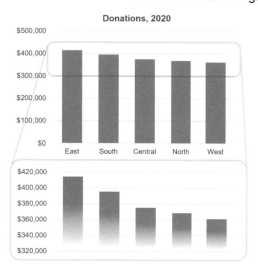

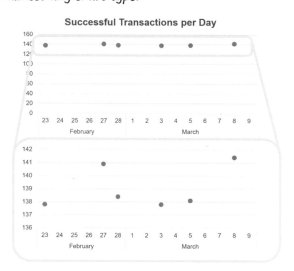

3.   If the distance from the values in the chart to zero seems truly irrelevant in the situation at hand (which is relatively rare), it's not necessary to extend the scale to zero or add an inset chart, unless we're designing a bar chart, which we'll discuss in more detail in the "Bar Charts" chapter later on.

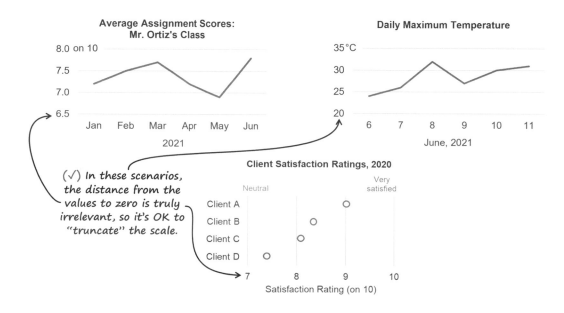

(✓) In these scenarios, the distance from the values to zero is truly irrelevant, so it's OK to "truncate" the scale.

So, those are the "works in something like 95% of situations" guidelines. What about the remaining situations?

More complex guidelines that cover more than 99% of situations:

While rare, there are situations in which the guidelines that we just saw won't lead you to the most effective design choice because there are additional factors that can sometimes affect when it does or doesn't make sense to truncate the scale in a chart. Those additional factors are summarized in the decision tree below, which I'm including in this book mostly to illustrate that there are a surprising number of factors that come into play if we want to make a good decision in virtually all situations about whether or not to truncate the scale.

Note that the decision tree below isn't intended to be self-explanatory, so don't worry about trying to decipher it. For those who feel like going down this particular rabbit hole, however, the full explanation can be found by visiting practicalreporting.com/pc-resources and clicking "Do I need to include zero in my chart's scale? (It's surprisingly complicated...)"

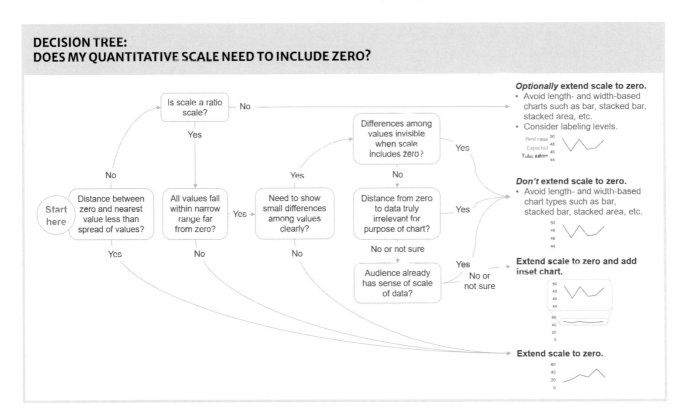

DECISION TREE:
DOES MY QUANTITATIVE SCALE NEED TO INCLUDE ZERO?

I decided to omit the full explanation of this decision tree from the book because the simpler guidelines that I provided earlier will cover the vast majority of situations that arise when making everyday charts.

> **Key takeaways: Extending the scale to zero**
>
> - By default, extend the quantitative scale to zero.
> - If the values in the chart all fall within a narrow range that's far from zero *and* it's important to feature the small differences among them, add an inset chart.
> - If the distance between zero and the values in the chart seems truly irrelevant (which is rare), it's OK to truncate the scale as long as the chart isn't a bar chart.

WHAT RANGE SHOULD MY QUANTITATIVE SCALE SPAN?

Now that we know when it is and isn't necessary to extend the scale to zero, what, exactly, should the upper and lower limits of our quantitative scales be?

The guidelines for making this important design choice depend on whether the values in our chart are all positive, all negative, or a mix of positive and negative values. Let's start by looking at the guidelines for charts that contain only positive values, and then see how those guidelines should be adapted if the values are all negative or consist of a mix of positive and negative values.

How to choose a lower quantitative scale limit:

When it comes to choosing a lower limit, there are three possibilities:

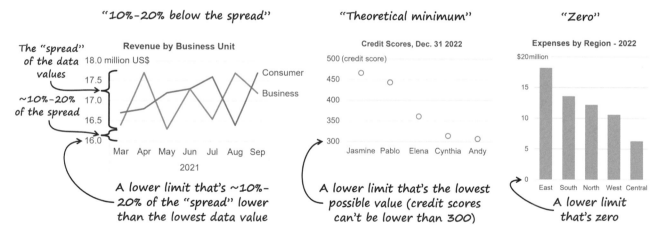

To determine which of the three types of lower limits to apply to a given chart, follow this decision tree:

DECISION TREE:
HOW TO CHOOSE A LOWER QUANTITATIVE SCALE LIMIT

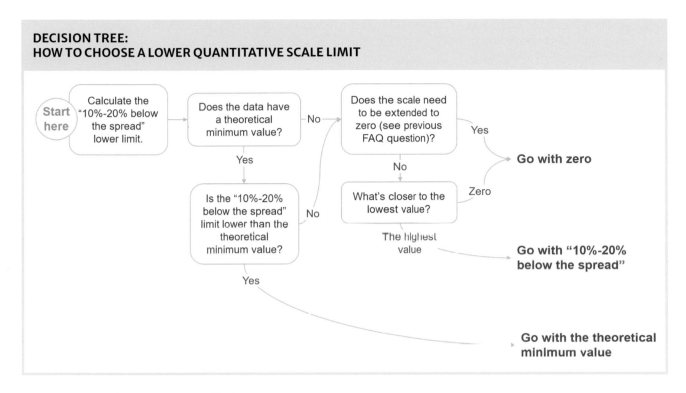

How to choose an upper limit:

This one is simpler: Choose an upper limit that allows some "breathing room" between the values in the chart and the edge of the chart. How much is "some" breathing room? I aim for roughly 10% to 20% of the distance between the highest value in the data and the lower limit that was just chosen in the previous step:

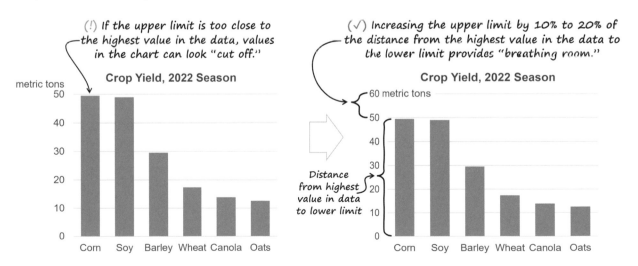

If the data in the chart has a theoretical maximum value, and adding the 10% to 20% breathing room pushes the upper limit beyond that theoretical maximum, we should cut the scale off at the theoretical maximum:

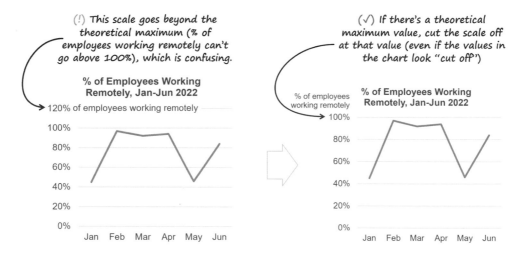

As I mentioned earlier, the guidelines above assume that all the values in a chart are positive. Things are slightly different, however...

If all the values in the chart are negative:

All of the guidelines above still apply, but "upside down" (use the decision tree to find the *upper* limit instead of the lower limit, and give the chart "breathing room" for the *lower* limit unless it would extend below a theoretical minimum).

If the chart contains both positive and negative values:

In this case, things are actually very simple: Just add 10% to 20% of the spread of the values as breathing room both above and below the values in the chart. If there's a theoretical maximum and/or minimum value, cut the scale off at the theoretical maximum and/or minimum.

Key takeaways: Choosing the upper and lower limits of a quantitative scale

- If all values in a chart are positive, choose a lower limit that's about 10% to 20% below the spread of the values, the theoretical minimum, or zero, based on the decision tree in this chapter. Choose an upper limit that's about 10% to 20% above the distance from the lower limit to the highest value in the chart.

- If all values in a chart are negative, choose an upper limit that's about 10% to 20% above the spread of the values, the theoretical maximum, or zero, based on the decision tree in this chapter. Choose a lower limit that's about 10% to 20% below the distance from the upper limit to the lowest value in the chart.

- If the values in a chart are both positive and negative, add 10% to 20% of the spread of the values both above and below the values in the chart to determine the upper and lower limits.

> • If the values in a chart have a theoretical maximum and/or minimum value, avoid extending the quantitative scale beyond of the theoretical maximum and/or minimum.

CAN I JUST LABEL ALL THE VALUES IN THE CHART DIRECTLY AND THEN REMOVE THE QUANTITATIVE SCALE ALTOGETHER?

Basically, can we do this?

Hopefully, this chart illustrates both the question and the answer. Labeling all the values in a chart *does* make the quantitative scale unnecessary, but it can also clutter up a chart. A better solution is to add a table below or beside the chart, which makes for a less cluttered look but still allows the audience to see exact values:

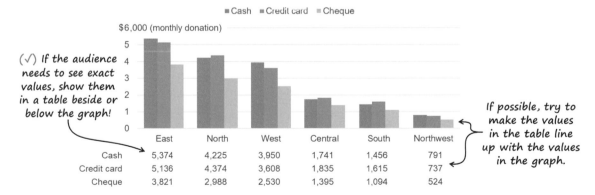

Adding a table beside or below a graph delivers the best of both worlds: a clean, uncluttered graph plus exact values if the audience needs them. For whatever reason, this solution rarely occurs to chart creators, and I regularly see headache-inducing graphs that are crammed full of number value labels.

Now, there *is* a situation in which I do think it makes sense to label the values directly in the chart and omit the quantitative scale, specifically, when there are relatively few values in a chart:

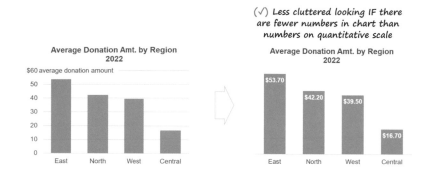

The rule of thumb that I use is, "Go with whatever option results in fewer numbers in the chart." For example, in the scenario above, there are seven numbers in the quantitative scale in the chart on the left (0, 10, 20, etc.), but only four numbers in the value labels in the chart on the right ($53.70, $42.40, etc.), so I'll go with the version on the right, labeling the values directly in the chart and removing the scale.

Key takeaway: Labeling values in a chart

- Avoid labeling values directly in charts. If the audience requires exact values (which is rarer than most chart creators assume), add a table below or beside the chart, except...
- If there are fewer values in the chart than labels on the quantitative scale, consider labeling the values directly and omitting the quantitative scale.

HOW MANY INTERVALS SHOULD MY QUANTITATIVE SCALE HAVE?

In most situations, it's best to go with fewer (i.e., wider) intervals because this makes for a cleaner-looking chart:

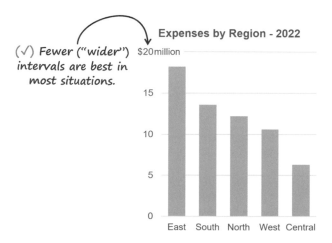

The cost of this cleaner look is that using fewer intervals doesn't allow the audience to visually estimate the values in the chart with very high precision (What, exactly, are expenses in the North region?). In my experience, however, very high precision isn't required in most situations.

Most situations aren't *all* situations, though. If the insight that we need to communicate were, for example, that expenses for the North region are over $12 million, the chart above doesn't offer enough precision to see whether the bar for the North region is above $12 million or below. In that case, we'd need to increase the number of intervals to provide the necessary level of precision to communicate that insight:

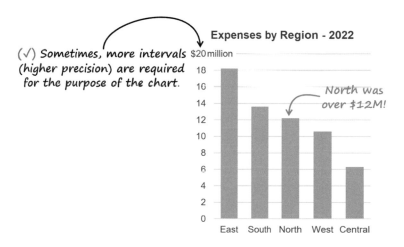

Don't go crazy, though…

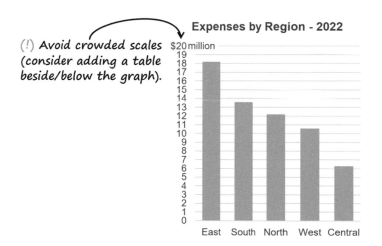

Although this last version of the chart above offers very high precision, it's also very visually busy. If the insight that needs to be communicated requires that much precision, consider adding a table of exact values below or beside the graph, as we saw in the previous FAQ question, instead of cramming a large number of intervals into the quantitative scale.

> ### Key takeaway: Deciding how many intervals to include in a quantitative scale
>
> • Include just enough intervals in the quantitative scale to provide the level of precision needed for the chart to do its specific job.

We just spent 26 pages talking about quantitative scales. WTH? Admittedly, that seems a little crazy, but I hope it's clear why we spent so much time on this topic. Quantitative scales are surprisingly tricky to get right, and problems with them are among the most common reasons why charts flop with, or accidentally mislead, audiences.

Now that you know the guidelines for formatting quantitative scales, you'll probably start to notice that *deliberately* violating quantitative scale guidelines is probably the single most common way that unscrupulous chart creators intentionally try to mislead audiences. If you want to really pull the wool over your audience's eyes, then, do the opposite of what I recommend in this chapter. Except don't do that.

As promised, let's summarize everything that we learned in a handy...

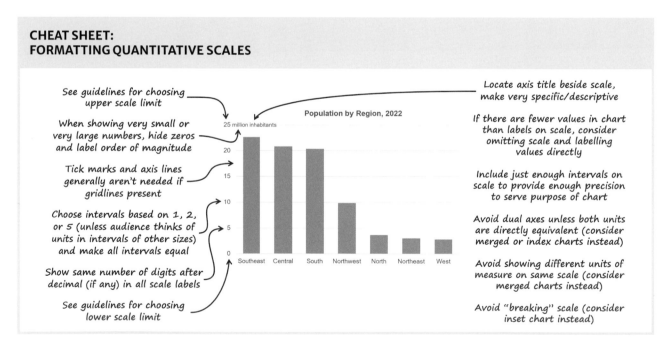

CHEAT SHEET:
FORMATTING QUANTITATIVE SCALES

Alright, we've now covered categorical and quantitative scales, so let's move on to the final type of scale that we'll use in everyday charts, that is...

TIME SCALES

The majority of everyday charts include a scale of time—days, months, quarters, years, etc. Unfortunately, though, many dataviz software products do a poor job of formatting time scales by default. For example, going with a software product's default time scale formatting might result in something like this:

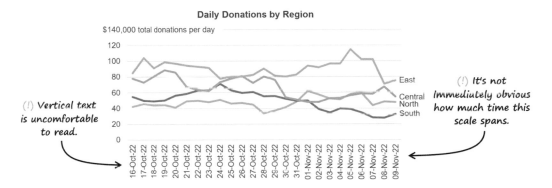

As we saw in our discussion of categorical scales, it's a bit uncomfortable to read text vertically. It's also not immediately obvious what span of time is being shown in this scale, which covers the latter half of October and the beginning of November.

Can we use the "rotate the chart 90°" trick that we saw in the "Categorical scales" section to at least make the time labels horizontal?

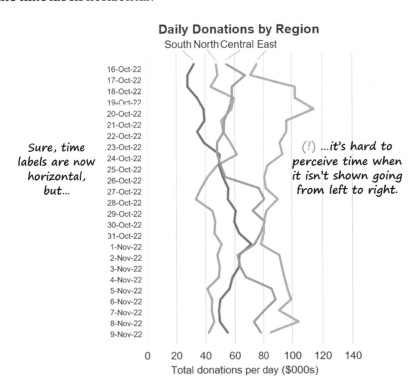

All the text in this chart is now horizontal, but... ouch! Trying to see patterns of change in the resulting vertical lines in this chart is a bit painful. For a variety of evolutionary and cultural reasons, most audiences find it easier to read charts that show time going from left to right, not top to bottom (or in any other direction). For a detailed explanation of why this might be true, visit practicalreporting.com/pc-resources and click "What direction should time go in charts?" Even without that explanation, you can probably see for yourself that time "doesn't compute" for most of us when it's shown from top to bottom or in any direction other than left to right.

As with any good guideline, there are exceptions—two, in fact:

1. **When showing time in a table:**

   When we see data as a table of numbers rather than in a graph, our brains don't think in the same spatial way, so showing time going from top to bottom or from left to right in a table is equally intuitive for most audiences. (We'll talk more about tables later on in the "Tables" chapter.)

(✓) OK to show time going left to right or top to bottom in tables

	Jan	Feb	Mar	Apr	May	Jun	Jul
East	$528,236	$579,630	$500,978	$455,963	$460,510	$505,698	$474,754
West	$274,593	$251,035	$239,350	$222,108	$213,256	$178,000	$168,527

	East	West
Jan	$528,236	$274,593
Feb	$579,630	$251,035
Mar	$500,978	$239,350
Apr	$455,963	$222,108
May	$460,510	$213,256
Jun	$505,698	$178,000
Jul	$474,754	$168,527

For very long or very wide tables, it can be useful to show time going from bottom to top or right to left so that the most recent values are easier to find, i.e., at the top or left-hand side of the table:

Expenses (US$), 2022 YTD

	East	West
Most recent day ⇨ 19-May	109,929	70,404
18-May	106,209	71,791
17-May	99,993	67,029
16-May	97,644	68,248
15-May	102,557	74,331
14-May	109,050	71,948
13-May	83,924	67,685
12-May	103,262	87,475
11-May	107,797	74,715
10-May	85,066	70,615
9-May	113,123	64,120
8-May	97,520	70,174
7-May	93,165	65,819
6-May	106,016	59,940
5-May	104,285	72,910
4-May	112,154	77,393

Make the non-standard sort order visually obvious, though!

For very long tables, showing time bottom to top or right to left can make more recent values easier to find.

2. **When showing more than one time scale:**

Check out this cool "heatmap" chart that shows the average number of babies born on each day of the year in the United States. It shows all sorts of interesting patterns, like the fact that more babies are born in late summer than mid-winter, and that mothers are less likely to deliver on the 13th of each month:

(✓) It's OK for time to go top to bottom when showing more than one time scale.

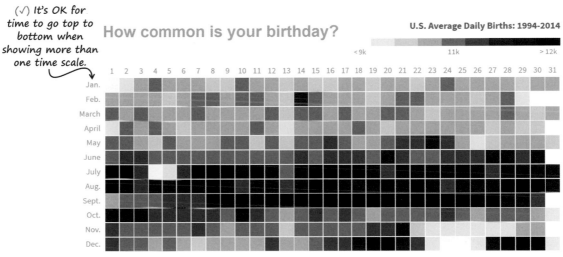

Reproduced with kind permission from Matt Stiles

This chart also has a time scale that goes from *top to bottom* (the scale of months on the left-hand side). The chart creator had to do this because the left-to-right axis was already used for the scale of days. In order to keep time horizontal, the chart creator would have had to have made the chart a single, 366-cell row of colored squares, which wouldn't be nearly as informative.

Key takeaways: Direction of time in charts

- In graphs, generally avoid showing time going in directions other than left to right.
- Time can go in other directions in tables, or in charts with more than one time scale.

Let's return to the original line chart with the vertical time scale labels that we saw earlier because we still haven't figured out how to make that time scale easier to read. If rotating the whole chart 90° isn't a good idea, are there other ways that we could make the time scale in that chart easier to read? If we tell our dataviz software to make the time scale labels horizontal, it might make them look something like this:

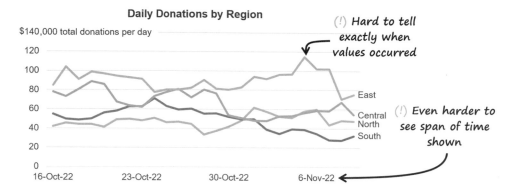

As you can see from my purple callouts, I don't think this a great way to format a time scale either. Is there a better option? Yes. In my experience, "multi-level" time scales are almost always easiest to read:

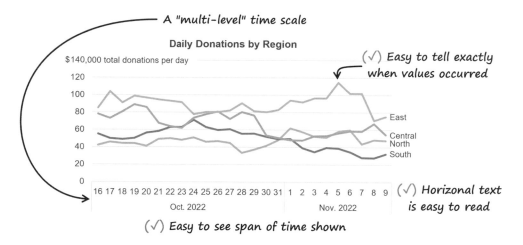

As far as I can tell, multi-level time scales are all upside compared with other ways to format time scales. The labels are horizontal (easy to read), it's easy to see what span of time is being shown, and it's easy to visually associate points in the chart with points in time on the scale. Multi-level time scales work with any units of time (seconds over minutes, months over quarters, etc.) and can support more than two "levels," e.g., days over months over quarters.

What if there isn't enough room on a multi-level time scale to show the labels for all time periods? Fortunately, most software products are smart enough to start hiding intermediate labels, for example, every second label, in order to avoid creating a mess of overlapping labels:

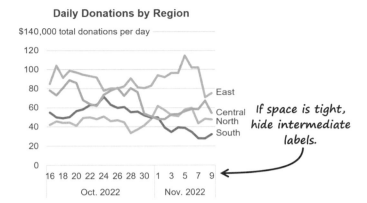

Happily, many software products now support multi-level time scales as a built-in feature; just Google "multi-level time scale in [name of software that you're using]" if you're unsure of whether or how your particular product supports them.

Key takeaway: Multi-level time scales

- Consider formatting time scales in graphs as multi-level time scales.

BTW, now that we've covered multi-level time scales, we now have three tricks for avoiding diagonal or vertical text in charts:

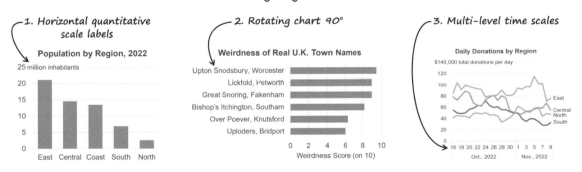

Using these tricks, I've personally managed to avoid diagonal or vertical text in every single chart that I've created in recent years. I'm not saying that diagonal or vertical text is *never* needed, but, if you find yourself making a chart that contains non-horizontal text, ask yourself whether you can use one of these three tricks to make the text horizontal.

Before summarizing what we've learned about formatting time scales, it's important to mention these…

Two common time scale formatting problems

Have a look at the line chart below. Although it might look OK at first glance, it's potentially very misleading. Take a moment and try to spot the problem:

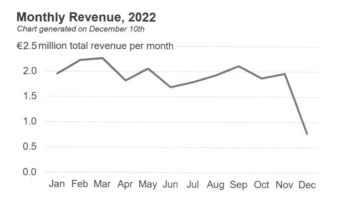

It looks like this chart is showing some pretty bad news, i.e., that revenue collapsed in December. On closer inspection, though, we might notice that the subtitle of this chart says that it was generated on December 10th, so the month of December *isn't finished yet*. Of course December's revenue is lower! There are still 21 days of potential revenue to go! Is revenue really collapsing, then? No. But the chart above certainly makes it *look* like revenue is collapsing, and there's a risk that the audience won't notice the date in the subtitle and will panic unnecessarily.

To avoid this risk, we could simply end the chart with the last complete period (i.e., November) and not show a value at all for incomplete periods (i.e., December). If, however, we need to show a value for an incomplete period for some reason, we need to make it very visually obvious that the incomplete-period value is *different* from the values for complete periods in order to avoid seriously misleading our audience:

This is an important problem to be aware of because most dataviz and business intelligence software will happily generate a chart like the first (misleading) one above if asked to show "the last 12 months of revenue," without any warnings that some values represent incomplete periods.

> **Key takeaway: Showing values for incomplete periods**
>
> • If a time scale includes incomplete time periods, either don't show the incomplete periods or make values for incomplete periods visually distinct from values for complete periods.

Let's have a look at the second common problem that I see with time scales. Can you spot a problem with the chart below?

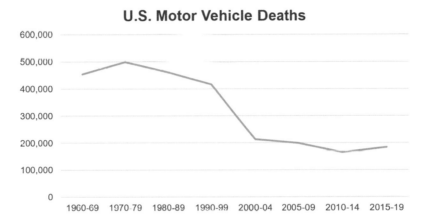

At first, it looks like motor vehicle deaths plummeted from the 1990s to the 2000s. On closer inspection, though, you may notice that the intervals in the time scale *aren't equal*. The first four intervals are 10 years long, but the last four intervals are just 5 years long. Of course there will almost certainly be fewer deaths during 5-year intervals than during 10-year intervals! Does that mean that deaths actually plummeted in early 2000s? Unh-uh.

If all the time intervals are made equal (e.g., all intervals of 10 years), the true pattern of change emerges:

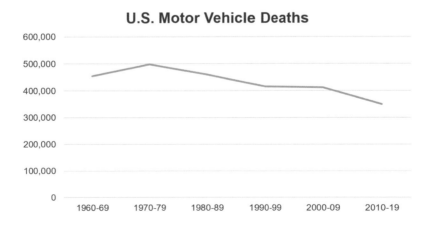

Yes, deaths declined, but not nearly as dramatically as the first chart suggested. When a time scale has been divided into *ranges* of time (a.k.a. "intervals" of time) all time intervals should be equal in order to avoid misrepresenting the data.

> ### Key takeaway: Interval scales of time
>
> - When time scales are divided into intervals, ensure that all time intervals are equal.

Alright, let's recap what we've learned about time scales in a…

CHEAT SHEET:
FORMATTING TIME SCALES

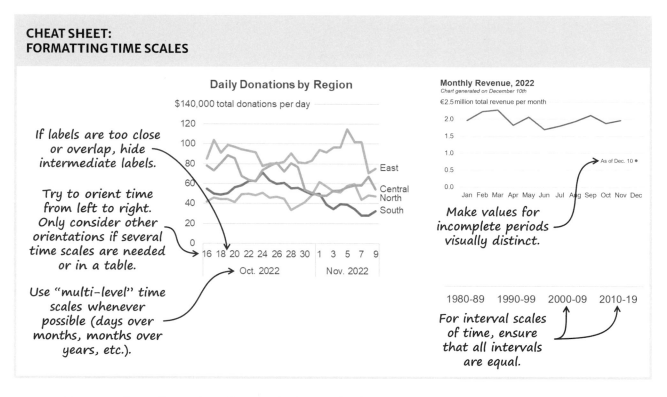

This caps off our discussion of categorical, quantitative, and time scales. It's amazing how many guidelines and common design mistakes are related to parts of a chart that most chart creators think of as straightforward (if they think about scales at all). Hopefully, it's now clear that scales are very much something that we need to think about when making charts, and poorly formatted scales are a major reason why charts flop or mislead audiences.

On to another important aspect of chart design. Chart creators tend to think about this one more than scales, but it still has plenty of potential for poor design choices; it's…

Chapter 3

Color

CHOOSING COLORS FOR a chart might seem simple, but, unfortunately, many charts feature poor color choices. By "poor," I don't mean color choices that look ugly (although that certainly happens and is a consideration); I mean color choices that make charts unobvious, confusing, or even misleading. Unlike in other types of graphics (cartoons, logos, etc.), color in charts communicates specific information. A chart with poor color choices, then, is liable to communicate confusing or incorrect information.

In the bad old days (pre-2010-ish), a major reason why so many charts had poor color choices was that the default color *palettes* (a palette is the set of colors used in a chart) in many dataviz software products were less than ideal. Those palettes often contained high-saturation colors (100% red, 100% blue, etc.), which were, well, a little intense:

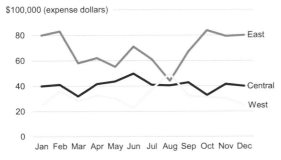
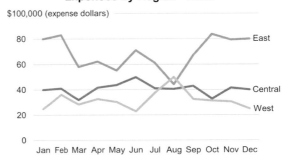

Happily, the default color palettes of most dataviz software products are pretty decent nowadays (with a few unfortunate exceptions). If you find that your software product's default color palette is too saturated, though, there are plenty of free online tools that recommend good color palettes; visit practicalreporting.com/pc-resources, and click "Color resources" for suggestions.

> **Key takeaway: High-saturation colors**
>
> • Generally, avoid color palettes with high-saturation colors because they tend to be less comfortable to look at than low-saturation colors.

Unless we're particularly picky (and some chart creators definitely are), the default color palettes that come with most major dataviz software products will work fine for most everyday charts. However, those products offer several *types* of color palettes to choose from and the software can't make that choice for us, so we'll need some guidelines to help us make that decision. Let's start with…

SINGLE-COLOR PALETTES

Many charts only need a single color, in which case the choice is pretty simple: just pick a nice, neutral, easy-on-the-eyes color:

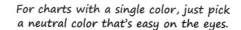

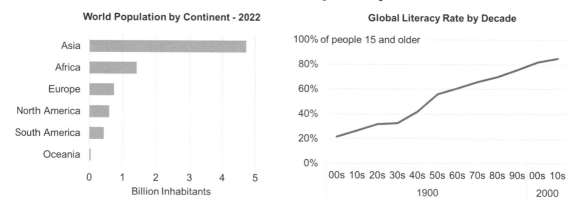

When a chart is perfectly clear with a single color (as in the examples above), avoid the temptation to add more colors to make the chart more "visually interesting":

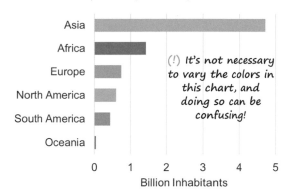

Because color in charts conveys specific information, the audience will be left wondering what the different colors in the chart above mean (Different units of measure? Some kind of highlighting?) until they figure out that the colors don't mean *anything* in the chart above.

Another example:

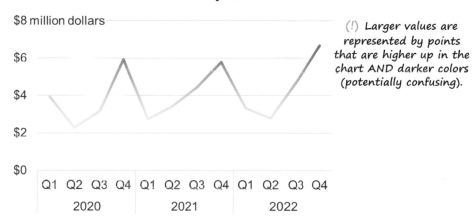

In this chart, darker color shades represent larger values, but larger values are *already* represented as points on the line that are higher up in the chart. As with the multi-color bar chart above, the audience will try to figure out the what the different color shades in this line chart mean (Perhaps a second variable, other than donation dollars, is being represented by lighter/darker color shades?) until they realize that the different color shades represent the *same* information that's already represented by the heights of the points.

In "Part 6: Making charts less boring," we'll see plenty of effective ways to make charts interesting. Using different colors for no reason isn't one of them.

> **Key takeaway: Varying colors for no reason**
>
> • If a chart is clear with a single color, avoid varying the colors to make it more "visually interesting."

For many charts, though, there are *good* reasons to use more than one color, and that's where things get a bit more involved, so let's talk about…

MULTI-COLOR PALETTES

There are three important *types* of multi-color palettes that are needed for everyday charts:

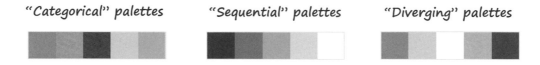

Probably the most common color-related problem that I come across is charts that use the wrong type of multi-color palette, for example, a chart with a categorical palette that would have been more effective with a sequential one, or a chart with a sequential palette that would have been more effective with a diverging one. It's worth spending a few pages, then, on learning when to use and not use these different types of color palettes, beginning with…

Categorical color palettes

The most common color palettes in everyday charts are "categorical" palettes (also called "qualitative" or "rainbow" palettes, but I'm going to stick with "categorical" in this book). A categorical palette is a set of colors with different "hues," such as blue, orange, red, and green.

Examples of categorical palettes

Most of the charts that we've seen so far in this book have categorical palettes:

Charts with categorical color palettes

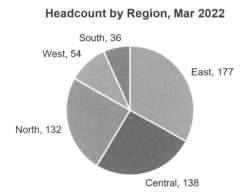

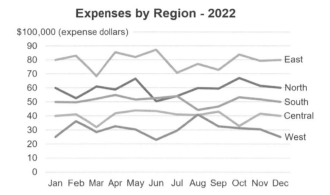

It made sense to use a categorical palette in these situations because the categories in these charts are *non-sequential*, meaning that they can be listed in any order. If the categories are *sequential*, however, we might want to use one of the other two types of palettes that we'll see in a moment.

Note that the colors in a categorical palette should be *balanced*, i.e., all colors should attract the same amount of visual attention. In the bad old days, the default categorical palettes of some software products were *unbalanced*, with some colors drawing a lot more visual attention than others, whether or not the chart creator was trying to draw attention to anything in the chart:

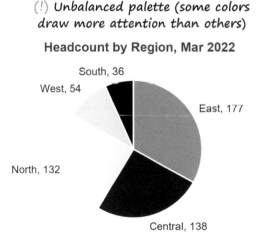

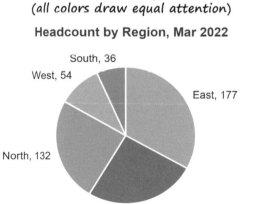

Thankfully, most (not all) modern dataviz software products come with balanced categorical color palettes built in.

If we *want* to highlight an individual shape in our chart (a bar, a line, a pie slice, etc.), amping up the color of that shape is an effective way to do it; we'll see that and other ways of highlighting individual parts of a chart in "Part 5: Making charts obvious." Highlighting should be deliberate, though, not random, as in the chart above on the left.

> **Key takeaways: Categorical palettes**
>
> · Generally, use a categorical palette to identify non-sequential categories.
> · The colors in a categorical palette should be balanced.

Now, let's have a look at the second of the three types of color palettes that are needed in every-day charts, that is…

Sequential color palettes

Let's look at another scenario: In this one, we're an investment firm with three portfolios of investments and we want to show that one of those portfolios contains more high-risk assets, so we design this stacked bar chart to communicate that:

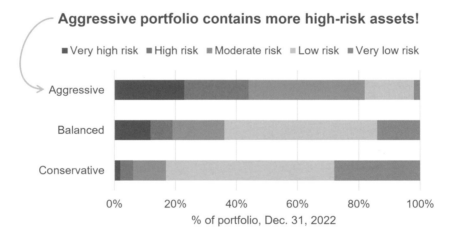

This chart works; the audience can get an idea of how much of each portfolio is made up of assets with different levels of risk.

Just for fun, though, let's try switching the categorical palette in this chart to a *sequential* palette, i.e., a palette in which all colors have the same hue (blue, in the chart below), but different *shades* (a.k.a. "intensities"):

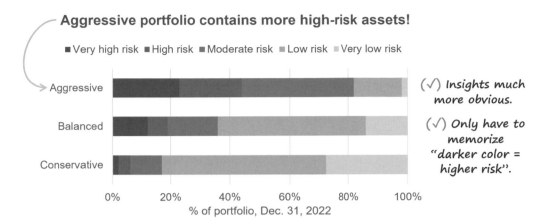

Huh! Suddenly, this chart seems a lot more obvious and easier to read. Even before the audience reads any of the text, they'll notice that the top bar contains a lot more of "something" than the other two bars. When the audience starts reading the text in the chart, they learn that that "something" is "high-risk assets." Was that as visually obvious in the first version of this chart with the categorical color palette? Nope.

The "sequential palette" version of this chart also requires less cognitive effort to read than the "categorical palette" version because, in the "categorical palette" version, the audience had to memorize five essentially random colors in order to interpret the chart. In the "sequential palette" version, the audience just has to remember that darker colors represent higher risk, which is easier to remember than five random colors.

Why did switching to a sequential scale improve this chart so much? Because the categories in it are sequential ("Very high risk," "High risk," "Moderate risk," etc.). **When a chart has sequential categories, using a sequential palette usually makes it easier to read and more obvious to understand.**

Note that categories that are "greater" (e.g., investments with greater risk) are typically represented by darker color shades. Against a dark background, however, this perception can get reversed, with *lighter* shades looking "greater":

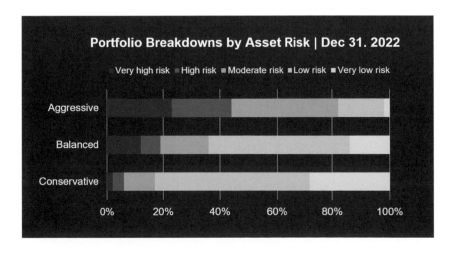

Sequential palettes work well with sequential categories, but we should avoid using sequential palettes with *non*-sequential categories. Why? Well, consider the chart below, which uses a sequential color palette to identify non-sequential categories (i.e., regions):

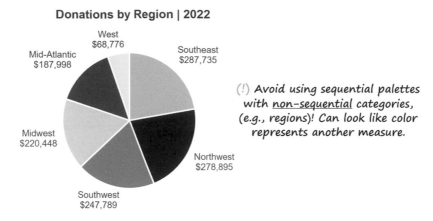

Donations by Region | 2022

(!) Avoid using sequential palettes with <u>non-sequential</u> categories, (e.g., regions)! Can look like color represents another measure.

Using a sequential palette with non-sequential categories such as regions can be confusing. Because audiences perceive darker shades as representing greater quantities, in the pie chart above, it looks as if the Northwest had "more of something" than the Southeast because the Northwest slice has a darker shade of blue. That's wrong, however, because the color shades in this chart were randomly assigned. Yes, eventually, the audience will figure out that the colors don't actually mean anything in this chart, but why impose that extra cognitive step on them? A categorical palette would be less confusing in this case because the colors in a categorical palette *don't* suggest different quantities.

As with any good guideline, there's an exception to this one: Let's say that we need to show how much of each of four crops were produced by five countries, but we also want to compare the *continents* that those countries belong to:

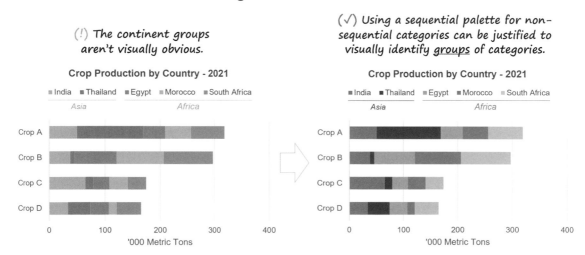

(!) The continent groups aren't visually obvious.

(✓) Using a sequential palette for non-sequential categories can be justified to visually identify <u>groups</u> of categories.

Using different shades of the same hue (i.e., a sequential palette) is an effective way to identify groups of categories (in the example above, countries grouped by continent), as long as it's visually obvious that the color shades don't represent quantities or sequential categories in the chart. In the previous chart on the right, for example, two design elements make it visually obvious that the colors represent groupings of categories, not quantities or sequential categories:

1. The design of the legend clearly shows that different color shades represent countries, not quantities.

2. The shades of orange are "out of order" (the darkest shade of orange is in the middle).

Key takeaways: Sequential palettes

- When the categories in a chart are sequential, consider using a sequential color palette to identify them.
- Avoid using sequential color palettes to identify non-sequential categories except when identifying groups of non-sequential categories.
- Sequential palettes can also be used to represent quantities. Darker (higher-intensity) shades are generally perceived as representing larger quantities except when shown against a dark background.

On to the third and final type of color palette that's needed in everyday charts, that is…

Diverging color palettes

To learn about diverging color palettes, let's look at another scenario. In this one, we work for an African company that ships products to countries all over the continent. The management team is interested in the average time that it takes for products to be shipped to each country, and we decide to show the data like this (we'll learn more about maps later in the book; I just want to focus on the color palette for now):

Average Shipping Time (Days) by Country, 2022

When we discuss this map with the management team, it becomes apparent that they expect shipping to take about seven days, so they're *delighted* when it only takes three days. In the chart above, though, a shipping time of three days is represented as light red, i.e., it looks like a *problem*, but that's not how the audience thinks about it at all.

In light of this new information, we decide to redesign this chart using a *diverging* color palette, with shades of green for shipping times that are shorter (i.e., better) than the seven days that the audience was expecting and shades of red for shipping times that are longer:

Average Shipping Time (Days) by Country, 2022

(✓) Diverging palette better reflects dividing point that audience perceives in data (i.e., expected shipping time of seven days)

Shipping Time (Days)

3   7   11

Ah! Now the chart accurately reflects how the management team *really* thinks about this data. The "good news" regions are visually distinct from the "bad news" regions.

Diverging color palettes are basically two sequential palettes stuck together, usually with a neutral "dividing color" (often white or gray) in between. **Diverging palettes are a good choice when the audience considers values on one side of a dividing point in the data to be categorically different than values on other side.** In the "shipping times" scenario, for example, we discovered that the audience thought of shipping times that were shorter than seven days as being categorically different than shipping times that were longer than seven days, so it made sense to use a diverging color palette with seven days as the dividing point.

Note that the decision of whether to use a sequential palette or a diverging palette depends entirely on how the *audience* thinks about the data. We can stare at the data all day long, but that won't tell us whether we should use a sequential or diverging palette. We must "get in the audience's head" and figure out whether or not they think that there's a dividing point in the data. Note that the dividing point isn't necessarily in the middle of the range of the data; it could be zero, the average of all the values, the threshold at which someone gets a bonus, or any other point:

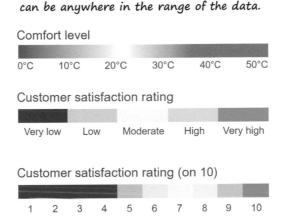

The dividing point in a diverging palette can be anywhere in the range of the data.

Comfort level

0°C   10°C   20°C   30°C   40°C   50°C

Customer satisfaction rating

Very low   Low   Moderate   High   Very high

Customer satisfaction rating (on 10)

1   2   3   4   5   6   7   8   9   10

Note that, in all of the diverging palette examples in this section, I've avoided the classic "traffic light" palette of red-yellow-green. This is because values that are close to the dividing point in a diverging palette are usually of *least interest* to the audience, i.e., they're average, expected, normal, etc., and using an attention-grabbing color like yellow (a.k.a. "amber") to represent values that require little or no attention doesn't make sense. It makes more sense to use an unremarkable color such as white or gray, or to simply make those values transparent.

> **Key takeaways: Diverging color palettes**
>
> - Consider using a diverging color palette when the audience thinks of values on one side of a dividing point in the data as being categorically different from values on the other side.
> - Avoid using bright colors like yellow/amber for values that are at or near the dividing point in a diverging palette.

"SPECIAL" COLORS

There are a few colors that most audiences perceive as being "special" or distinct from other colors. This should be taken into account when choosing colors in a palette.

Gray, black, and white

In charts with categorical palettes, most audiences perceive black and gray (and white, if the chart has a dark background) as being "distinct" from other colors like blue, orange, green, etc., so it's generally best to reserve those colors for categories that are distinct from other categories in the chart, such as averages, totals, "all others," or missing values:

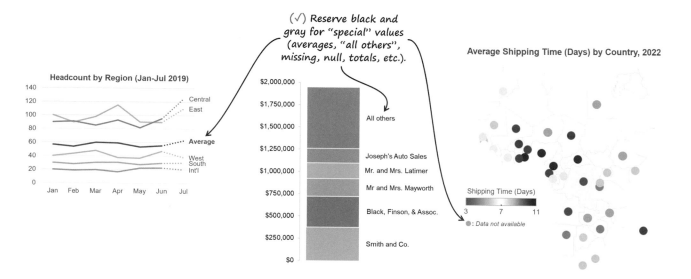

This is why I generally try to avoid categorical palettes that include black or gray as "regular" colors. Unfortunately, however, the default categorical palettes in many dataviz software products include gray, so we might need to manually edit the palette to replace gray with another color.

Key takeaway: Gray, black and white

- Avoid using gray, black, and white as "regular" colors in a categorical palette. Reserve those colors for "special" values, such as averages, totals, "all others," or missing values.

Red and green

Audiences in many cultures associate red with "bad" and green with "good" (a notable exception is some Asian cultures). This cultural convention is extremely useful when designing charts because adding red and/or green to charts can help audiences interpret them quickly and easily, and can make insights and key takeaways (especially problems) a lot more obvious:

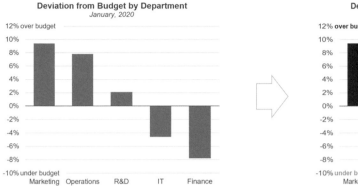

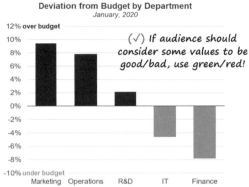

Note that, if red and green indicate good and bad values in a chart, those colors can no longer be used as "regular colors" in that chart's palette. That's why, as a general rule, I try to avoid using red as a "regular color" in categorical palettes even when red *doesn't* represent "bad" in the chart. This just eliminates the risk that the audience might think that, for example, a red line in a line chart is "bad." For whatever reason, using green as a regular color in a categorical palette seems to be less problematic, at least in my experience.

We'll talk more about using red and green in "Part 5: Making charts obvious" later in the book. For now, I just want to point out that they're "special" colors.

Key takeaway: Red and green

- In most cultures, red is associated with "bad" and green is associated with "good," which is often useful when designing charts.

Now that we have a good handle on the basics of choosing colors, let's look at…

FIVE COMMON COLOR CHOICE PROBLEMS

Unfortunately, you'll see these color choice problems all over the place once you know what they are:

- Using colors that aren't colorblind-friendly
- Using palettes with too many colors
- Using colors inconsistently
- Failing to use "known" colors
- Using externally imposed color palettes

Let's start with…

Problem 1: Using colors that aren't colorblind-friendly

Roughly 4% of the general population has some form of colorblindness (or, more accurately, "color vision deficiency" because most of them do perceive color to one degree or another). The proportion can be as high as 8% among certain demographic groups, so it's definitely something to be aware of.

If we take the map of shipping times that we saw earlier and simulate how it might look to someone with a common form of colorblindness, it looks like this:

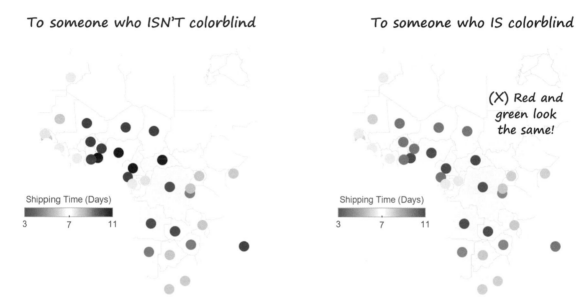

What can we do to ensure that our charts can be read easily and accurately by colorblind audiences? Two suggestions:

1. **Test your charts in a colorblindness simulator.**

   Visit practicalreporting.com/pc-resources and click "Color resources" to get links to online tools that allow users to upload a screenshot of a chart (or any other image), which the tool will then display back to the user as it would appear to someone with colorblindness (that's how I got the image above on the right). Checking charts using this simple test before publishing them is a good practice.

   If we discover that a chart that we've created *isn't* colorblind-friendly and if we know or suspect that members of our audience are colorblind, we can then...

2. **Use a colorblind-friendly color palette.**

   Some dataviz software products now come with built-in palettes that are labeled as colorblind-safe. If your software product doesn't have such palettes, you can get colorblind-safe palettes by visiting practicalreporting.com/pc-resources and clicking "Color resources." If we apply one of these colorblind-safe palettes to the shipping times chart, we might get something like this:

A chart with colorblind-safe colors

Shipping Time (Days)

3   7   11

People with most types of colorblindness have difficulty with green and red but can tell blue and orange apart. The disadvantage is that people *without* colorblindness might no longer immediately recognize some values as "good" and others as "bad" because blue and orange don't have the same intuitive associations as red and green among most audiences.

If the chart that you're making will being shown on a web page or in a software product (as opposed to being printed or shown on a presentation slide), an ideal solution is to make two versions of the chart: one that uses a more intuitive (but potentially color-blind-unsafe) palette, and one that uses a colorblind-safe palette that's potentially less intuitive. In the website or software product, show the first chart version by default, but allow the user to switch to the colorblind-safe version using a checkbox, dropdown menu, or similar user interface control. More work, yes, but this does offer the best user experience for everyone.

Key takeaways: Accounting for colorblindness

- If you know or suspect that members of your audience are colorblind, test your charts in a colorblindness simulator before showing them to the audience.
- If a chart cannot be read easily or accurately when viewed in a colorblindness simulator, consider changing the color palette to a colorblind-safe color palette or offering a colorblind-safe version of the chart as an alternative to the original.

Problem 2: Using palettes with too many colors

For both categorical and sequential palettes, things can get dicey when there are more than seven or eight colors because we start to get colors that are similar to one another:

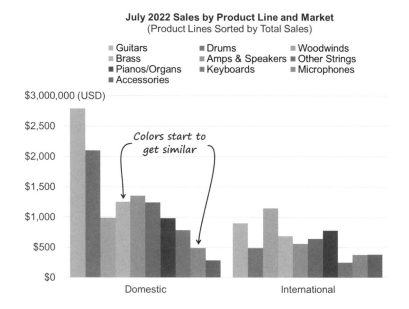

Depending on the design of the chart, having similar colors may or may not be a problem. For example, this 13-color line chart works fine because the categories are directly labeled and not in a legend (more on legends shortly), and because colors that are similar to one another are always far apart in the chart:

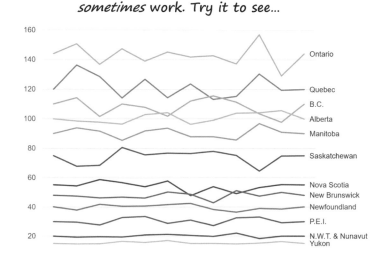

What if we need to show more than seven or eight categories in a chart and the chart doesn't work well when we try it with more than seven or eight colors? A few suggestions:

1. **Try to reduce the number of categories.** *If possible...*

   - Remove categories that aren't essential to the insight being communicated.

   - Merge categories into category groups.

   - Merge less important categories into an "All others" category.

2. **Try a "multi-hued" sequential or diverging palette.**

   If our chart has, say, nine or ten sequential categories, we could use a "multi-hued" sequential palette, such as the one shown below, which includes blue, green, and yellow hues:

   Because of the special way this palette was designed, it still looks like a sequence even though it contains different hues. One advantage of multi-hued sequential palettes is that they make it easier to tell the colors apart, so we can get away with a few more than seven or eight colors (there are nine in the palette above, but it's still easy to tell them apart). Many people (including me) also think that they tend to look nicer than single-hued sequential palettes.

   We can use the same multi-hue trick to get away with more colors in a diverging color palette, as well:

   The downside of multi-hued palettes is that they're more mathematically complex to generate than single-hued palettes, so your software product may or may not offer them as built-in palettes. If your dataviz software doesn't have multi-hued palettes built-in, visit practicalreporting.com/pc-resources and click "Color resources" for links to online resources that provide multi-hued palettes that you can import into your software product.

Key takeaways: Too many colors in chart

- Generally, try to avoid categorical or sequential palettes with more than seven or eight colors, especially in charts with legends.
- If more than seven or eight categories need to be shown, try to reduce the number of categories, or try a multi–hued palette if the categories are sequential.

Problem 3: Using color inconsistently

When making charts for a report, presentation, dashboard, or anything else that contains multiple charts, try to use the same colors for the same categories in all charts. If the West region is purple in one chart, try to make the West region purple in *all* charts. Sometimes this is possible, and sometimes it's not, depending on the number of categories, the number of charts, and other factors, but try to apply this guideline whenever you can.

> **Key takeaway: Using colors consistently**
>
> - When presenting multiple charts in a presentation, report, etc., try to use the same colors to represent the same categories in all charts.

Problem 4: Failing to use "known" colors

Occasionally, an audience might already associate the categories in a chart with specific colors before they've even seen our chart. For example, maybe the audience associates political parties, sports teams, or countries in our chart with specific colors. Obviously, in those situations, we should try to use those "known" colors because they reduce or eliminate the need for the audience to memorize colors in order to read the chart. In fact, using colors that *differ* from ones that the audience already associates with the categories in a chart may confuse the audience or cause them to misread the chart.

We need to be mindful, however, that some audiences might be offended if the colors in a chart are colors that are traditionally associated with specific races, genders, or other demographic groups. In those situations, it may be better to use random colors.

> **Key takeaway: Using known colors**
>
> - If the target audience for a chart already associates the categories in a chart with certain colors, use those colors in the chart, if possible.

Problem 5: Using "brand" colors

If you work in a larger organization, you might be told to use the organization's brand colors in all publications, including charts. As you can probably imagine after reading this chapter, being forced to always use the same color palette, regardless of whether the categories in a chart are sequential or non-sequential, how many categories there are, and so on, will inevitably result in charts that are confusing at best and misleading at worst. This can be especially problematic if the brand colors include green or *gulp* red.

The only advice I can offer in such situations is to push back and try to explain to the powers that be (often, someone in the marketing department) that being forced to use brand colors will make for confusing and potentially misleading charts. Share some examples from this chapter of the book with them, if they'll listen. You might succeed and you might not, but fight the good fight.

Let's recap what we've learned about choosing colors in a handy…

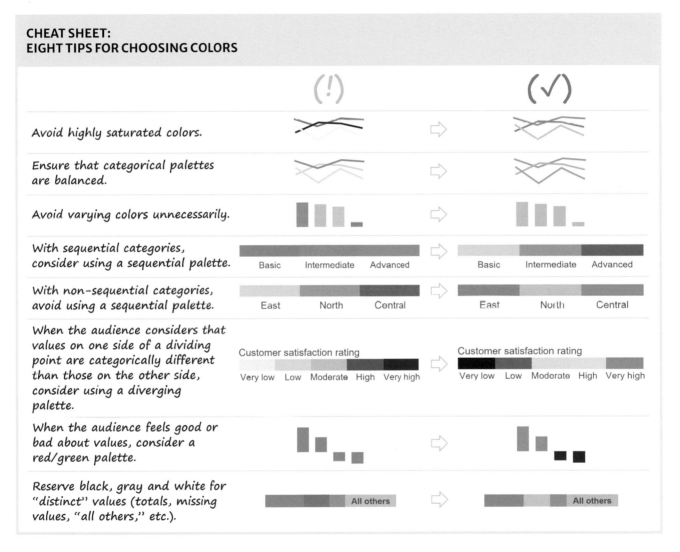

CHEAT SHEET:
EIGHT TIPS FOR CHOOSING COLORS

Avoid highly saturated colors.

Ensure that categorical palettes are balanced.

Avoid varying colors unnecessarily.

With sequential categories, consider using a sequential palette.

With non-sequential categories, avoid using a sequential palette.

When the audience considers that values on one side of a dividing point are categorically different than those on the other side, consider using a diverging palette.

When the audience feels good or bad about values, consider a red/green palette.

Reserve black, gray and white for "distinct" values (totals, missing values, "all others," etc.).

Before leaving color behind, I want to mention a challenge that, thankfully, is getting less common with each passing year, which is…

Adapting charts to be shown in black and white

Oh no! We've just discovered that our chart will be printed, photocopied, or (God forbid) faxed on a black and white device. As you can imagine, there's a good chance that this will make it impossible to read our chart correctly. Unfortunately, there's no magic-bullet solution in these situations, but there are a variety of techniques that we can use to redesign charts so that they can still be read correctly in black and white. Visit practicalreporting.com/pc-resources and click "Adapting charts to be shown in black and white" for suggestions.

There's lots more that we could talk about when it comes to color, but those are the essential guidelines for making good everyday charts, in my experience. On to…

Chapter 4

Legends

LEGENDS (ALSO CALLED "KEYS") are pretty straightforward, but there are a few ways in which chart creators design them sub-optimally. Let's have a look at the most common legend problems so that we can avoid them in our own charts.

It's important to understand that, when a chart has a legend, the audience must *memorize* the colors (or, sometimes, symbols) in the legend before beginning to interpret the chart. Sure, that generally doesn't require a huge amount of cognitive work, but it's still work. Legend design guidelines, therefore, generally focus on minimizing or eliminating that cognitive work.

In fact, the first guideline that I'll offer about legends is that **the best legend is no legend at all**, which eliminates any legend-related cognitive work altogether:

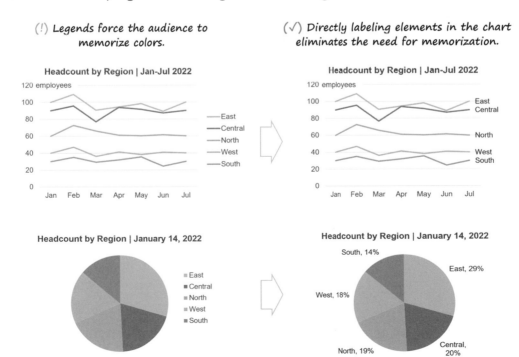

If we can avoid forcing the audience to memorize anything in the first place, that's a win. Although this might seem like an obvious improvement, I see charts all the time that have legends even though labeling the lines, bars, or other elements directly in the chart would be completely doable. This probably has something to do with unfortunate dataviz software defaults, which often add legends when direct labeling is both possible and preferable.

Sometimes, though, labeling elements directly in a chart isn't possible, or it results in a cluttered chart. For example, a clustered bar chart could get a bit messy if we were to label each bar directly:

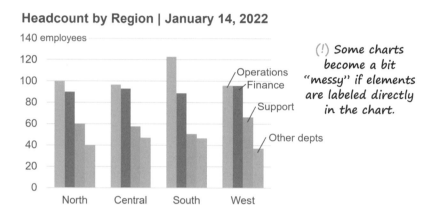

In this situation, we're probably better off with a legend. There are a few things that we can do to make it a little easier for the audience to associate colors in the legend with colors in the chart, though. Specifically, we can try to make the legend "match" the colors in the chart as closely as possible. For example, in the clustered bar chart below on the left, neither the sequence of colors in the legend nor the direction of the legend matches the sequence and direction of the colors in the chart:

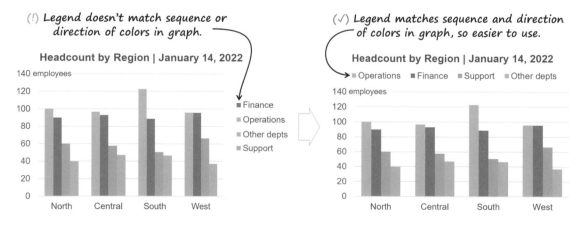

Rearranging the legend so that it matches both the sequence and the direction of the colors in the chart as closely as possible makes it easier for the audience to associate items in the legend with elements in the chart.

Another situation that might require a legend is one in which a chart is dynamically generated, such as on a live dashboard. This creates a risk that category labels will overlap if they're directly beside elements in the chart:

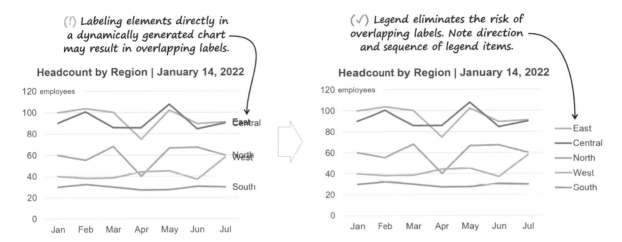

Note that, in this example, we're still applying the "try to match the sequence and direction of colors in the legend with the colors in the chart" guideline. In the chart above on the right, the sequence of colors in the legend matches the chart (well, it matches the final month in the chart anyway because that's probably the month of greatest interest), and the direction of colors in the legend (top to bottom) is the same as that of the colors in the chart.

In workshops, participants often ask about whether to position the legend above, below, to the left, or to the right of the chart area. This is the convention that I use:

- For most charts, I position the legend above the chart area (but underneath the chart title) because the legend must be read *before* the elements in the chart can be understood.

- For line charts showing time, I tend to position the legend to the right of the chart (as in the line chart above on the right) because this makes it easier to associate the items in the legend with the lines in the chart. Why not put the legend on the left? Because, in most time series charts, the values of greatest interest are the most recent values, which are on the right-hand side in a standard line chart.

Having said all this, I doubt that it would confuse anyone if the legend were located below or to the left of the chart area.

> ### Key takeaways: Legends
>
> - Whenever possible, avoid using a legend and label bars/lines/etc. directly.
> - When a legend is necessary, try to match the colors in the legend to the sequence and direction of the colors in the chart as closely as possible.
> - Usually, position the legend above the chart area or, for time series charts, closest to the most recent values (usually, to the right).

There's no cheat sheet for legends because the guidelines for them are pretty straightforward and fully captured in the previous "Key takeaways" block.

On to…

Chapter 5

Formatting numbers, dates, and text in charts

NOTHING ROCKET SCIENCE-Y in this chapter, just some guidelines to avoid the most common number, date, and text formatting problems in charts.

Choosing typefaces

Choosing a typeface (what many people refer to as a "font") can be highly subjective, but, when it comes to everyday charts, it's generally best to avoid stylized typefaces and stick to simple ones that are optimized for easy reading:

(!) More stylized, somewhat less legible typefaces	(✓) Simple, highly legible typefaces
Brush Script	Arial
Elephant Pro	Helvetica
Elegant Script	Calibri
`Courier New`	Verdana

It's also generally a good idea to avoid typefaces that have "proportional-width" numerals (e.g., the "1" is narrower than the "8") and instead to choose a typeface in which all numerals have the same width (a.k.a. "monospaced" or "tabular" typefaces):

(!) Typefaces with "proportional" number widths (harder to compare values)		(✓) Typefaces with "monospaced" numbers (easier to compare values)	
Barlow Condensed	Candara	Arial	Calibri
31,751.71	31,751.71	31,751.71	31,751.71
91,775.33	91,775.33	91,775.33	91,775.33
69,986.60	69,986.60	69,986.60	69,986.60
72,819.45	72,819.45	72,819.45	72,819.45
57,757.13	57,757.13	57,757.13	57,757.13
26,810.08	26,810.08	26,810.08	26,810.08

Typefaces with monospaced numerals make columns of numbers easier to read and compare because the tens, hundreds, thousands, etc., all "line up" vertically.

In everyday charts, it's also generally best to avoid typefaces with "non-lining figures" because, although they're fine in paragraphs of text, they tend to make numbers slightly harder to read in tables and graphs:

(!) In typefaces with "non-lining figures," some numbers "stick out" slightly above or below the others.	(✓) Favor typefaces with "lining figures," i.e., the tops and bottoms of all numbers align.
Candara: 1 2 3 4 5 6 7 8 9 0	Arial: 1 2 3 4 5 6 7 8 9 0
Georgia: 1 2 3 4 5 6 7 8 9 0	Calibri: 1 2 3 4 5 6 7 8 9 0

If we're not sure whether a typeface has monospaced, lining numerals, we can open a spreadsheet and type out the digits "1234567890" in a cell, and then "1111111111" and "8888888888" in the two cells below it. When the typeface is applied to all three cells, if the contents of all three cells are the same width, the typeface is monospaced. If the characters in the cell with "1234567890" in it all have the same height, the typeface has lining numerals.

FYI, the text and numbers in most of the chart examples in this book use the "Arial" typeface. Other typefaces that work well for everyday charts include Helvetica, Calibri, Verdana, and Lucida Sans.

As we've seen, I also use a "handwritten" typeface for chart callouts such as the purple ones that occur throughout this book (that typeface is called "Segoe Print"). I use that very distinct typeface for comments to make them obviously distinct from the chart itself. There are other ways to make comments visually distinct; the point is that it's important that the audience is able to immediately tell the difference between the chart itself and the chart creator's comments *about* the chart.

Choosing text styles

Everyday charts tend to look cleaner when they contain few text styles, a "style" being size, color, bolding, italicization, etc. In most cases, two to four styles of a single typeface should do it:

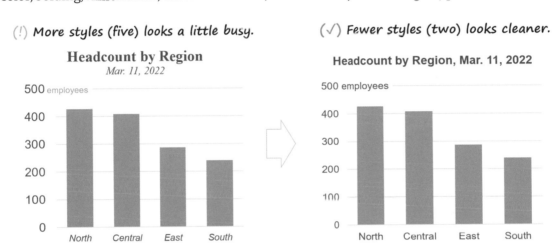

We should also be sure that all text in our charts is large enough to be read comfortably by our audience, especially if they might have vision challenges. For the same reason, we should avoid choosing text colors that are similar to the background color on which the text appears, e.g., light gray text on a white background.

Key takeaways: Typefaces and text styles

- For everyday charts, choose a simple, highly legible typeface with monospaced numerals and lining figures, such as Arial, Helvetica, Calibri, Verdana, or Lucida Sans.
- Make comments in charts visually distinct from chart labeling.
- Minimize the number of text styles in a chart (two to four styles is typically plenty).
- Avoid text that's too small to read comfortably by the audience, or that has a color that's too similar to the background color on which the text appears.

Formatting numbers

HIDING DIGITS

When showing numbers with more than four digits, consider hiding digits to give the chart a less cluttered look and make the numbers easier to read. Obviously, **it's crucial to make the fact that digits have been hidden very visually obvious** to avoid the audience seriously misinterpreting the data:

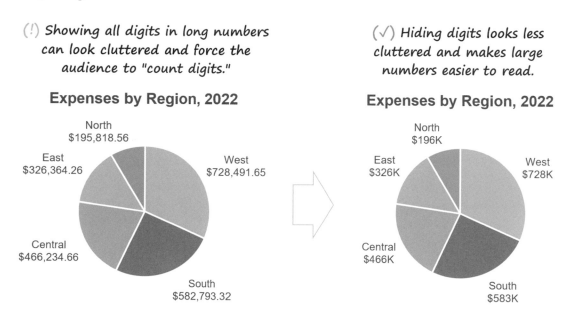

Before hiding digits, we need to make sure that the audience doesn't genuinely need to see all the digits. For example, if some numbers are very close to one another, and the specific job of the chart requires seeing the small differences between them, it might be necessary to show all the digits. Or, if the chart will be submitted to a government authority, we might be legally required to show all the digits. In those cases, we can still keep long numbers out of our graph by moving them to a separate table beside or below the graph, as we saw back in the "Quantitative scales" section.

Note that conventions for abbreviating thousands can vary by region, and even by organization ("K" versus "'000s" versus "M"), and there can also be differences in how millions and billions are abbreviated. If we're not sure what our audience is used to seeing, we'll need to do a bit of research.

SEPARATING DIGITS INTO GROUPS OF THREE

When a chart shows large numbers and we must show all the digits of those numbers, we should insert a "separator" character, such as a comma or space, between each group of three digits to the left of the decimal point to make the large numbers easier to read:

(!) Showing long numbers without separators forces the audience to "count digits."

(√) Adding separators makes numbers easier to read.

	Inhabitants
Country A	5477210
Country B	214185727
Country C	71243105

	Inhabitants
Country A	5,477,210
Country B	214,185,727
Country C	71,243,105

	Inhabitants
Country A	5 477 210
Country B	214 185 727
Country C	71 243 105

Note that audiences in different parts of the world use different characters as separators; some use commas, others use periods, and yet others use spaces. If we're not sure what separator character our target audience is used to seeing, we'll need to do some research beforehand.

Key takeaways: Formatting numbers

- Generally, only show enough digits to support the specific insight or answer that the chart is intended to communicate. If digits are hidden, make this very visually obvious (add "K", "M" "000s", etc.).
- When it's necessary to show numbers with many digits, separate the digits into groups of three to make them easier to read.

Formatting dates

Unfortunately, the date format that audiences find most intuitive varies from one region to the next, and even from one organization to the next, so we might need to do a bit of research to figure out which date format our audience is used to reading. If we're certain that our audience always expects dates to be shown in a specific format, great! We should use that. But if it's less clear, we might need to make an educated guess. When making educated guesses, I favor date formats that:

- Show months as alphabetic characters (e.g., "Aug" or "August") rather than month numbers (e.g., "08") because:
  a. Most audiences find month names more intuitive than month numbers.
  b. The audience can immediately tell which characters in a date represent the month, as opposed the day or year (which are always numbers, not alphabetic characters).

- Show years as four digits rather than two because this makes it immediately clear which part of a date is the year. For example, "22" could be either the 22nd day of the month or the year 2022, but "2022" is clearly the year.

(!) May be ambiguous or misinterpreted	(✓) Likely to be interpreted easily and correctly
10-Feb-07	10-Feb-2007
10-02-2007	Feb.10, 2007
20070210	2007-Feb-10
02/10/07	February 10, 2007

When we're showing a *column* of dates, there are some additional considerations that narrow our date format choices. In order for a column of dates to be read quickly and easily:

- The day of the month should always have two digits, with a zero added if the day only has one digit, e.g., "2" becomes "02."

- The month should always have the same number of characters (usually, three alphabetic characters).

- The year should always have the same number of digits (ideally, four).

The reason that these additional criteria apply when choosing a date format for a column of dates is that, if we choose a date format that meets all of them, our column of dates will be easy to read because the days, months, and years will "line up" vertically:

(!) Days, months and years don't line up vertically (a bit harder to read).		(✓) Days, months, and years line up vertically (easier to read).
October 23, 2021	Saturday, October 23, 2021	23-Oct-2021
December 2, 2021	Thursday, December 2, 2021	02-Dec-2021
December 16, 2021	Thursday, December 16, 2021	16-Dec-2021
January 14, 2022	Friday, January 14, 2022	14-Jan-2022
February 10, 2022	Thursday, February 10, 2022	10-Feb-2022
March 11, 2022	Friday, March 11, 2022	11-Mar-2022
April 30, 2022	Saturday, April 30, 2022	30-Apr-2022

Eagle-eyed readers may have noticed that the years in the right-most column above don't line up *perfectly*. This is because the typeface that I used (Arial) has monospaced *numerals*, but its *alpha-*

betic characters have variable widths (e.g., the "i" is narrower than the "w"), so the three-letter months are slightly different widths. To my eye, this isn't the end of the world, but, if we want everything to line up *perfectly,* we'd need to switch to one of the few fully monospaced typefaces such as Courier New, Lucida Sans Typewriter, or Cascadia, which have monospaced numbers *and* monospaced alphabetic characters:

```
23-Oct-2021
02-Dec-2021
16-Dec-2021
14-Jan-2022
10-Feb-2022
11-Mar-2022
30-Apr-2022
02-May-2022
```

In a column of dates in a fully monospaced typeface (Cascadia), the days, months, and years line up perfectly but the typeface looks a little "computer-y."

The tradeoff is that fully monospaced typefaces are generally designed for technical applications like writing code, so they tend to look kind of computer-y and are slightly less comfortable to read. I'll leave it to you to pick your poison.

Note that, when it comes to formatting date labels on scales in graphs, as we saw back in our discussion of time scales, I favor "multi-level" time scales. In multi-level time scales, the days, months, years, etc., are "split up," so most of these date format guidelines don't apply, and we have more options when choosing typefaces.

Key takeaways: Formatting dates

- If the audience is used to a certain date format, use it.
- When selecting a date format, favor formats that show months as alphabetic characters and years as four digits.
- When showing a column of dates, favor date formats in which the days, months, and years always have the same number of characters.

Like I said, nothing rocket science-y in this chapter, just a few tips to help avoid the most common number, date, and text formatting problems in charts. As usual, let's recap what we've learned in a…

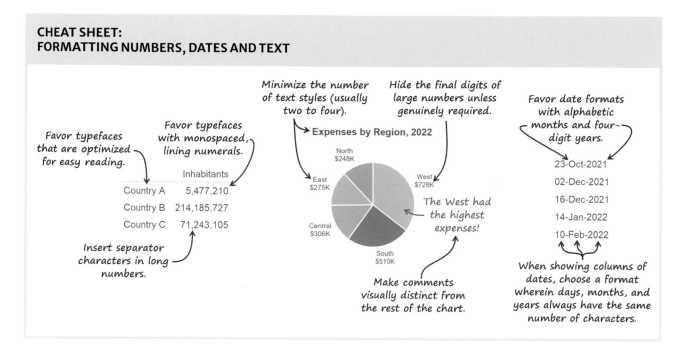

**CHEAT SHEET:
FORMATTING NUMBERS, DATES AND TEXT**

Favor typefaces that are optimized for easy reading.

Favor typefaces with monospaced, lining numerals.

Insert separator characters in long numbers.

Minimize the number of text styles (usually two to four).

Hide the final digits of large numbers unless genuinely required.

Favor date formats with alphabetic months and four-digit years.

Make comments visually distinct from the rest of the chart.

The West had the highest expenses!

When showing columns of dates, choose a format wherein days, months, and years always have the same number of characters.

A final word about general chart formatting guidelines

I hope it's now obvious that the general formatting guidelines in this part of the book are anything but "just cosmetic." Especially when it comes to things like quantitative scales and color palettes, poor formatting choices can—and often do—confuse audiences or fundamentally misrepresent the data in charts.

Having said that, poor formatting choices *also* reliably produce fugly charts:

(!) *Charts with poor formatting choices look unprofessional and are unpleasant to read.*

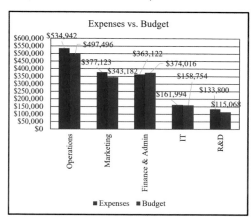

(✓) *Charts with good formatting choices are "non-ugly," look professional, and are easy to read.*

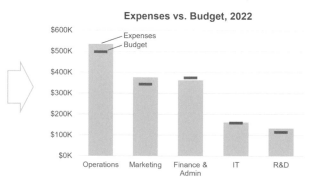

Poorly formatted charts like the previous one on the left are more than just ugly; they can cause credibility problems. When an audience sees a chart like that, they may think to themselves, "Whoever created this chart clearly knows nothing about designing charts, so what *other* skills are they lacking? Was the data handled correctly? Should I even trust this chart?"

Charts don't need to be beautiful in order to be credible, however. When it comes to everyday charts (as opposed to infographics or data art), just creating charts that are "non-ugly" is plenty good enough. By following the formatting guidelines in this part of the book, anyone can create non-ugly charts—no artistic talent required, which is good news for people like me:

Finally, a quick reminder that, as I mentioned at the beginning of this part of the book, there are other important formatting guidelines that we didn't see in this part because they're specific to particular chart types (bar charts, line charts, maps, etc.). We'll see those in "Part 2: Choosing a chart type," which, happily, is coming up next.

PART

2

Choosing a chart type

In this part of the book, we'll see 30 chart types that are regularly needed when creating everyday charts, i.e., the "vocabulary" of dataviz. If you look at the page counts in the table of contents of this book, you'll see that this is, by far, the longest part of the book. Why are we going to spend so much time talking about how to choose a chart type? A few reasons:

1. *To create effective everyday charts, we need to know about a surprisingly wide variety of chart types.*

2. *Choosing a chart type is a lot trickier than most chart creators realize.*

3. *Chart creators frequently make poor chart type choices, making charts unobvious, confusing, or misleading.*

Let's kick off this part of the book with a closer look at each of these reasons.

WHY ARE WE GOING TO SPEND SO MUCH TIME ON CHOOSING A CHART TYPE?

Let's start with…

1. To create effective everyday charts, we need to know about a surprisingly wide variety of chart types.

When writing this book, I cut all the chart types that, in my experience, aren't regularly needed for everyday charts, and there were about 30 left. Will you need all of those chart types in your day-to-day work? Well, once we've learned when each type is needed, yes, I suspect that you *will* use most of them regularly. Will your audiences be familiar with all of these chart types? No, there will probably be a few that will be new to them, but, as we'll see, those chart types are needed to show certain types of data accurately, and using a more familiar chart type in those situations would misrepresent the data. Not to worry, though, because I'll provide helpful tips for quickly and easily teaching audiences how to read chart types that might be new to them.

What if you only need a small number of different chart types for your particular work? Well, that's like saying, "I only need a small number of words when I speak." If we always use the same small handful of words, we'll be hard to understand, and miscommunications will abound. The same thing applies to charts: Always using the same small handful of chart types will make our charts hard to understand and will vastly increase the risk of accidentally misleading our audience.

Note that I'm not saying that we should use a wide variety of different chart types to make our reports or presentations more interesting. Randomizing chart types to "spice things up" is *not* a good way to get audiences more interested in our charts and will almost certainly result in charts that are harder to read or that pose a higher risk of misrepresenting the data. As we'll see in "Part 6: Making charts less boring" later in the book, there are much more effective ways to get our audiences interested in our charts.

Also, note that there are hundreds of other useful chart types beyond the ones that we'll see in this book, but they generally aren't needed for everyday charts and are only needed in advanced data analysis, data art, or in specialized domains such as mineral exploration or genomics.

2. Choosing a chart type is a lot trickier than most chart creators realize.

As we'll see, it's not unusual to have to take 5, 6, or even 10 factors into account when choosing a chart type. Many chart creators aren't aware of this complexity, however, and assume that chart-choosing guidelines are as simple as, for example, "Always use a line chart to show data over time," or "Always use a pie chart to show the breakdown of a total." As we'll see, there are many situations in which simple guidelines like those result in obviously bad chart type choices. I've tried to keep the chart-choosing guidelines in this section as simple as possible, but the bottom line is that choosing a chart type is always a multi-factor decision that can't be usefully summarized in simple, single-sentence rules.

The fact that most chart creators underestimate how tricky it is to choose a chart type probably explains why…

3. Chart creators frequently make poor chart type choices.

Unfortunately, after reading this book, you'll notice poor chart type choices all over the place. Again, sorry about that. Making a poor chart type choice is like using the wrong word in a door knob, though: There's a good chance that the audience will be left confused or misled.

> **Key takeaways: Choosing a chart type**
>
> - About 30 chart types are needed regularly when creating everyday charts.
> - Most chart creators don't realize how tricky and multi-factored choosing a chart type is, so they routinely make poor chart type choices.
> - A poor chart type choice will leave audiences confused or misled.

The 30 or so chart types that we'll see in this book can be organized into the eight groups listed below. (Don't worry if you're not sure what some of these group names mean; this is just a preview of what we'll see in this part of the book.)

Line charts and other chart types for showing *data over time*

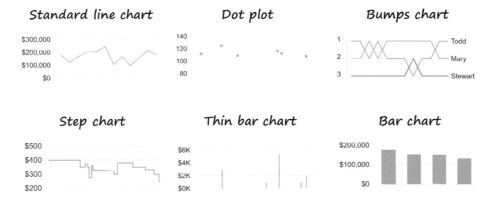

Chart types for showing *change between two time periods*

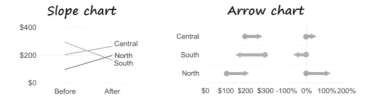

Note that the "showing data over time" group of chart types is special because, as we'll see on the next two pages, there are *additional* time-related chart types in other chart type groups.

Pie charts and other chart types for showing the *breakdown of a total (or totals)*

Single totals

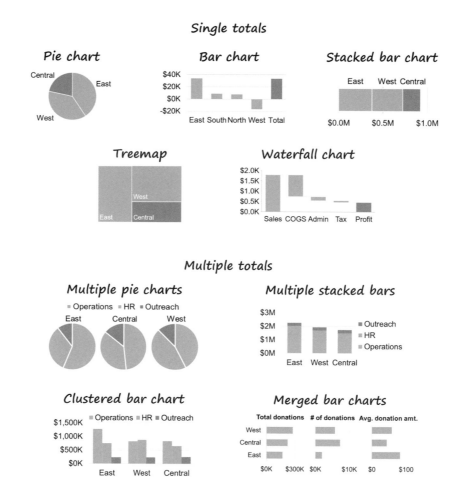

Multiple totals

Chart types for showing breakdowns of totals *changing over time*

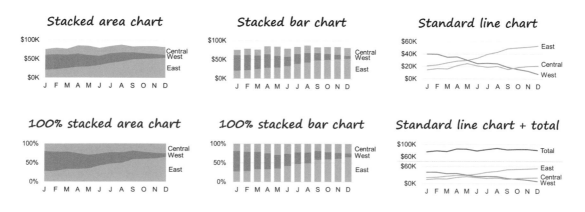

Maps

Choropleth map

Colored dots on map

Tile map

Bubbles on map

Bars on map

Bar chart

West
South
East
North

0K   5K   10K   15K

Maps for showing *values changing over time*

Lines on map

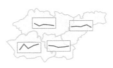

Bar charts

Bar chart

$200,000

$100,000

$0

Stacked bar chart

East   West Central

$0.0M $0.5M $1.0M

Clustered bar chart

■ Operations ■ HR ■ Outreach

$1,500K
$1,000K
$500K
$0K

East   West   Central

Merged bar charts

Total donations   # of donations Avg. donation amt.

West
Central
East

$0K $300K $0K $10K $0 $100

Tables

Table

Monthly Sales by Salesperson

	Jan	Feb	Mar
Joe P.	$553K	$473K	$490K
Lisa Q.	$489K	$401K	$521K
Kim J.	$459K	$422K	$482K

Table with graphical elements

Monthly Sales by Salesperson

	Jan	Feb	Mar
Joe P.	$553K	$473K	$490K
Lisa Q.	$489K	$401K	$521K
Kim J.	$459K	$422K	$482K

We'll end this part of the book with a short discussion of combo charts (charts that combine two or more different types in the same chart) and about a dozen chart types that I recommend avoiding when creating everyday charts.

The first step in choosing a chart type is to figure out which of these groups our chart will fall into. This is usually pretty obvious once we understand what all of these groups are. After that, figuring out which chart type to use *within* a group is considerably more involved.

Let's start with…

Chapter 6

Line charts and other ways to show data over time

Really? Do we really need an entire chapter (and a pretty long one, at that) about one of the simplest, most common chart types? How many ways can there be to screw up a line chart?

WELL, AS WE'LL see, quite a few. A surprising number of line charts that I see "in the wild" fail to make key insights obvious or—worse—misrepresent the underlying data; they're actually one of the *hardest* chart types to design effectively.

The first, perhaps surprising, thing that we're going to learn about line charts is that there's a variety of different *types* of charts for showing data over time beyond "standard" line charts, so let's talk about…

ESSENTIAL CHART TYPES FOR SHOWING DATA OVER TIME

Each of these chart types is the best way—or, in certain cases, the **only** way—to represent a given series of values over time (a "time series") accurately:

Standard line chart

For showing patterns of change in summary values that occur at regular intervals of time

Dot plot

For showing time series that are missing many values

Bumps chart

For showing changes in rank among values that occur at regular intervals of time

Step chart

For showing *persistent* values that occur at irregular intervals of time

Thin bar chart

For showing individual (not summarized) values that occur at irregular intervals of time

Bar chart

For drawing attention to individual time periods when showing values that occur at regular intervals of time

Many chart creators aren't aware of these different types of charts for showing data over time and always use "standard" line charts (the first type in the above examples). Although standard line charts are often the best choice, we'll see many situations in this chapter in which they *can't* represent the data accurately and a less common type of time series chart *must* be used. I want to be clear that I'm not saying that using a standard line chart in those situations would be "less clear" or "not ideal," I'm saying that it **could seriously misrepresent the data**. Many chart creators are unaware of this, however, and I regularly see standard line charts that misrepresent data because a different chart type should have been used in that situation.

If you're unfamiliar with some of these chart types, don't sweat it; we're going to learn about all of them in this chapter, as well as ways to quickly educate our audience when we end up needing to use a chart type that may be unfamiliar to them.

Underneath each chart type example above, I mentioned the type of time series data that that chart type is designed to show. (Don't worry if you're not sure what those types of time series data are; we're going to see examples of all of them in this chapter.) As you can see, different types of time series data require different types of charts, so, in order to determine which type of time series chart to use, we need to be able to recognize which type of time series data we're dealing with.

This also means that, unlike most other chart design decisions that we'll see in this book, choosing a chart type for showing time series data is based mostly on the *nature of the data to be shown*. The specific job of the chart is a consideration, but it's not the *main* consideration when choosing a chart type to show data over time.

Although figuring out which type of time series data we're dealing with isn't rocket science, it can get a bit technical. Happily, there's a cheat sheet at the end of this section with a handy decision tree that summarizes exactly how to determine what type of time series data we're dealing with. Here's a preview of that decision tree, but don't worry if you're not sure what some parts mean; it will be much easier to understand and use after you've read this chapter:

DECISION TREE:
CHOOSING A CHART TYPE TO SHOW DATA OVER TIME

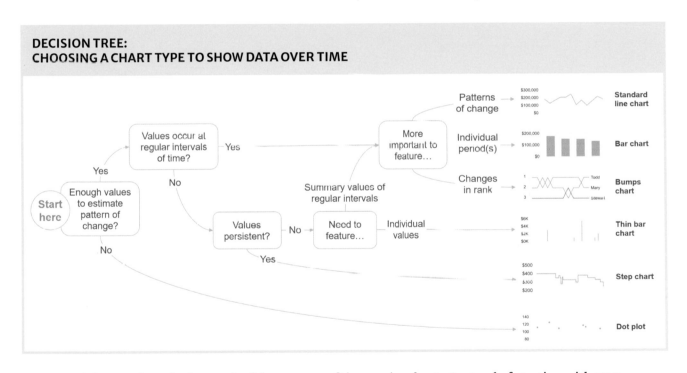

Let's have a closer look at each of these types of time series charts. Instead of starting with standard line charts, I want to start with dot plots, for reasons that will become clear in a moment.

Dot plots

Our organization has experienced a serious server failure, resulting in the loss of our "Expenses" data for all but 6 of the last 31 days. As a result of this data loss, a standard line chart of the last 31 days of daily expenses now looks like this:

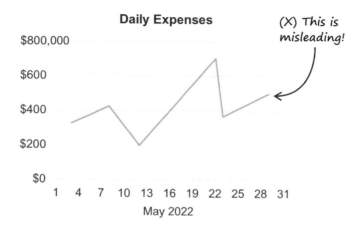

The line in this chart shows a pattern of change, but we don't really know what the pattern of change was because we're missing so many values (values for 25 of the 31 days are missing). If we had values for *all* the days, the pattern of change might have looked like any of these, or innumerable other possible patterns:

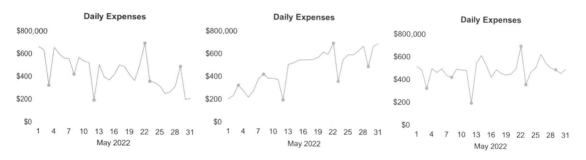

Connecting the points that we have in a standard line chart *did* show a pattern of change, however, even though we didn't have enough data to know what the pattern of change actually was. This is why I'd say that **using a standard line chart in this situation would be a mistake**, i.e., a design choice that poses a high risk of fundamentally misrepresenting the data. If we don't have enough values to know what the actual pattern of change was, the only safe way to show a time series is to remove the lines and leave only dot markers for the values that we *do* know, which gives us a "dot plot":

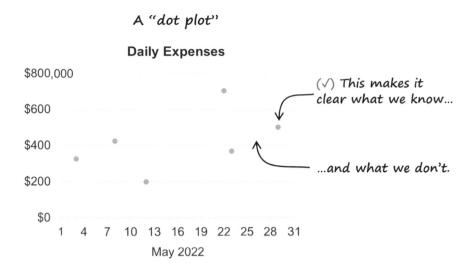

For those who are concerned about using a dot plot because it might be unfamiliar to their audience, I'll provide some tips shortly for quickly and easily teaching audiences how to read chart types that might be unfamiliar to them.

If you're not sure how to create a dot plot or any other chart type that I mention using your dataviz software product (Microsoft Excel, Tableau Desktop, etc.), just Google "how to create a dot plot in [name of your software product]," and you'll find many decent tutorial videos or articles.

Key takeaway: Dot plots

- When there are many missing values in a time series, a dot plot should be used because using a standard line chart (or any other chart type) in that situation can misrepresent the data by showing a pattern of change when there isn't enough data to know what the pattern of change was.

If we do have enough values to know (or, at least, confidently estimate) the true pattern of change in a time series, which chart type should you use? The most common choice will be...

Standard line charts

For example:

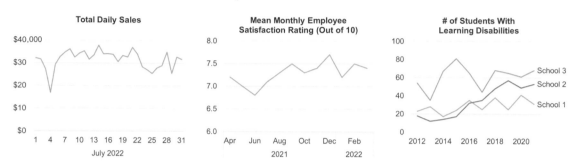

This chart type is so common that people usually just refer to it as a "line chart." To distinguish it from the other types of line charts that we'll see in this chapter, however, I'm going to call it a "standard line chart."

A standard line chart should only be used to show values that represent regular intervals of time (days, weeks, months, etc.), with exactly one value for each interval, for example:

- Daily revenue totals

- Weekly average employee satisfaction ratings

- Monthly median transaction values

In each of these examples, each regular interval of time (each day/week/month/etc.) is represented by exactly one value per interval (one value per day, one value per week, etc.). This is important because using a standard line chart with a time series that *doesn't* consist of one value per regular interval of time can be unclear or, worse, misleading, as we'll see shortly.

> **Key takeaways: Standard line charts**
>
> - Standard line charts should only be used to show values that represent regular intervals of time with exactly one value per time interval.
> - Don't use a standard line chart unless there are enough values to know the pattern of change. If there aren't enough values, use a dot plot instead.

Although standard line charts should only be used to show values that represent regular intervals of time, that doesn't mean that they're the *only* way to show that type of time series data. Two important alternatives to standard line charts are bar charts and *bumps charts* so let's have a look at those, starting with…

Bar charts (for showing data over time)

You've almost certainly seen data over time shown as a bar chart before:

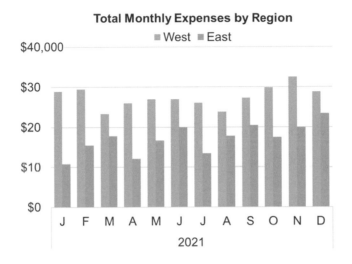

Generally, there's no problem with showing data over time as bars, as long as each bar represents a regular interval of time (a day, a month, etc.), as with standard line charts. A standard line chart, however, makes patterns of change, such as spikes, dips, and cycles, a bit more obvious than bars do:

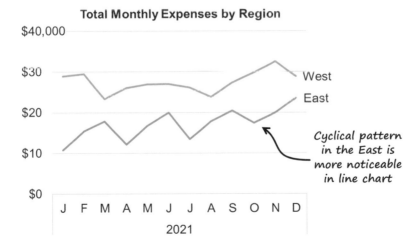

As we can see in the line chart above, patterns of change such as the cyclical quarterly pattern in the East region are more obvious than in the original bar chart version, which begs the question: Why would we ever use bars to show time series data if lines make patterns of change clearer?

Well, **bars are a better choice if we want the audience to focus on individual time periods rather than the overall pattern of change.** For example, if we wanted to illustrate an insight such as "October donations were under $160K (20% lower than September)" in the chart below, a bar chart will make that insight a bit more obvious:

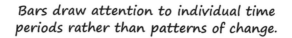

Bars draw attention to individual time periods rather than patterns of change.

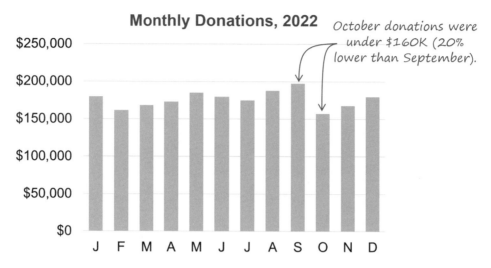

Bars would be a better choice in this situation because bars prompt the audience to focus in on *individual time periods* (which this insight is about) rather than the overall pattern of change (which isn't even mentioned in this insight). Admittedly, this is a subtle difference, and using a standard line chart to communicate this kind of insight wouldn't be "wrong" because the audience could still compare individual periods relatively easily.

Key takeaways: Using bar charts to show values over time

- Consider using a bar chart rather than a standard line chart when the audience should focus on individual time periods, rather than overall patterns of change.
- When showing data over time, it's more common to want the audience to focus on patterns of change rather than individual time periods, so lines are often a better choice than bars to show values that represent regular intervals of time.
- Only use bar charts with time series data that consists of values that represent regular intervals of time, such daily revenue totals, average monthly customer satisfaction, etc.

Now that we know when to use bar charts instead of standard line charts to show time series data, let's look at the other important alternative to standard line charts, that is…

Bumps charts

> What the # $ *% is a bumps chart?

Bumps charts are a less common chart type and may be unfamiliar to many audiences. As we'll see, though, there are certain types of insights that are far more obvious in bumps charts than in standard line charts, for example…

Let's say we needed to show that, in terms of medal count, the Netherlands lost ground to other countries during the Olympics. If we were to show the medal counts over time as a standard line chart, we'd get this:

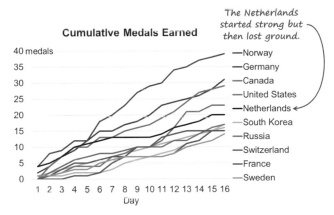

Does it look like the Netherlands "lost ground" in this chart? Not really. In fact, it looks like the Netherlands *went up*. Yes, the audience might, with a certain amount of effort, realize that the Netherlands actually lost ground relative to other countries, but that's not visually obvious at all. This chart would be fine if we wanted to say something about the number of medals each country won throughout the Olympics, but that's not the insight that we needed to communicate in this scenario.

We could, instead, show this data in a *bumps chart* that features changes in *rank*, rather than changes in quantity:

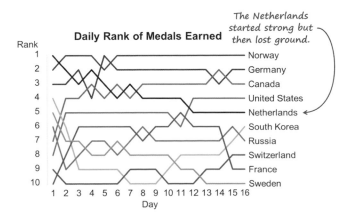

Instead of showing the actual number of medals that each country won, this bumps chart shows how each country's rank changed over time (based on medal count). The fact that the Netherlands lost ground relative to other countries is now far more visually obvious than it was in the standard line chart.

> **Key takeaways: Bumps charts**
>
> • If the insight to be communicated is more about changes in rank than changes in quantity, consider using a bumps chart instead of a standard line chart.
> • Only consider using a bumps chart for values that represent regular intervals of time.

When I show bumps charts in training workshops, participants regularly tell me that they'd hesitate to use them in practice because their audience isn't familiar with them. That's a completely legitimate concern; there's no point in showing an audience a chart that they won't understand. It's also a real problem, though, because the more familiar chart type that the audience would understand in this scenario (i.e., a standard line chart) doesn't communicate the insight that the audience needs to know (i.e., that the Netherlands lost ground to other countries). What to do?

In practice, it happens fairly often that familiar chart types *can't* say what we need to say about the data, and we *must* use a less familiar chart type. In these situations, I use several tricks to help audiences quickly and easily grasp new chart types. These tricks aren't specific to showing data over time and so are a bit of a tangent, so let's learn about them in a…

> **Sidebar: Explaining unfamiliar chart types to audiences**
>
> As a general rule, we should use familiar chart types and techniques whenever possible. Audiences for everyday charts almost always just want information and don't want to learn how to read new chart types. If we can avoid asking them to learn how to read a new chart type, then, that's generally a win. Indeed, some audiences may even get annoyed if we show them a chart type that's not familiar to them.
>
> Does this mean that we should never show potentially unfamiliar chart types to an audience? No. As we just saw, there are situations in which familiar chart types *can't* communicate what the audience needs to know about the data. **Showing a chart that's familiar to the audience but that doesn't actually communicate what they need to know about the data is a waste of everyone's time**, so, in those situations, we pretty much *have* to show them an unfamiliar chart type.
>
> There are tricks, however, that we can use to help audiences quickly and easily grasp potentially unfamiliar charts types. Three tricks that I often use are…

1. **Reveal the elements in the unfamiliar chart type one at a time** to build up an understanding of the chart in the mind of the audience in *steps*. For example, we could explain a bumps chart to an audience in steps, like this:

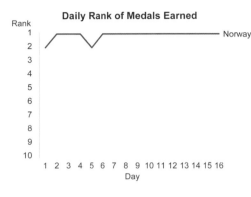

"This tells us that Norway had the highest medal count for most of the Olympics, only dropping to second place twice."

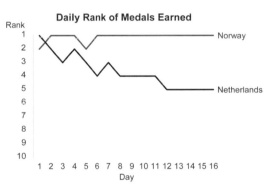

"This tells us that the Netherlands started off with the most medals, but then was overtaken by other countries and dropped down in the standings."

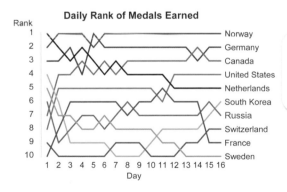

"When we add in the rest of the countries, we can see how their *rank* changed throughout the Olympics."

I call this the **"gentle reveal"** trick.

2. **Start by showing the familiar-but-uninformative chart**, then explain why it's not telling the audience what they need to know. Then, reveal the unfamiliar—but more informative—chart. For example:

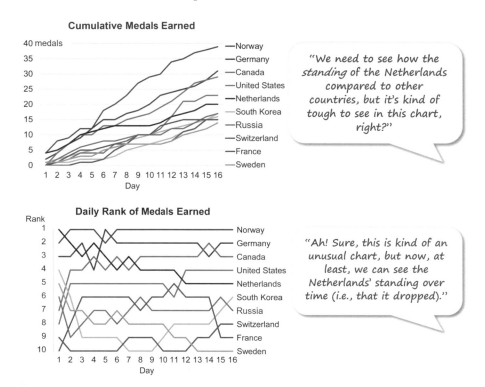

I call this the **"bait-and-switch" trick**. (I used this trick to introduce bumps charts to you at the beginning of this section.)

3. **Include a few "duh insights."** When we're not in a position to explain to an audience how to read a potentially unfamiliar chart (e.g., when the chart is in a report that the audience will read on their own), we can include a few of what I call "duh insights":

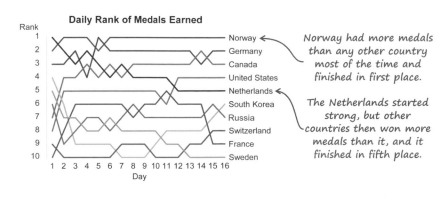

"Duh insights" are insights that would be very obvious to anyone who already knows how to read that chart type (hence the "duh") but that are very helpful to readers who aren't familiar with that chart type and who must figure out how to read it on their own.

> ### Key takeaways: Teaching audiences to read unfamiliar chart types
>
> - When creating everyday charts, whenever possible, try to stick to chart types and techniques that are familiar to the audience. Sometimes, however, familiar chart types can't communicate what the audience needs to know about the data, so a chart type that's unfamiliar to the audience must be used.
> - When introducing a chart type that's unfamiliar to the audience, use the "gentle reveal," "bait-and-switch," and/or "duh insights" tricks to quickly teach the audience how to read the unfamiliar chart type.

Alright, let's get back to looking at different chart types for showing data over time, the next one being...

Step charts

For example...

Examples of step charts

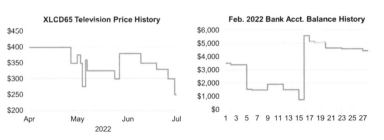

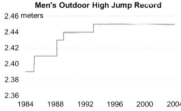

Why did I decide to use a step chart (also called a "stepped line chart") in the scenarios above? Two reasons:

First, unlike the time series that we've seen so far in this chapter, the values in the time series in these scenarios occur at irregular intervals of time. For example, the price of the TV in the first scenario can change five times in one day and then stay the same for three weeks.

Second, unlike the daily/weekly/monthly/etc. values that we saw earlier, the price of a TV *remains in effect* until the next value occurs. For example, if the price of a TV increases from $380 to $400, the new price of $400 remains in effect until the next price change occurs. This is why I call it a "persistent" time series. Persistent time series data is different than something like a "daily sales total" time series, in which, if the daily sales total for one day is $104,762, that value doesn't "persist" into the following day if there's no value for the following day.

Irregular, persistent time series are actually fairly common, and include...

- The inventory level of a product
- The current highest bid on an auction item
- A bank's prime lending rate
- A bank account balance

Step charts show irregular, persistent time series correctly:

If we were to show an irregular, persistent time series as a standard line chart, it would have several problems:

One problem with this standard line chart is that it makes it look like there was a price at the beginning of April ($400) and then nothing until the end of April when the price was $350. That's not what happened, however. This TV *did* have a price between the beginning of April and the end of April: It was $400 the whole time. Indeed, this TV had a price continuously throughout the entire period shown, but that's not what the standard line chart suggests.

For the above reason alone, a standard line chart shouldn't be used for irregular, persistent time series, but there's another problem with using a standard line chart for this kind of data: I've seen readers with less chart-reading experience interpret a chart like the one above to mean that, for example, the price of the TV *steadily declined* from $400 at the beginning of April to $350 at the end of April. That, for example, the price in mid-April was around $375. But it wasn't; it was $400 in mid-April. The step chart shows that correctly, but a standard line chart doesn't.

Key takeaways: Step charts

- Consider using a step chart to show irregular, persistent time series values.
- Avoid using standard line charts to show irregular, persistent time series values.

When I show step charts in my training workshops, participants sometimes object that their audience is unfamiliar with them and may get confused when they see them. If you have that same concern, you can use the "gentle reveal," "bait-and-switch," or "duh insights" tricks that we saw earlier to explain step charts (or any other chart type). In situations when we need to use a step chart or any other chart type that we know or suspect is unfamiliar to the audience, though, we should ask ourselves if we absolutely have to show a chart in the first place. This is an important point but a bit of a tangent, so let's tackle it in another...

Sidebar: We don't always need to show a chart

When presenting insights that are based on data, we often automatically assume that we *must* present a chart of that data to the audience. However, if we just need to communicate that, for example, the price of the XLCD65 TV dropped from $400 in April to $250 in July, we don't actually *need* a chart to say that; a bullet point or two would do it:

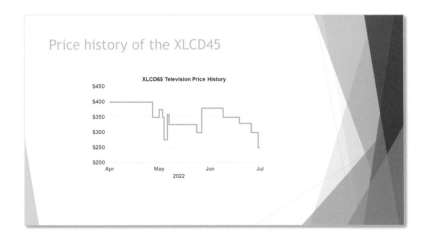

If communicating a given insight would require showing a potentially unfamiliar chart type...

...consider just showing the insight as prose (text) instead.

Price history of the XLCD45

▸ Was at $400 in April, then dropped to $250 by July.

In these situations, we should probably have a chart in our back pocket, perhaps on a hidden slide or as a report appendix that can be shown if the audience asks for more detail or supporting evidence. If the audience doesn't need that detail, however, we can save them time and cognitive effort by presenting the insights as text—especially if showing the insight as a chart would require us to explain an unfamiliar chart type.

Key takeaways: Communicating insights in prose instead of charts

- When an unfamiliar or complex chart would be needed to communicate an insight, consider communicating the insight as text instead (if the insight can be communicated adequately in a small number of words).
- Have charts available as optional resources (hidden slides, report appendices, etc.) in case the audience requests more detail.

Let's look at the final important chart type for showing data over time, that is...

"Thin bar" charts

For example:

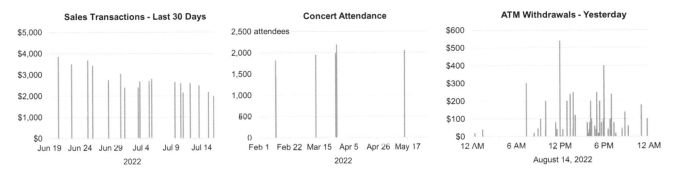

Examples of thin bar charts

Why did I choose to show the time series above as thin bar charts? Two reasons:

1. Like the type of time series that we saw previously for step charts, the values in these charts occur at irregular intervals of time.

2. *Unlike* the time series that we just saw for step charts, the values in these charts aren't persistent. In the first chart above on the left, for example, when a sales transaction occurs, the value of that transaction doesn't persist until the next sales transaction occurs. There's just a sales transaction that takes place at a single point in time, and then nothing until the next sales transaction occurs.

If we use a standard line chart to show an irregular, non-persistent time series like this, it's confusing at best, misleading at worst:

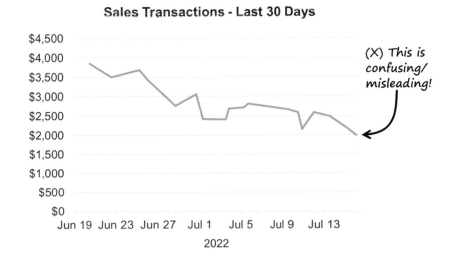

As a standard line chart, it looks like sales are declining. If, however, we summarize (a.k.a. "aggregate") the individual sales transactions into weekly sales totals, we see that the overall trend of sales is actually *increasing*:

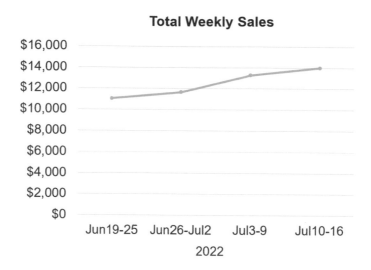

This is why we don't usually see time series such as individual sales transactions shown as a thin bar chart. Instead, the individual values are usually summarized into regular intervals of time (daily totals, weekly averages, etc.), and those summary values are shown as a standard line chart that makes it much easier to see patterns of change accurately.

Sometimes, however, individual values *do* need to be shown instead of daily/weekly/etc. summary values. For example, maybe we need to show attendee counts at a series of concerts that occurred at irregular intervals of time. Summarizing those values into weekly/monthly/etc. averages or totals would hide the attendee counts for individual concerts. In that case, then, we should use a thin bar chart:

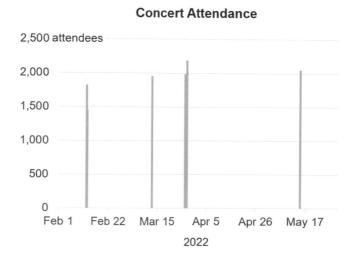

Key takeaways: Thin bar charts

- Consider using a thin bar chart to show irregular, non-persistent time series when it's necessary to show individual (not summary) values.
- Avoid using a standard line chart to show irregular, non-persistent time series.

> Wow. That's a lot of chart types and factors to consider. How do I choose a chart type for showing data over time in practice?

That's where this handy-dandy decision tree comes in, which summarizes all of the key take-aways that we saw in this section, to quickly guide us to an expert-level chart type choice:

DECISION TREE:
CHOOSING A CHART TYPE TO SHOW DATA OVER TIME

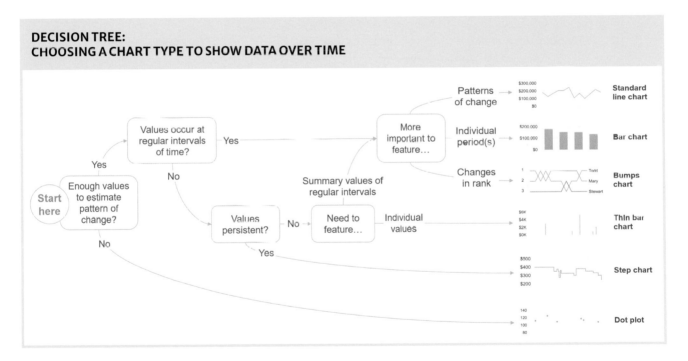

Note that this decision tree only applies to time series that…

- Contain more than two time periods and…
- Don't represent the breakdown of a total changing over time.

We'll address both of those situations in the next sections.

Yeah, I know, we've spent a lot of time talking about showing data over time, but we're not done with it yet! There are several important additional types of time-related charts that we'll see later in the book:

Charts for showing change between just two time periods (in the next section):

Time will also come back to haunt us in later chapters:

Charts for showing the *breakdown of a total* changing over time in the "Pie charts and other ways to show the breakdown of a total" chapter:

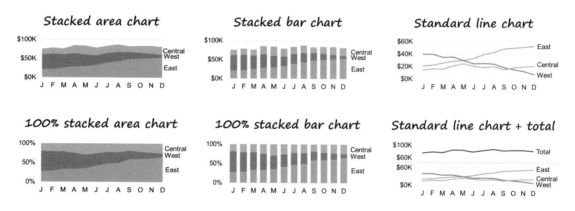

Charts for showing *values with locations* changing over time in the "Maps" chapter:

For now, let's look at…

COMPARING TWO TIME PERIODS

If our time series data contains values for just two time periods (two days, two months, etc.), we can, in theory, use any of the chart types that we've seen so far. In practice, however, I generally use just one chart type in these situations, and it's a type that we haven't seen yet.

"In the wild," the most common way that I see this kind of data shown is as a clustered bar chart:

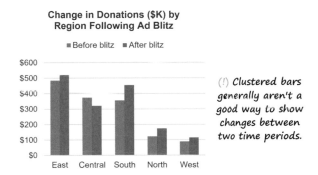

(!) Clustered bars generally aren't a good way to show changes between two time periods.

Generally, this isn't a great way to compare two time periods, however:

- If the chart labels were blurred out, the chart above would just look like five groups of two values, i.e., there's nothing about it that visually suggests values increasing or decreasing over time. As we saw earlier in this chapter, bars prompt the audience to think of values as discrete and independent from one another, not as patterns of change (increases, decreases, etc.). Yes, in a clustered bar chart like this, the audience can figure out that they're looking at changes over time; it's just not immediately obvious.

- A bigger concern is that it's not immediately obvious which categories (e.g., which regions) increased and which ones decreased. Yes, again, the audience will figure it out, but other chart types make increases and decreases more obvious, such as…

Slope charts

A slope chart is just a line chart with two points in time:

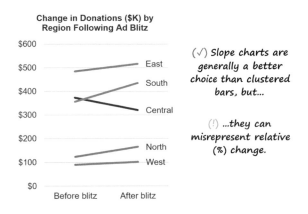

(✓) Slope charts are generally a better choice than clustered bars, but…

(!) …they can misrepresent relative (%) change.

Ah! Now, it's more obvious that we're looking at values that are increasing or decreasing over time. The fact that four of those values increased and one decreased is also a lot more obvious in the slope chart above. (Did you notice that insight in the clustered bar chart?)

Although slope charts are almost always a better choice than clustered bar charts when showing change between two time periods, they have a subtle but very important problem that few chart creators realize: Slope charts make large changes among smaller values look artificially small.

> WTH are you talking about?

For example, in the slope chart we just saw, if I were to ask you which region improved its performance the most, you'd probably say the South region because its line has the steepest upward slope. Yes, the South region *did* improve by about 28% (from $356K to $455K), but the North region improved by 41% (from $123K to $174K)! Uh-oh. For a more detailed discussion of this problem, visit practicalreporting.com/pc-resources and click "The problem with slope charts." The bottom line (pun intended) is that this is a big enough concern that I now avoid using slope charts in most situations. Is there an alternative that doesn't have this perceptual problem? Yes, we could use…

Arrow charts

(✓) Arrow charts can show both absolute and relative change.

Change in Donations by Region Following Ad Blitz

There we go. Now, the audience can see which regions raised the most donations overall (East and South), but, in the right-hand "relative change" chart, the audience can also clearly see that the North region improved its donation performance the most (i.e., *not* the South region).

If the insight that we need to communicate is only about absolute changes (e.g., changes in donation dollars), then the right-hand chart of relative changes isn't necessary. In my experience, however, many audiences don't understand the difference between absolute and relative change unless they see them side by side. For example, if only shown the arrow chart on the left (change in dollars) and asked, "Which region improved its performance the most?" the vast majority of audiences will answer, "The South region," which is *wrong*. Very few will answer "Well, the South region increased the most in absolute terms, but it's not clear which region improved its performance the most in relative terms." In practice, therefore, I almost always include the second chart of relative changes to make sure that the audience doesn't misinterpret the data in the chart.

If the insight to be communicated only concerns relative (percentage) change, however, just showing an arrow chart of percentage changes is unlikely to cause problems.

Arrow charts also have other advantages over slope charts, such as being able to show more categories without turning into a mess of crisscrossing lines and being able to show values that are very close to one another clearly, which can be a challenge in slope charts where the value labels can overlap. Having said that, I would add that there are some relatively rare, special cases in which slope charts can work, such as showing changes in rank between two time periods. However, arrow charts can also be used in most of those cases, as well.

> **Key takeaways: Showing changes between two time periods**
>
> • When showing changes between two time periods, arrow charts are less likely to be misinterpreted than clustered bar charts or slope charts.
> • Avoid showing absolute changes between two time periods without also showing relative (percentage) changes.

Now that we've covered all the major chart types that we're likely to need when showing data over time, let's move on to some important tips for…

FORMATTING LINE CHARTS

First off, a quick reminder that all the formatting guidelines that we saw in "Part 1: General formatting guidelines" (choosing colors, formatting quantitative scales, etc.) apply to line charts, as well as all other chart types. In this section, we'll see a few *additional* formatting guidelines that apply only to line charts and not to other chart types.

Just as with the general formatting guidelines that we learned about earlier, line chart formatting guidelines serve more than just cosmetic purposes because poor line chart formatting choices can—and often do—result in confusing or misleading charts. Let's have a look at a few line charts with common formatting problems and then learn how to avoid those problems. As usual, at the end of this section, the guidelines that we cover will be summarized in a handy one-page cheat sheet.

Have a look at the line chart below. Although it might look fine at first, there's a problem with this chart. It's not obvious, but take a moment and see whether you can spot it (gold star if you can):

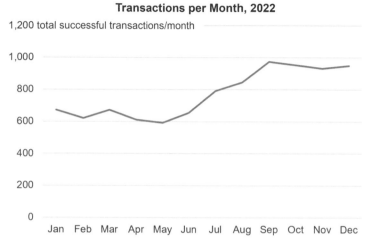

The problem has to do with the value for October, specifically, that the audience has no way of knowing if there actually *is* a value for October. The value for October could happen to be exactly midway between the September and November values, or it could be missing, and the dataviz software that was used to make this chart decided to just directly connect September to November, straight through the missing value in October. If the points on the line are marked off with dots, we can see that that's exactly what happened 😟

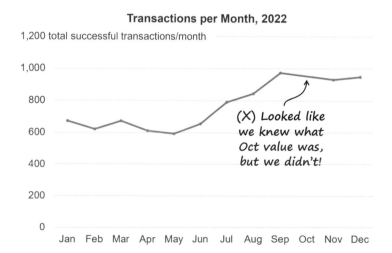

The original chart made it look like we knew what the value was for October, but, in fact, we had no idea what it was:

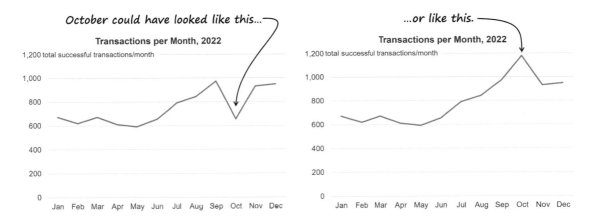

At least the software was smart enough to not do this:

Yes, unfortunately, some dataviz software still treats missing or null values as zero, but **zero isn't the same thing as "missing" or "null."** Zero means that we know what the value was: it was zero.

So how can we avoid misleading the audience when there are missing values in a line chart? One way that I've seen it done is to use dashed or dotted lines, like this:

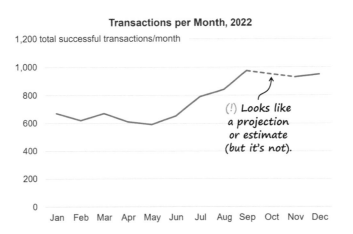

However, dashed or dotted lines usually suggest data of lower certainty, such as estimates or projections, whereas in this scenario, we don't have an estimate for October; we have no idea what it was. Therefore, using a dashed line is misleading because it suggests that we *do* have some idea what the value for October was. A safer way to handle missing values is to simply show them as gaps in the line:

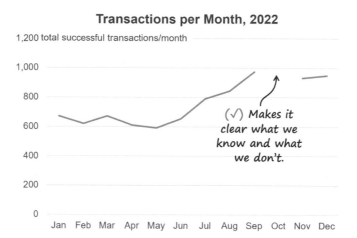

If there are multiple missing values, we can show multiple gaps. If a known value is surrounded by unknown values, we can mark off the points on the line with dot markers so that the known value is visible:

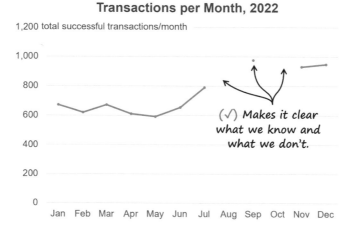

Note that point markers (e.g., dots) on lines are only necessary in relatively rare situations like the one above. Unless there's a specific reason to include them, point markers generally aren't necessary and add a bit of visual clutter. Also note that, if there are a lot of missing values, we should switch from a line chart to a dot plot as we saw in the previous section on choosing chart types for showing time series.

> ### Key takeaways: Handling missing values in line charts
>
> - Don't connect lines through missing values. Show missing values as gaps in lines instead.
> - Reserve dashed or dotted lines for values of lower certainty or importance (estimates, projections, targets, etc.).
> - If a value is surrounded by two missing values, add small point markers to the line.

There are a few other important line chart formatting guidelines to be aware of, so let's look at another scenario. Say we need to show how our organization's headcount has changed in the six regions in which it operates:

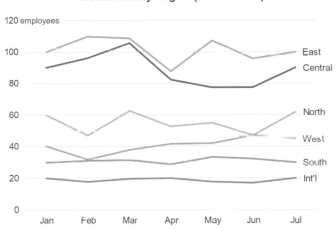

We need to draw attention to the Central region, so we decide to "tone down" the other regions by making their lines gray:

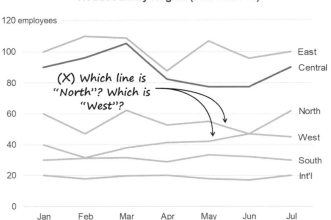

The "Central" line certainly pops out now, but because all the other lines are now gray, it's no longer possible to tell which is which when they cross. This is obviously a major problem. That's the main reason why, as a general rule, **avoid making lines in a line chart the same color**. There are a few exceptions to this guideline, and we'll see those shortly, but, most of the time, making lines the same color is risky.

> ### Key takeaway: Line colors in line charts
>
> • Generally, make lines in line charts different colors.

How could we visually highlight the "Central" line in the chart above in a less problematic way? There are lots of ways to highlight specific parts of a chart that we'll see later in "Part 5: Making charts obvious," but one way would be to make the Central line thicker than the others:

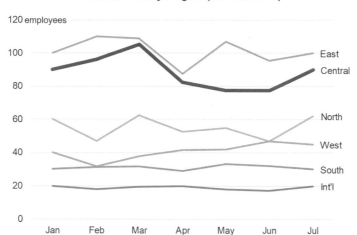

The Central line definitely "pops" now, and we're pretty pleased with this chart so we send it to the boss. We walk by the boss's desk the next day and are delighted to see a printout of our chart lying on their desk. Clearly, they found it to be useful! We're a whole lot less delighted when we see the actual printout, however:

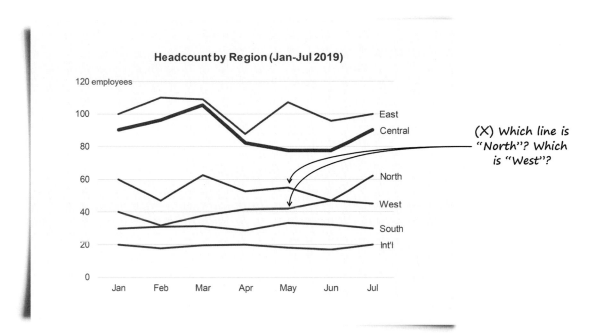

Crap. The printer (or, God forbid, fax machine) that printed our chart flattened all the colors to black, so the "which line is which?" problem is back again. What to do? Well, one common solution is to use different line *styles* to identify each line:

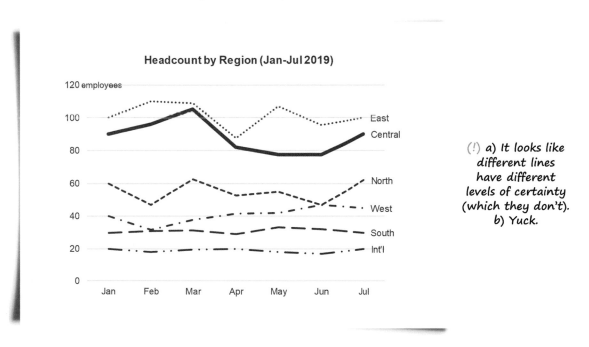

A "less bad" option is to use different marker symbols to identify different lines.

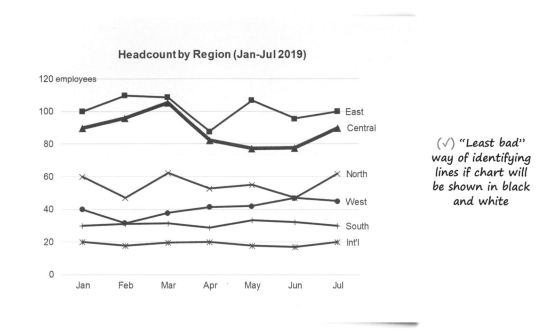

(√) "Least bad" way of identifying lines if chart will be shown in black and white

Definitely not pretty, but this is about as good as we're going to get when there's a risk that our line chart could be reproduced in black and white. If that's not a risk, don't add different marker symbols!

Key takeaway: Adding marker symbols to line charts

- If there's a risk that a chart will be reproduced in black and white, add markers with different symbols to identify lines in a line chart.

As usual, let's recap what we saw in this section with a handy...

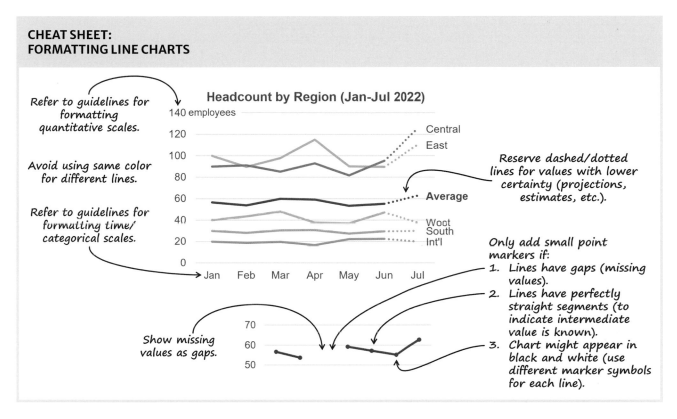

**CHEAT SHEET:
FORMATTING LINE CHARTS**

Refer to guidelines for formatting quantitative scales.

Avoid using same color for different lines.

Refer to guidelines for formatting time/ categorical scales.

Headcount by Region (Jan-Jul 2022)

Reserve dashed/dotted lines for values with lower certainty (projections, estimates, etc.).

Only add small point markers if:
1. Lines have gaps (missing values).
2. Lines have perfectly straight segments (to indicate intermediate value is known).
3. Chart might appear in black and white (use different marker symbols for each line).

Show missing values as gaps.

Believe it or not, we're *still* not done with line charts and showing data over time! There are some common questions about line charts that come up in workshops that we haven't touched on yet, so the final section on line charts is a...

LINE CHART FAQ

What are the common line chart questions that we haven't addressed yet? They are...

- "How many lines can I put in a line chart?"
- "What about vertical line charts? Bad idea?"
- "What about smoothed/curvy lines?"
- "Can I use line charts with scales other than time?"
- "Don't line charts misrepresent data by 'hiding' the values in between points?"

Let's start with...

How many lines can I put in a line chart?

Up to four or five lines is usually fine, i.e., there's little risk of ending up with an overly busy "spaghetti" chart. If we have more than four or five time series to show, the maximum number that can be shown depends on a few things, such as how much the lines intersect with one another:

(✓) If lines don't intersect much, 10+ lines can work, but...

(!) ...if lines intersect a lot, more than four or five lines can look like a "spaghetti chart."

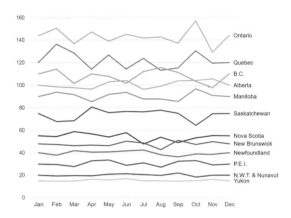

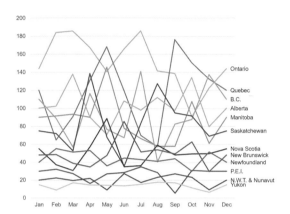

As we can see in the chart on the left, 10 or even more lines can work if the lines don't cross over one another very much and they can be directly labeled. However, if the lines *do* cross over one another a lot, the result is a spaghetti chart like the one on the right, so we need a different solution, such as splitting the lines into separate charts:

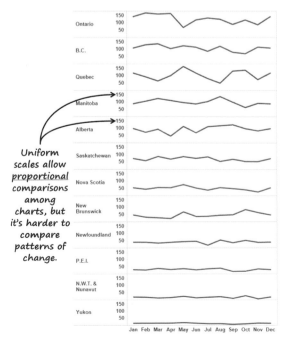

Uniform scales allow _proportional_ comparisons among charts, but it's harder to compare patterns of change.

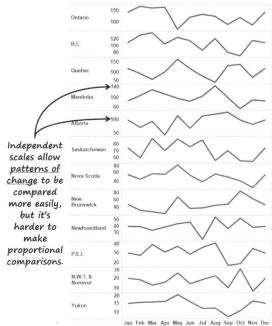

Independent scales allow _patterns of change_ to be compared more easily, but it's harder to make proportional comparisons.

The advantage of this solution is that we can stack 20 or perhaps even 30 line charts like this before things start to become overwhelming. The disadvantage is that it's harder to compare the individual lines with one another. For example, it's now harder to identify the months during which Ontario was higher or lower than Quebec, which would be easy to see if the lines overlapped.

I'm showing two versions of this solution because each makes it easier for the audience to notice different types of insights. The version on the left has *uniform scales*, meaning that each chart has the same scale (0 to 150, in this example). This allows the audience to see that, for instance, Ontario was always much higher than the Yukon. However, it's hard to compare the *patterns of change* of the smaller values (e.g., the Yukon) because they get "crushed" down close to the zero line.

If the insight or answer that we need to communicate is more about comparing patterns of change (spikes, dips, cycles, etc.) than making "proportional" comparisons, we'd want to use the version on the right, which has *independent scales*, meaning that the scale of each chart is different (Ontario is still 0 to 150, but the Yukon is now 0 to 20). This version makes patterns of change much clearer, but the audience can no longer make the "proportional" comparisons that are possible in the version on the left. Once again, the best design choice depends on what, exactly, we need to say about the data. Is our insight more about proportional comparisons or comparing patterns of change?

Let's keep pushing. What if, instead of needing to show data for the 13 Canadian provinces and territories, we needed to show data for 50 U.S. states plus Washington, D.C.? A stack of 51 line charts would probably be overwhelming, but we could use a *heatmap* instead:

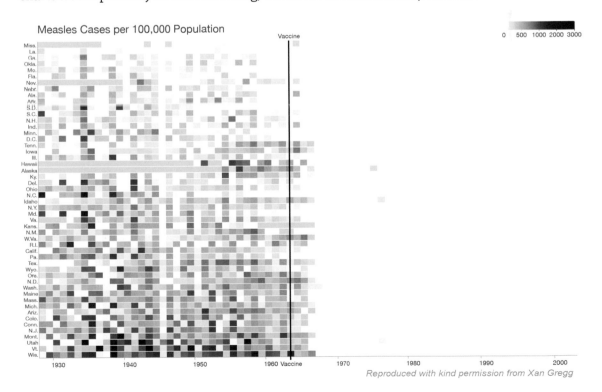

Reproduced with kind permission from Xan Gregg

As we saw earlier, the main advantage of heatmaps is that we can show considerably more values before things start to look overwhelming. However, as in the "stacked line chart" solution that we just saw, it's harder to directly compare one data series to another because the data series don't overlap in a heatmap. There's also the other disadvantage that we saw with heatmaps, which is that we lose precision: The audience can only estimate values in the chart very approximately because trying to match a color in the chart to a color in the legend is tricky. However, we can still show many interesting insights with this heatmap, such as the dramatic drop in measles cases in the years following the introduction of the vaccine.

> **Key takeaway: Showing many lines in a line chart**
>
> • When a regular line chart is too busy looking, consider using stacks of line charts or a heatmap.

What about vertical line charts? Bad idea?

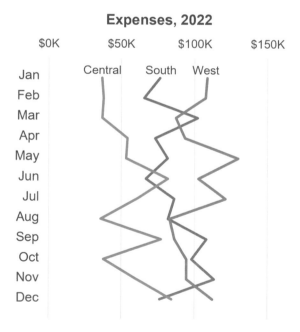

Usually, yes. There are several reasons why most readers find vertical line charts like the one above harder to read than horizontal line charts, but you can probably see for yourself that it's more "cognitively cumbersome" than a horizontal version would be.

There are a few rare situations in which a vertical line chart might be an effective choice, but those situations are unlikely to arise when creating everyday charts, so I don't think it's worth spending time on them in this book. For those who want to go down that particular rabbit hole, visit practicalreporting.com/pc-resources, and click "Are vertical line charts ever a good idea?" for a detailed article on that topic.

Key takeaway: Vertical line charts

- In everyday charts, generally avoid using vertical line charts except in rare special cases.

What about smoothed/curvy lines?

You've probably seen line charts with "smoothed" or "curvy" lines before:

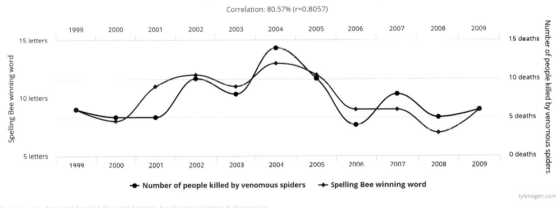

(BTW, this chart is from the Tyler Vigan's "Spurious Correlations" website, which is hilarious. Visit it immediately by going to practicalreporting.com/pc-resources and clicking "Spurious Correlations website").

Why would chart creators decide to smooth the lines in a chart? In most cases, it's simply because they think that it looks nicer. Opinions differ on whether or when it's OK to smooth lines; however, it's important to be aware of potential problems that smoothing can create.

The main concern with smoothed lines is the "overshooting" problem, whereby the line can end up going outside of the actual range of the data:

I've heard a few other concerns regarding smoothed lines, such as the risk that they might imply that there are "intermediate" values in between the actual values in the chart when there aren't any, or imply that the data is sampled from a continuous process like the temperature of a lake. Personally, I don't think that most audiences will perceive smoothed lines in those ways—especially if the points are indicated with small markers—but I'm not aware of any studies that support either opinion.

Another consideration with smoothed lines is that the *degree* of smoothing is subjective, i.e., the chart creator must decide whether to make the line segments straighter or curvier (assuming that the software being used doesn't force the chart creator to use hardwired smoothing settings, which some software does).

Should we avoid smoothing lines, then? My advice is "yes," especially for everyday charts when cosmetics aren't as high a priority as they are for charts that are created to entertain, inspire, etc. Even though I don't think that the risks of smoothed lines are as significant as some people make them out to be, I'm not aware of any actual *benefits* of smoothed lines aside from purely cosmetic ones. (And are smoothed line segments really that much prettier than straight ones?)

As with any good guideline, there are exceptions (two, in this case):

1. Smoothed lines are OK for lines that *don't connect the points in a chart*, such as trendlines, because the risks that I just mentioned aren't risks for those types of lines:

(✓) Smoothed lines are fine for lines that don't connect the points in a chart (trendlines, etc.).

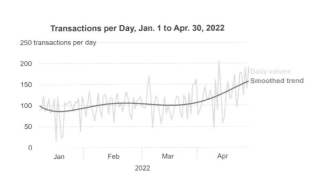

2. Smoothed lines are fine in bumps charts because the risks that I mentioned don't really apply when showing changes in *rank*, and a different smoothing algorithm can be used that forces the lines to be perfectly horizontal when they pass through each point, which eliminates the "overshooting" problem:

Smoothed lines are fine in bumps charts

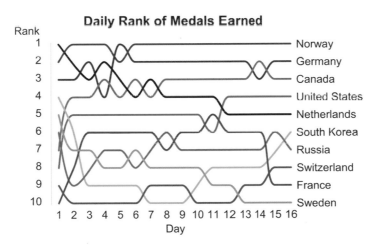

Key takeaway: Smoothed/curvy lines

- Avoid using smoothed lines in everyday charts, except for lines that don't go through points in the chart (e.g., trendlines) and for lines in bumps charts.

Can I use line charts with scales other than time?

Although the vast majority of line charts show values changing over *time*, line charts can be used with scales other than time as long as the scale is *sequential*. In the line chart below, for example, the scale is a sequential scale of employee categories, going from least to most senior:

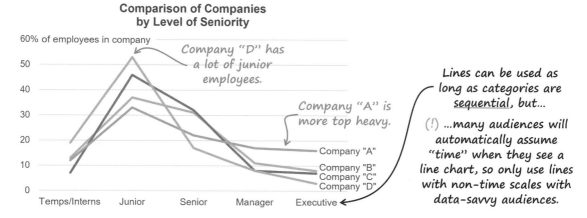

Technically, this chart works; however, I tend to avoid "non-time" line charts in practice. Why? As I mentioned in the purple callout above, many audiences assume that *all* line charts show values changing over time, and I've seen audiences get quite confused if the horizontal scale in a line chart *isn't* time. If the audience is very data savvy, they might not get confused by a non-time line chart, but most audiences aren't that data savvy.

What should almost always be avoided in everyday charts is using lines with *non-sequential* categories, such as the departments in an organization:

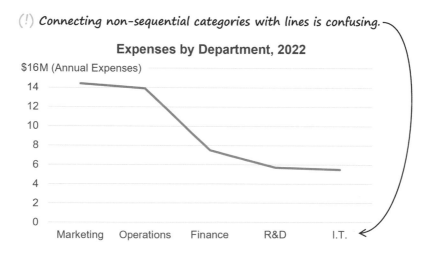

This chart looks "wrong" to most audiences because the line strongly suggests that the categories are connected in a sequence, but the scale of departments in the chart above is *non*-sequential; i.e., they can be listed in any order. In the chart above, for example, it looks like Marketing is "connected" to Operations in a sequence, but "not connected" to Finance, none of which is true. Also, as we saw a moment ago, many audiences assume that line charts automatically mean "time," so the audience's initial understanding of the chart above might be that "expenses have been decreasing over time," which is definitely not what's actually happening.

There are specialized chart types, such as *parallel coordinates plots*, in which it can make sense to connect non-sequential categories with lines, but those chart types are generally only used in advanced analysis, not for everyday charts.

> **Key takeaway: Using lines with scales other than time**
>
> • Avoid using lines with scales other than time unless the audience is quite data savvy or when conducting advanced analyses.

Don't line charts misrepresent data by "hiding" the values in between the points?

When I show a standard line chart like this in workshops…

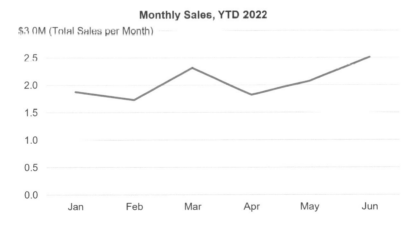

…participants sometimes object, saying something like, "This chart misleading. It looks like, for example, sales increased at a perfectly steady rate between the middle of February and the middle of March, but they almost certainly didn't. Sales typically bounce around from day to day, but this chart makes it look like they always increased or decreased at a perfectly steady rate in between the midpoint of each month."

I don't think that this is a valid concern, but the explanation gets a bit complicated. If you're curious, I've written up my reasoning in a detailed article that can be found by visiting practicalreporting.com/pc-resources and clicking "Are line charts liars?" The bottom line is that that I think that charts like the monthly sales one above are fine and don't hide information or misrepresent the data.

Finally, we've reached the end of our discussion of line charts and other ways to show data over time. I hope it's understandable why we spent dozens of pages on these chart types: because there are dozens of ways to mess them up. Ironically, the "simple" chart types like line charts and bar charts are the hardest to design effectively, and that's definitely also the case for the next "simple" chart types that we'll tackle, which are…

Chapter 7

Pie charts and other ways to show the breakdown of a total

ALONG WITH SHOWING values over time, showing the *breakdown of a total* is one of the most common tasks that most of us need to do with everyday charts.

There are three possible scenarios when showing the breakdowns of totals, each of which requires different chart types:

- Showing the breakdown of a *single* total
- Showing the breakdowns of *several* totals
- Showing the breakdown of a total *over time*

Let's start with…

SHOWING THE BREAKDOWN OF A SINGLE TOTAL

In this situation, many chart creators instinctively reach for a *pie chart*, but there are several other important chart types for showing the breakdown of a single total:

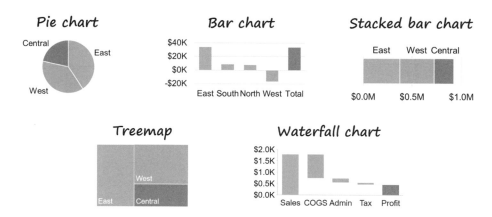

Although pie charts are *sometimes* the best choice for showing the breakdown of a total, there are many situations in which a pie chart *can't* represent the data accurately and when one of the other "breakdown of total" chart types *must* be used. I want to be clear that I'm not saying that using a pie chart in those situations would be "less clear" or "not the best choice"; I'm saying that it **could seriously misrepresent the data**. Many chart creators are unaware of this, however, and I regularly see pie charts that misrepresent data in situations where a different "breakdown of a total" chart type should have been used, such as a bar chart or a stacked bar chart.

Just as when we saw how to show data over time, we'll look at a series of scenarios to learn when to use different "breakdown of a total" chart types. We'll then recap what we learned in a handy, one-page decision tree that can quickly guide us to a good chart type choice in a wide variety of situations. Here's a preview of that decision tree:

DECISION TREE:
CHOOSING A CHART TYPE TO SHOW THE BREAKDOWN OF A SINGLE TOTAL

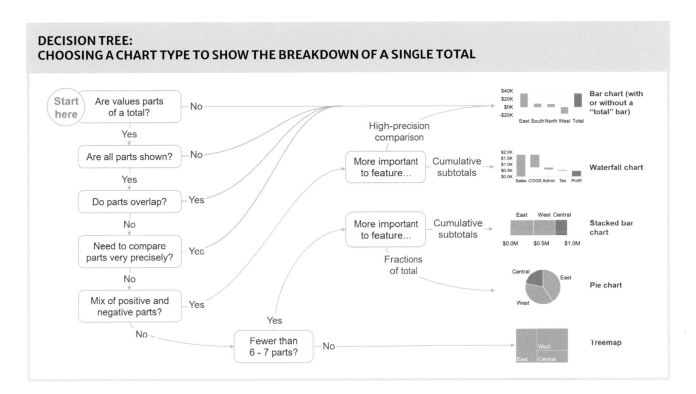

Before we look at some scenarios, I want to address what a significant number of readers are probably thinking/yelling right now…

Why are we even talking about pie charts?
Aren't they the devil's chart type?

Those who are new to the dataviz field might be surprised to learn that pie charts are quite controversial. As I write this in early 2023, and for many decades prior to that, the dataviz community has been split into two camps, with experienced chart creators in both:

1. **The "never-pie-charters,"** who believe that pie charts are *never* a better choice than bar charts, stacked bar charts, or other ways of showing the breakdown of a total.

2. **The "sometimes-pie-charters,"** who believe that there are situations in which pie charts can be the most effective choice.

The camp that I'm in is probably already clear, but I want to preface anything that I say about pie charts by emphasizing that, whichever position I take, a lot of people in the dataviz community will disagree with that position. You can, of course, decide which position to take for yourself, confident that, regardless of which one you choose, you'll be in good company.

Key takeaways: Controversy around pie charts

- There's widespread disagreement in the dataviz community regarding whether pie charts are ever a better choice than alternatives such as bar charts or stacked bar charts.
- There are several other major chart types for showing the breakdown of a total, all of which are needed in certain situations.

With that huge caveat out of the way, let's look at some scenarios to learn about the various chart types for showing the breakdown of a total.

Have a look at the following three ways of showing the breakdown of total donations to our charity, by donor. Which one do you think is the most effective way to show this data?

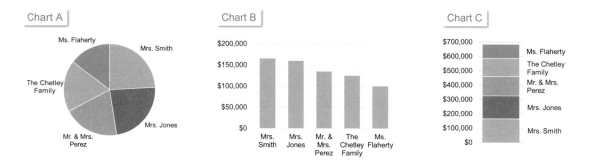

If you've been paying attention so far, you know that this is a trick question 🙂 As usual, the most effective design choice depends on the specific job that the chart is designed to do, i.e., the specific insight or answer that needs to be communicated about the data. Let's look at a few scenarios in which each of these chart types would be the most effective choice.

Which of the three charts below do you think best communicates this insight?

"Mrs. Smith contributed more than Mrs. Jones."

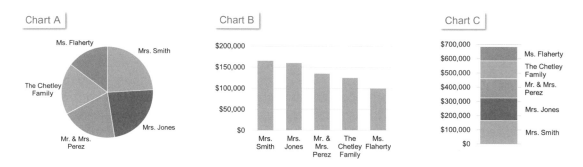

In the pie chart (Chart A), it's tough to tell whether the "Mrs. Smith" slice is bigger or smaller than the "Mrs. Jones" slice, so a pie chart doesn't offer enough precision to communicate this particular insight. That's the main concern that never-pie-charters have with pie charts: **Pie charts don't allow the various parts of a total to be compared with one another *precisely*.** The audience can make *rough* comparisons of the parts, such as seeing that Mrs. Smith (the blue slice) donated more than Ms. Flaherty (the dark green slice), but not the precise comparison that would be required to show that, for example, Mrs. Smith donated more than Mrs. Jones, because their slices are similar in size.

The stacked bar chart (Chart C) also doesn't allow for precise comparison of the parts: The audience can't compare the bar segments within the stacked bar precisely because the segments are all *offset* from one another, i.e., the bottoms of the bar segments are all at different heights, making it hard to precisely compare their lengths with one another.

Bar charts (for showing the breakdown of a total)

In the regular bar chart (Chart B), the bottoms of the bars are all nicely lined up, which allows their lengths to be compared precisely. This makes the bar chart the only option that provides enough precision to see that Mrs. Smith did, indeed, donate more than Mrs. Jones.

> **Key takeaway: Bars charts for showing the breakdown of a total**
>
> • If the insight or answer to be communicated about the breakdown of a total requires precise comparison of the parts, consider using a bar chart rather than a pie chart or stacked bar chart

Now, what if we needed to communicate a different insight about this same data; for example…

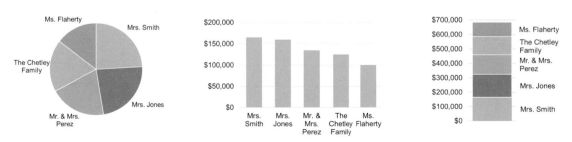

All of a sudden, the bar chart doesn't look like such a great choice anymore because it makes it quite hard to tell what *fraction of the total* the "Mrs. Smith" bar represents. A third? A quarter? A sixth? To try to figure that out, the audience would have to mentally stack all the bars on top of one another and try to imagine what fraction of that stack the "Mrs. Smith" bar would represent. In other words, the audience would have to try to reconstruct the stacked bar chart above on the right *in their head*. This would be super cognitively demanding and unlikely to produce accurate estimates of what fraction of the total each bar represents.

Therefore, to communicate this insight, the stacked bar chart would be a better choice than the regular bar chart. In the stacked bar chart, the audience can more easily see that Mrs. Smith represents *about* a quarter of all donations. But is it "almost a quarter"? Or a little more than a quarter? Hmm.

Pie charts

What about the pie chart? Huh! The pie chart makes it immediately clear that Mrs. Smith represents a little less than a quarter of total donations and so would be the best choice for communicating this insight (IMO, anyway). Now you know which camp I'm in: Yes, I believe that there *are* situations, such as the one above, in which a pie chart would be the most effective choice.

Pie charts have three strengths compared with bar charts and stacked bar charts:

1. As we just saw, **pie charts often make it easier to see what *fraction of the total* each part represents,** especially "familiar fractions," like one-half, one-third, and three-quarters (oddball fractions like five-twelfths might not be as obvious).

2. **Pie charts make it more immediately obvious that the chart is showing the *breakdown of a total*.** Regular bar charts can show values that are parts of a total (e.g., the breakdown of donations by donor) *or* values that aren't parts of a total (e.g., the % discount for various products). This forces the audience to perform the extra cognitive step of figuring out whether the values in a bar chart are or aren't parts of a total in order to correctly interpret the chart.

3. Using a pie chart suggests that the audience should **focus more on what fraction of the total each part represents and less on how the parts compare with one another**, which is useful if that's the type of insight that we need to communicate.

Never-pie-charters sometimes object that a bar chart with a "percentage of total" scale would make it easier to perceive what fraction of the total each part represents:

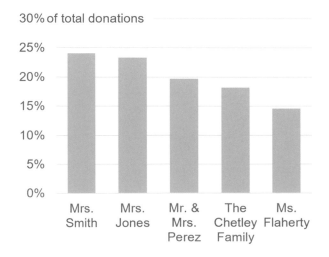

Yes, a "percentage of total" scale makes it easi**er** to get a sense of what fraction of the total each part represents but still not as easy as in a pie chart. In the bar chart above, the graphical elements (i.e., the bars) don't provide any sense of what fraction of the total each part represents, so the audience is forced to rely almost entirely on the non-graphical scale of percentages, which slows things down and makes things less intuitive: The audience must estimate the percentage value of each bar based on the (textual) percentage values on the scale and then convert those textual percentage values into mental representations of the parts of a total. That's certainly doable, but a pie chart skips most of those cognitive steps and shows fractions of a total in a way that's probably much closer to how we represent those kinds of quantities in our minds in the first place.

Sometimes, never-pie-charters argue that mentally converting textual "percentage of total" values into mental representations of parts of a total doesn't require much effort. I could turn that argument around, however, and argue that adding percentage value labels to a pie chart would allow the slices to be compared precisely without much cognitive effort:

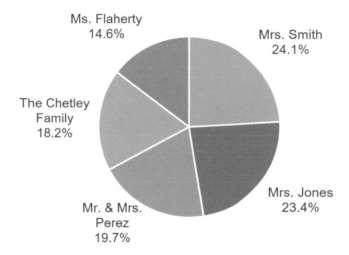

With the percentage values labeled, a pie chart's main weakness (i.e., the inability to compare parts precisely) disappears! I wouldn't actually make that argument, however, because perceiving quantities as textual value labels is much less efficient and less informative than perceiving quantities as *graphics* (shape size, shape length, color shades, etc.). As a general rule, **if a chart relies mostly on reading textual value labels rather than perceiving quantities as shapes, colors, etc., the chart should probably be redesigned** because the chart's graphics aren't actually helping the audience understand the data.

> **Key takeaway: Relying too much on value labels**
>
> - If a chart relies heavily on the audience reading textual value labels in order to do its job, it should be redesigned so that key insights are communicated primarily by graphics (bars, lines, pie slices, etc.).

There are also the other advantages of pie charts that I mentioned before, i.e., that they make it more immediately obvious that the chart is showing the breakdown of a total than bar charts do, and pie charts tell the audience to focus on fractions of the total rather than comparison of parts in situations when that's what we want the audience to do.

> **Key takeaway: When to use pie charts**
>
> • If the insight or answer to be communicated about the breakdown of a total is primarily about what fraction of the total each part represents, consider using a pie chart rather than a regular bar chart or stacked bar chart.

Let's try another, different insight that we might need to communicate about the previous donation data:

"Mrs. Smith and Mrs. Jones account for over $300K in donations."

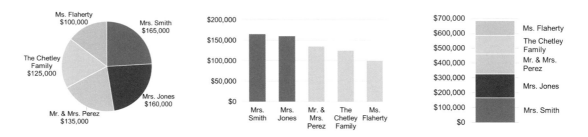

For this insight, the pie chart isn't looking like such a great choice anymore because it would force the audience to do some math in their heads (add $165,000 plus $160,000 and then determine whether the total is more than $300,000). Doing that math isn't the end of the world, but, as a general rule, we don't want our audiences to be doing any kind of math in their heads when reading our charts. (That's what computers are for!) **If we discover that our audience is doing mental calculations when reading one of our charts, that's a big hint that we should probably redesign that chart.**

The bar chart also forces the audience to do some mental math in order to perceive this insight: They must visually estimate the value of the "Mrs. Smith" bar, then visually estimate the value of the "Mrs. Jones" bar, and then add those two values together in their heads to see that the total is more than $300,000.

Stacked bar charts

In the stacked bar chart, the audience can easily see that the "Mrs. Smith" and "Mrs. Jones" bar segments together are more than $300,000—no mental math required.

> ### Key takeaway: Stacked bar charts for showing parts of a total
>
> - If the insight or answer to be communicated about the breakdown of a total is primarily about *a subtotal of multiple parts*, consider using a stacked bar chart rather than a regular bar chart or pie chart.

Note that pie charts can also show how multiple parts compare with the other parts or the total, but only *as a fraction of the total*. For example, in the scenario above, if we had wanted to communicate that "Mrs. Smith and Mrs. Jones account for *almost half* of all donations" (rather than "more than $300,000 in donations"), the pie chart would be a better choice.

OK, we've actually been kind of lucky so far, because, in all the scenarios that we've seen, the number of parts was pretty low, i.e., fewer than six or seven parts. In the real world, however, we might not be so lucky; we might end up needing to show totals with 10, 15, or perhaps even 100 parts, so we should probably talk about…

Showing totals with a large number of parts

Let's say that we needed to show a breakdown of donations by country, but there are 15 countries:

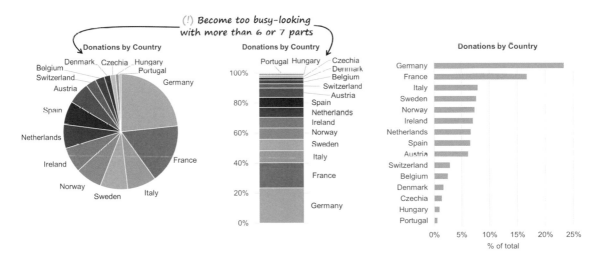

As we can see, pie charts and stacked bar charts generally become busy-looking spaghetti charts when there are more than about six or seven parts. The bar chart on the right, however, is still easy to read, **so bar charts can show a larger number of parts without looking overly busy.** In fact, we could even use what dataviz expert Stephen Few calls a "wrapped bar chart" to show donations for 100 countries!

WRAPPED BAR CHARTS

A wrapped bar chart is basically a huge bar chart that's been sliced into sections so that it fits within a smaller space. Although there's a lot going on in this wrapped bar chart, it's still pretty readable:

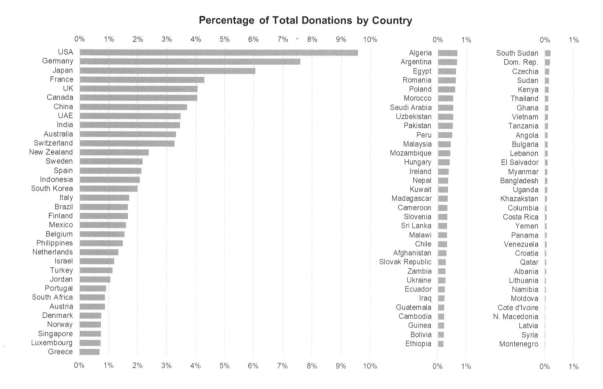

But what if we needed to show what *fraction of total donations* each of these 100 countries represented? As we saw earlier, bar charts don't show "part of total" insights as well as pie charts or stacked bar charts. A 100-slice pie chart would be an unintelligible mess, however, and same with a 100-segment stacked bar chart. Are we stuck? No, there are good options in situations like these, but they require a chart type that we haven't seen yet, specifically...

TREEMAPS

A treemap of donation values for 100 countries would look something like this:

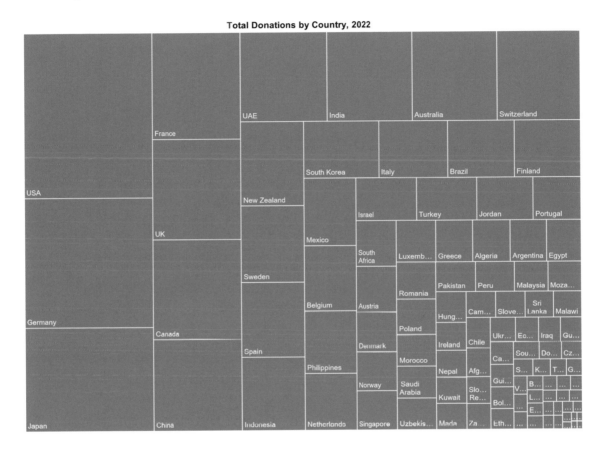

In this treemap, the size of each rectangle represents the amount that each country donated. The main strength of treemaps is that they can show many values without becoming spaghetti charts, but, as with every chart type, there are downsides:

- Treemaps are a **less common chart type**, so we might need to use the "gentle reveal," "bait and switch," and/or "duh insights" tricks that we saw earlier to explain them to our audience.

- Compared to a wrapped bar chart, a treemap makes it easier to get a sense of what part of the total each part represents, but it's still **not as easy as it is in a pie chart** (What fraction of the total above is the USA? A tenth? A fifteenth? A twentieth?).

- Like pie charts and stacked bar charts, **treemaps allow the parts to be compared with one another with only low precision**. For example, we can clearly see that Germany donated more than the UK, but it's hard to estimate how much more. Twice as much? Three times as much?

- In treemaps, **smaller parts often end up being represented as rectangles that are too small to show the name of that part** (e.g., the countries in the bottom right of the treemap above). This problem can be at least partially solved if the treemap is being viewed in a software product or web page that shows a tooltip when the user hovers over a rectangle in the treemap, but that's not ideal if, for example, the user is trying to find a specific country, and it's not possible at all if the treemap is being shown in a screenshot or printout where tooltips aren't available.

Pie charts perform better on most of these fronts and are much more familiar to most audiences, so I'd **only use a treemap if there were too many parts to show comfortably in a pie chart.**

One potentially useful "bonus feature" of treemaps is that they do a good job of showing *hierar-chies* of parts. For example, if it were important to show which continent each country belonged to, we could add that information easily in a treemap:

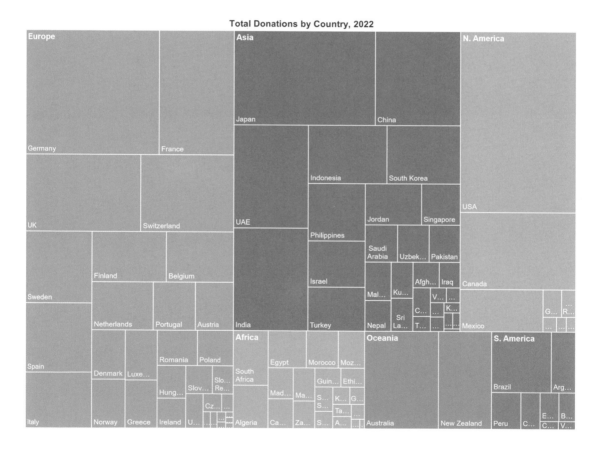

> ### Key takeaways: Treemaps
>
> - When showing the breakdown of a total with many parts and the (rough) fraction of the total that each part represents needs to be featured, consider using a treemap.
> - If there are few enough parts to fit comfortably in a pie chart, consider using a pie chart instead of a treemap.

I should mention at this point that, in some situations, we can "cheat" and show a pie or stacked bar chart when there are more than six or seven parts. How? Well, if we're lucky, we can get away with lumping less-important parts together into a single "All Others" category, thereby reducing the number of parts sufficiently for pie and stacked bar charts to become viable options again:

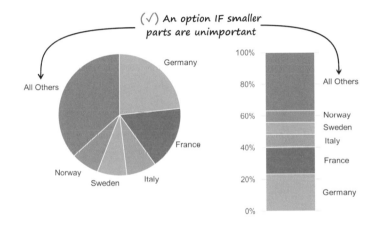

There's another useful trick that I use fairly often when showing the breakdown of a total as a bar chart or stacked bar chart: For those chart types, we always need to decide whether to show a quantitative scale of absolute values (dollars, employees, etc.) or percentages of total. It can be tricky to make this choice because both can be relevant to the insight or answer that needs to be communicated, so I'll sometimes include both scales, like this:

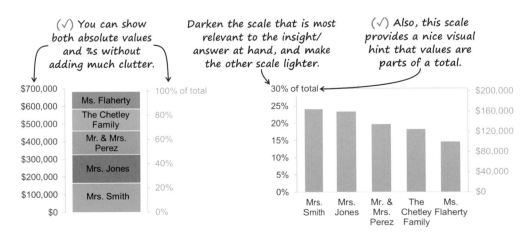

Including both scales doesn't create too much visual clutter and allows us to communicate insights about absolute values *and* percentages of the total in the same chart. Yes, this results in a dual-axis chart like the ones that we saw when we were discussing quantitative scales, but the two scales are always directly equivalent in these situations, so using dual axes is fine.

Key takeaways: Showing a total with more than six or seven parts

- Pie charts and stacked bar charts generally start to look too busy if there are more than six or seven parts.
- Bar charts or wrapped bar charts can show a large number of values without looking overly busy.
- When there are more than six or seven parts to show and the insight to be communicated is about fractions of the total or a subtotal of parts, consider using a treemap.

We're starting to get a better idea of when it makes sense to use different chart types to show the breakdown of a total, but there are a few additional factors that can come into play when deciding which chart type to use in a given situation. Let's look at a few more scenarios to learn what those factors are.

Have a look at the three charts below and then take a moment to decide which one you think best answers this question:

"What was the breakdown of average donation amounts by region?"

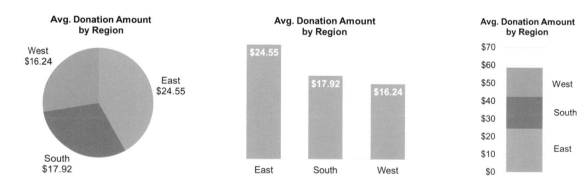

The twist in this scenario is that the values are *average* donation amounts, which can't be represented correctly in pie charts or stacked bar charts. In the pie chart on the left, for example, it looks like the East is a little over a third of… what, exactly? A third of "total average donations"? Adding up the average donations for the three regions gives us about $58, but that number doesn't mean anything. It's not the overall average donation amount for all regions, which would be something like $20. In other words, these values aren't parts of a meaningful total. Therefore, **pie charts only make sense when the values *are* parts of a meaningful total.**

The stacked bar chart on the right has the same problem: Because these values aren't parts of a meaningful total, they can't be added together, i.e., they can't be "stacked." The top of the stack makes it look like the "average donations" total was about $58, but, as we just saw, that's a nonsensical number. Therefore, **stacked bar charts also only make sense when the values are parts of a meaningful total.**

What's left? The regular bar chart, which can show pretty much any type of values, whether they're parts of a meaningful total or not. There's a cost for this flexibility, however, which is that, when audiences see a bar chart, they have to figure out whether it's showing the breakdown of a total or a set of values that don't add up to a meaningful total, which adds extra cognitive steps.

To determine whether the values in our data are parts of a meaningful total or not, we just need to ask ourselves whether the sum of the values would be a meaningful number. If it wouldn't be, we should avoid using a pie or stacked bar chart to show those values. Same goes for treemaps, which only make sense when showing parts of a meaningful total.

> **Key takeaways: Showing values that aren't parts of a meaningful total**
>
> - Avoid using pie charts, stacked bar charts, or treemaps to show values that aren't parts of a meaningful total.
> - For values that aren't parts of a meaningful total, consider using a regular bar chart.

Next scenario: Take a moment to decide which of the three charts below best answers the following question:

"How did each of our top three donors compare to the overall total?"

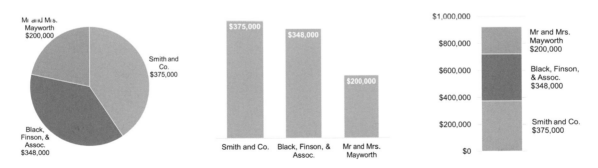

The wrinkle in this scenario is that only the *top three* donors are shown. This means that there are more than three donors, i.e., not all of the parts of the total are being shown. We don't know how many donors there are, but we do know that there are more than the three that are being shown.

This is a problem for the pie chart, because it makes it look like, for example, "Smith and Co." represents over a third of *all* donations. But is that perception accurate if all donations aren't included the chart? Nope. Based on the data that's being shown, we *don't know* what fraction of the total any of these donors represents because we don't know what the total is. Therefore, **pie charts misrepresent the data unless all of the parts of the total are included in the chart.**

Yes, technically, "our top three donors" could be considered to be "a total" (i.e., the total of our top three donors), but it's not the "overall total" that's referred to in the question above the three charts, which the audience would almost certainly consider to be "total donations for *all* donors" (not just the top three).

The stacked bar chart on the right has the same problem: In that chart, it looks like total donations (the top of the stack) were a little more than $900,000, and Smith and Co. accounted for a little over a third, but we know that neither of those statements is true. Therefore, **stacked bar charts also misrepresent the data unless all of the parts of the total are included in the chart.**

Treemaps have similar problems when all of the parts of a total aren't included, so what's left? Regular bar charts. There's nothing about a regular bar chart that visually suggests that all parts of a total are being shown. A bar chart could be showing some or all parts of a total (or values that aren't even parts of a total in the first place). The cost of this flexibility is that, when audiences see a bar chart, they need to figure out whether all the parts of a total are being shown or not, which adds extra cognitive steps.

Key takeaways: Showing some of the parts of a total

- Avoid using pie charts, stacked bar charts, or treemaps if all the parts of a total aren't included in the chart.
- If all the parts aren't included, consider using a regular bar chart.

Next scenario: Which chart do you think best answers the following question?

"What fraction of our total net donations does each region represent?"

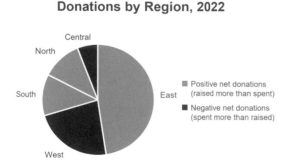

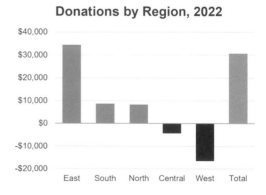

The twist in this scenario is that the parts consist of a *mix of positive and negative values*: Some regions had positive net donations (raised more than they spent), and others had negative net donations (spent more than they raised—ouch!).

Even though the question that we're trying to answer has to do with fractions of the total, a pie chart doesn't make sense when the parts consist of both positive and negative values. For example, the pie chart above makes it look like the East accounted for almost half of total donations, but look at the bar chart on the right; does the bar for the East look like it's about half of the gray "Total" bar? Not at all. Therefore, **pie charts can't be used to show a mix of positive and negative parts,** and treemaps don't work either for similar reasons. In pie charts and treemaps, the parts can be all positive or all negative (e.g., if all regions had negative net donations) but not a mix of positive *and* negative parts.

Again, what are we left with? A regular bar chart, like the one above on the right. Even though bar charts don't show fractions of a total nearly as well as other chart types, they're the only option that shows the data correctly in this scenario, so we have no choice but to use a bar chart in this case.

Stacked bar charts can work with a mix of positive and negative parts, but I struggle to think of scenarios in which a stacked bar chart would be more useful than a standard bar chart or a waterfall chart (which we'll cover in the next section):

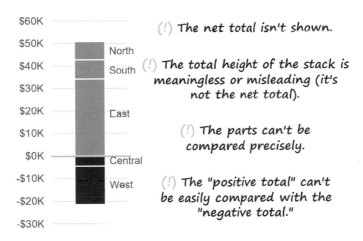

Key takeaways: Showing parts that consist of positive and negative values

- Avoid using pie charts, stacked bar charts, or treemaps to show a mix of positive and negative parts.
- If a total consists of a mix of positive and negative parts, consider using a regular bar chart or waterfall chart (see below) instead.

OK, so what the heck are...

Waterfall charts

A waterfall chart is like a stacked bar chart, but with the parts "slid apart." Why would we want to do that? The main reason is that it allows *cumulative subtotals* to be shown when the parts consist of both positive and negative values:

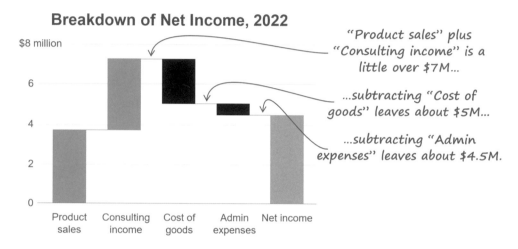

A "waterfall chart" can show cumulative subtotals of positive and negative parts.

While this situation doesn't come up all that often in general, it comes up all the time when showing financial data in particular. As with all chart types, there are, of course, downsides to waterfall charts. The main one is that the audience can't compare the parts with one another *precisely*. For example, if the main insight that we need to communicate is that "Product sales" exceeded "Consulting income," the waterfall chart above doesn't offer enough precision to allow us to show that because the bar segments are offset from one another (the bottoms of the bars are all at different heights), which makes them hard to compare precisely. If that were the main insight that we needed to communicate, we'd need to fall back on a regular bar chart, which offers enough precision to see that "Product sales" did, indeed, slightly exceed "Consulting income":

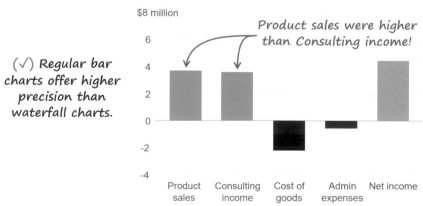

> **Key takeaway: Waterfall charts**
>
> - If the parts of a total consist of positive and negative values, it's necessary to show cumulative subtotals, and it's not necessary to compare the parts with one another precisely, consider using a waterfall chart.

Before we leave behind the topic of charts to show the breakdown of a single total, there's a common design problem that I see in many "breakdown of a total" charts that we haven't discussed yet, which is…

Showing parts that overlap

Another scenario: Which of the following charts do you think best answers the following question about the breakdown of a car dealership's sales?

"What fraction of total sales does each type of vehicle represent?"

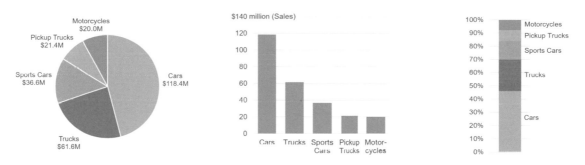

The wrinkle in this scenario is that some of the parts *overlap*. For example, "Cars" overlaps "Sports Cars" (which are a subset of "Cars"), and "Trucks" overlap "Pickup Trucks" (which are a subset of "Trucks"). In the pie chart, however, these look like separate, discrete categories even though they're *not*. This is confusing at best and misleading at worst. For example, the pie chart makes it look like Cars accounted for less than half of the dealership's sales, but can we say that if the "Sports Cars" pie slice is part of the "Cars" pie slice? Nope.

The stacked bar chart has the same issue; it shows "Sports Cars" as a separate, discrete category from "Cars" even though "Sports cars" are *included within* "Cars." The stacked bar chart makes it look like Cars accounted for about 45% of sales but, as we just saw, that's not correct. Unfortunately, showing overlapping categories as discrete pie slices or stacked bar segments is a fairly common design problem.

The bar chart, at least, is basically accurate. It's not ideal, however, because the overlapping nature of the categories isn't obvious. Is there a better option? Yes. If we do a bit of math, we can "un-overlap" the categories and represent them accurately:

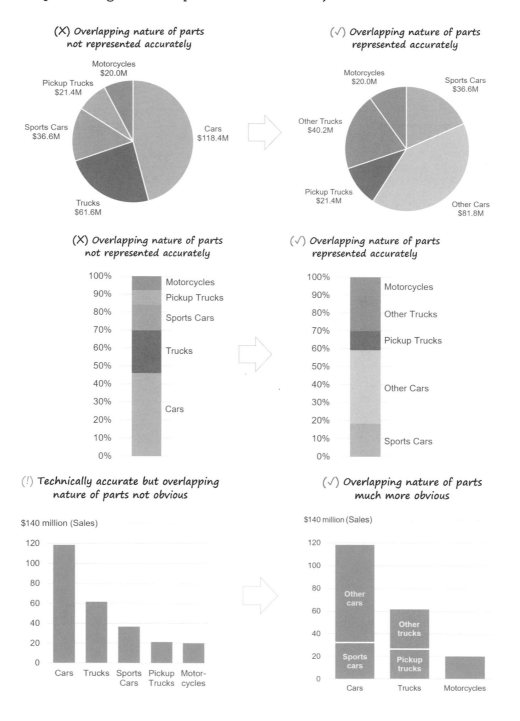

(X) *Overlapping nature of parts not represented accurately*

(✓) *Overlapping nature of parts represented accurately*

(X) *Overlapping nature of parts not represented accurately*

(✓) *Overlapping nature of parts represented accurately*

(!) *Technically accurate but overlapping nature of parts not obvious*

(✓) *Overlapping nature of parts much more obvious*

The overlapping relationships in these examples are relatively simple, but overlapping relationships can get much more complex and involve categories that, for example, partially overlap, or that overlap more than one other category. It can be tough to figure out how to represent these more complex overlapping relationships as graphs, which makes it tempting to just show a table of numbers or a very simple graph that doesn't reflect the overlapping relationships at all:

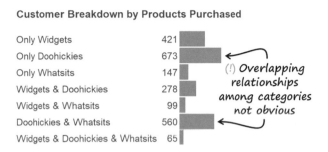

This isn't very helpful to audiences, however, because it forces them to figure out on their own how all of these categories relate to one another. With some time and creativity, we might come up with something more informative, like this:

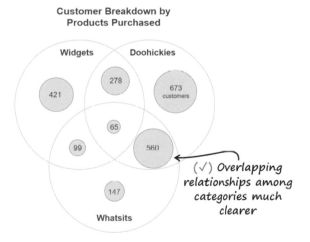

How did I figure out how to represent these overlapping relationships in this way? Unfortunately, that would be hard to distill as specific guidelines because there are many different types of relationships that can exist among categories, each of which would require different types of graphics to represent. This is one of those rare times in this book, then, when the most I can offer is "judgment and experience." Sorry. I'll only do that one or two more times.

> ### Key takeaway: Overlapping categories
>
> - Be careful when showing categories that overlap in pie charts, stacked bar charts, and treemaps. If categories overlap, either "un-overlap" them using calculations, or make the overlapping relationships as visually obvious as possible.

There you have it! We just saw a variety of different chart types for showing the breakdown of a total and when to use each. As with showing data over time, chart type choice can—and often does—make or break a chart when it comes to showing the breakdown of a total and requires a surprising number of factors to be taken into account. Happily, all of those factors are summarized in this handy cheat sheet, which I hope makes a lot more sense now than it did before reading this chapter:

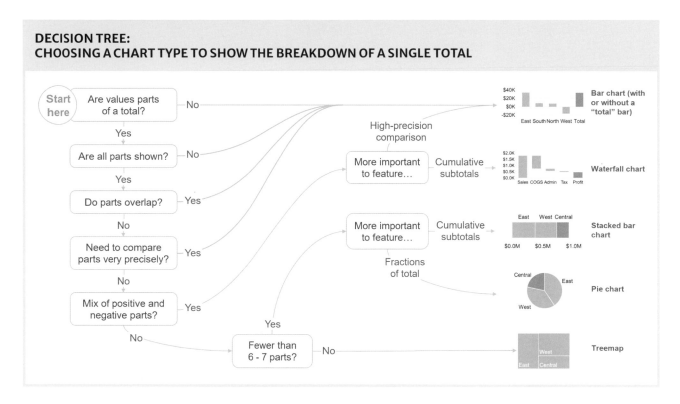

Now that we have a good handle on how to show the breakdown of a *single* total, let's move on to…

SHOWING THE BREAKDOWNS OF *SEVERAL* TOTALS

In the last section, we saw chart types for showing the breakdown of a single total. In practice, we also often need to show the breakdowns of *several* totals, in which case our data might look something like this:

Breakdowns of several totals

Regional Expenses by Department (2022)

	East	Central	West
Operations	$1,276,652	$843,329	$824,423
HR	$754,998	$654,669	$879,321
Finance	$565,789	$654,884	$317,774
Outreach	$237,889	$248,999	$235,798
PR	$175,998	$154,434	$142,663
Development	$98,776	$87,662	$91,442
Total	$3,110,102	$2,643,977	$2,491,421

There are four important chart types for showing this type of data, two of which we've seen already, and two of which we haven't discussed yet:

Multiple stacked bar charts

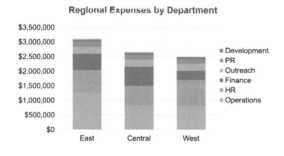

Multiple pie charts

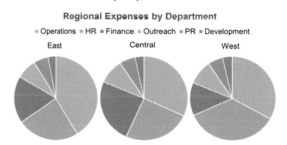

Clustered bar charts

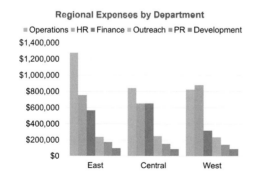

Merged bar charts

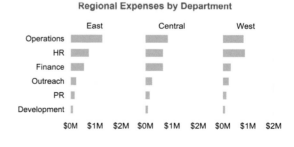

As usual, the choice of chart type depends mostly on the specific insight or answer that we need to communicate about the data. As we did in the last section, we'll learn about when it makes sense to use each of these chart types by considering a series of scenarios and then summarize what we've learned in a decision tree.

First scenario: Have a look at the four charts below, each of which shows a breakdown of total expenses for three regions (i.e., three totals) by department. Take a minute or two to decide which one best shows the following insight:

"Operations expenses in the Central region were lower than HR expenses in the West region."

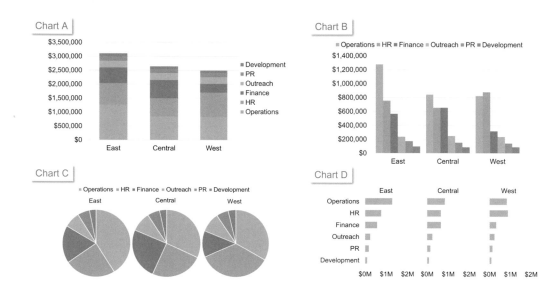

Clustered bar charts

The *clustered bar chart* (Chart B) is the only option that allows parts of different totals (i.e., different departments within different regions) to be compared *precisely*, which is required for this insight:

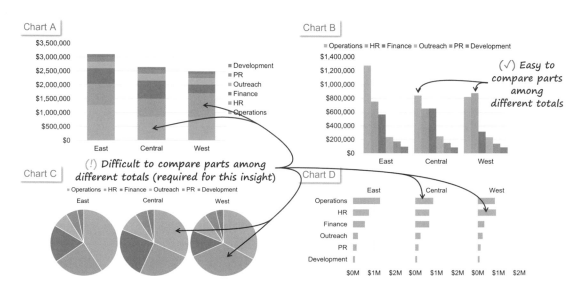

Key takeaway: Clustered bar charts

- When showing the breakdown of several totals and the insight to be communicated is primarily about how parts compare with one another among different totals, consider using a clustered bar chart.

Now, let's assume that we need to say something different about this data. Have another look at the four charts on the previous page and decide which one best answers the following question:

"Which region had the highest overall expenses, and which departments were the big spenders within each region?"

Multiple stacked bar charts

The clustered bar chart isn't such a great choice now because, in that chart, it's very hard to see—much less compare—the *totals* for each region, which is required to answer this question. The multiple stacked bars (Chart A), however, allow the audience to compare region totals easily and precisely. Although the parts within stacked bars can't be compared precisely, we only need to see the "big spenders" for this insight, so precise comparisons aren't needed:

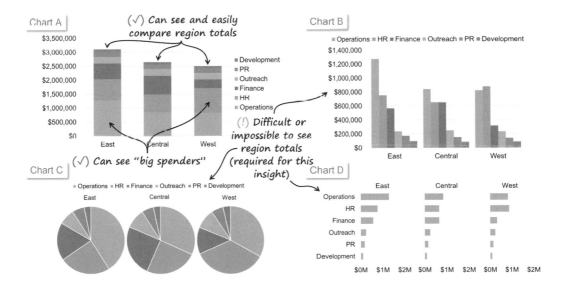

Key takeaway: Multiple stacked bars

- When showing the breakdown of several totals and the insight to be communicated is primarily about how the totals compare, consider using multiple stacked bars.

Let's try a different insight. Which of the four charts on p. 148 best communicates the following?

"Operations accounted for more than a quarter of expenses in every region (and we don't care how the regions compared with one another)."

Multiple pie charts

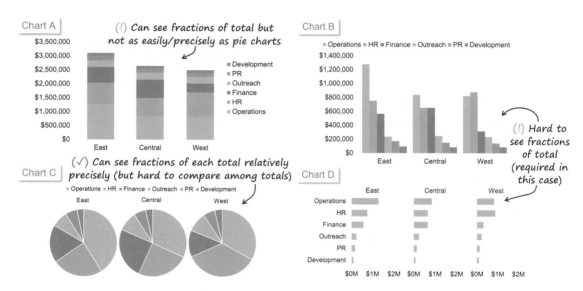

A few important comments about this scenario:

- Note that it's rare in practice that "…we don't care how the parts (e.g., departments) compared among totals (e.g., regions)." When showing breakdowns of multiple totals, we usually *do* care about how the parts compare among different totals. Pie charts, however, make it difficult to make almost *any* kind of comparison among different totals, which means that **showing multiple pie charts is rarely the best option.**

- Also, note that only fractions of each total can be seen when showing several pie charts, so **comparisons of absolute values (dollars, employee counts, etc.) aren't possible.** These two reasons are probably why…

- Saying that several pie charts can be an effective choice is **absolute blasphemy to many never-pie-charters,** who believe that the only thing worse than a pie chart is several pie charts. I believe, however, that there are rare cases like the one above when multiple pie charts could be the most effective choice.

Key takeaways: Multiple pie charts

- When showing the breakdown of several totals and the insight to be communicated is exclusively about what fraction of the total the parts of each total represent, consider using multiple pie charts.

- If anything other than very rough comparisons of parts among the totals is required (which it usually is), multiple pie charts should be avoided.

For this next scenario, let's keep the same chart types but change the data up a bit. Take a moment to consider which chart option best answers the following question:

"How did the three most expensive departments compare within each region?"

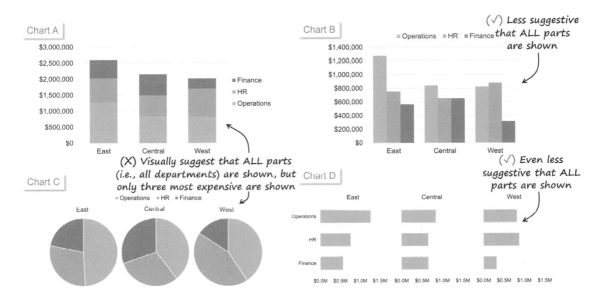

Merged bar charts

As you can see from my purple callouts, we basically have the same issue that we saw in the previous section when we were looking at the breakdown of a single total: In this scenario, we're not showing all of the parts (i.e., all of the departments), only the three most expensive ones. We don't know how many departments there are, but we know that there are more than three. As we saw in the previous section, stacked bar charts and pie charts are misleading unless they include *all* of the parts of a total (e.g., all of the departments). In the pie charts, for example, it looks like Operations accounted for about half of expenses in the East. Can we say that if we're not showing all the departments? Nope.

The clustered bar chart (Chart B) shows this data accurately, but I worry that audiences still might assume that all departments are being shown, i.e., that there are only three departments. In my experience, merged bar charts (Chart D) are a safer option when all of the parts aren't being shown because, to my eye, anyway, merged bar charts don't visually imply whether all of the parts are being shown or not (I'm not aware of any studies that back this up, however).

BTW, as we've seen a few times now, **merged bar charts and other types of merged charts are very useful in many situations**, but it often doesn't occur to chart creators to use them. Because merged charts are so useful, we're going to see them a few more times in this book.

Key takeaways: Merged bar charts

- When showing the breakdown of several totals and not all parts are being shown, avoid using multiple pie charts and stacked bar charts.
- Clustered bar charts or, better yet, merged bar charts are safer options in those cases.

Alright, final scenario in this section: In this one, we need to show some data for a charity's three regions. Specifically, we need to show Average Donation Amount, Donor Satisfaction Rating, and Average Household Income for each region. Because we're showing three completely different measures with different units of measurement (donation dollars, satisfaction ratings, and household income dollars), there's only one safe chart type option:

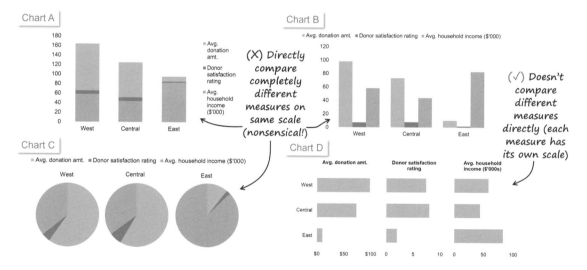

The stacked bar, clustered bar, and pie charts all show the values on the same quantitative scale, but, as we saw in the discussion of quantitative scales back in Part 1, showing values with different units of measurement on the same scale leads to nonsensical conclusions about the data, for example:

- In the stacked bar chart, it looks like the three values for the West region add up to a little over 160… 160 whats, exactly? Clearly, we can't stack different measures like Average Donation Amount, Donor Satisfaction Rating, and Average Household together.

- In the clustered bar chart, in the West region, it looks like Average Donation Amount was almost twice as high as Average Household Income ($'000s). Does that make any sense? None at all.

- In the pie charts, in the West, it looks like Average Donation Amount accounted for over half of… what, exactly?

The merged bar chart, on the other hand, shows each measure on its own separate scale, avoiding any of the nonsensical conclusions that we see in the other charts. Like I said, merged charts can be useful in many situations.

> ### Key takeaways: Showing different units of measurement for multiple totals
>
> - Avoid showing values with different units of measurement (donation dollars, satisfaction ratings, etc.) as stacked bar charts, clustered bar charts, or multiple pie charts.
> - Consider using merged bar charts to show values with different units of measure.

We've now seen four important chart types and when to use each to show the breakdowns of several totals. As usual, a variety of considerations must be taken into account when choosing a chart type for a given situation, all of which are summarized in this handy…

DECISION TREE: CHOOSING A CHART TYPE TO SHOW THE BREAKDOWNS OF SEVERAL TOTALS

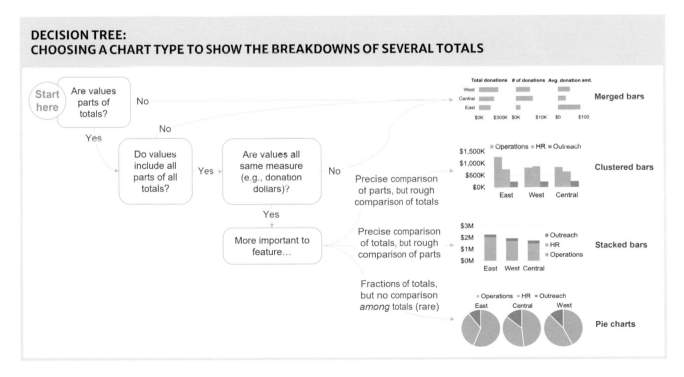

We've now seen how to show the breakdown of a single total and how the show the breakdown of multiple totals. There's one more major type of "breakdown of total" situation that arises all the time in practice, which is…

SHOWING THE BREAKDOWN OF A TOTAL *OVER TIME*

Most of us need to show the breakdown of a total *over time* pretty often. In those situations, our data might look something like this:

Data that represents the breakdown of a total over time

Donations ($000s) by Region - 2022

	Jan	Feb	Mar	Apr	May	Jun	Jul	Aug	Sep	Oct	Nov	Dec
East	14.0	20.0	19.8	14.9	14.0	19.6	24.2	25.6	25.7	23.8	26.3	22.4
West	12.0	17.3	18.8	10.5	10.0	13.6	26.5	25.5	27.8	8.0	3.2	4.6
North	7.4	8.3	7.0	8.7	6.0	7.1	7.0	6.7	11.2	7.3	9.2	7.9
South	10.0	8.8	12.8	5.1	5.3	7.9	9.6	14.6	22.4	1.0	10.3	6.0
Total	43.4	54.4	58.4	39.3	35.3	48.1	67.3	72.4	87.1	40.1	49.0	40.9

Showing this kind of data requires new chart types, some of which we haven't seen yet:

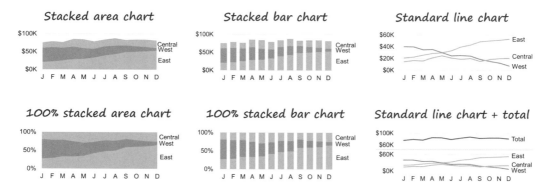

Which chart type should we use to show "breakdown of a total over time" data? This particular design choice depends entirely on the specific job of the chart, i.e., the specific insight or answer that we need to communicate about the data. That's why, in all the scenarios that we'll see in this section of the book, *the data is always the same* (i.e., the donation data in the table above). What changes in each scenario is the type of insight or answer that we need to communicate about the data, which determines which chart type we should use.

When it comes to choosing a chart type to show the breakdown of a total over time, I have good news and bad news. Which do you want first?

> The bad news. Everyone always wants the bad news first.

The bad news is that it can be quite tricky to select a chart type in these situations. Based on the specific insight or answer that we need to communicate, we'll need to take multiple factors into account in order to choose a chart type, such as:

- Is the pattern of change of the *total* relevant to the insight to be communicated? Or only the patterns of change of the parts?

- Is it more important to show the *actual values* (dollars, employees, etc.) of the parts, or the percentage of the total that each part represents?

- Is it more important to see what *fraction of the total* each part represents or to precisely compare the parts with one another?

- Is the insight to be communicated more about *overall patterns of change* (spikes, dips, cycles, etc.) or about specific, individual periods (particular days, months, etc.)?

- Does the insight to be communicated require comparing a subtotal of *two or more parts* (e.g., the North region plus the East region) to the other parts or the total?

> Ugh. What's the good news?

The good news is that, even if we don't choose the most effective chart type for the situation at hand, there's still a pretty good chance that the audience will get enough value from the chart for it to be useful to them, so we don't need to sweat it too much.

A bonus piece of good news is, that, as usual, there will be a cheat sheet at the end of this section that summarizes all the guidelines that we'll cover, and that can quickly guide us to a good chart type choice in a wide variety of situations. Here's a preview, but it will be easier to understand after you've read this section:

DECISION TREE:
CHOOSING A CHART TYPE TO SHOW THE BREAKDOWN OF A TOTAL OVER TIME

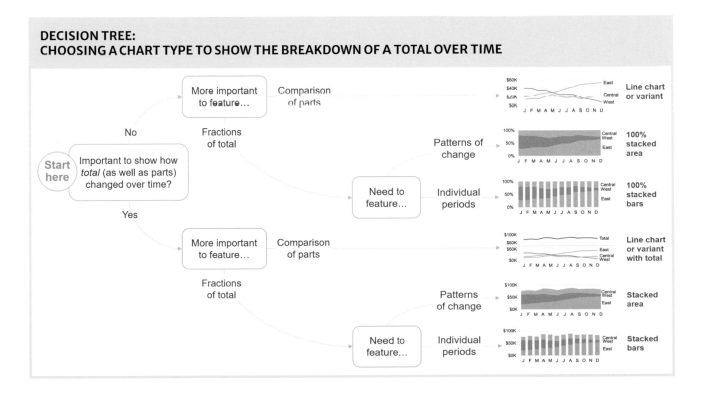

Now that that's out of the way, let's have a closer look at the six chart types for showing the breakdown of a total over time and when to use each. Each chart type example below has callouts that point out the strengths (✓) and weaknesses (!) of that chart type, along with an example of an insight that would be communicated effectively by that chart type in *blue "handwritten" typeface*.

Let's start with…

Standard line charts

We probably won't be using a standard line chart very often to show the parts of a total over time, but there are times when it's sufficient to say what we need to say about the data:

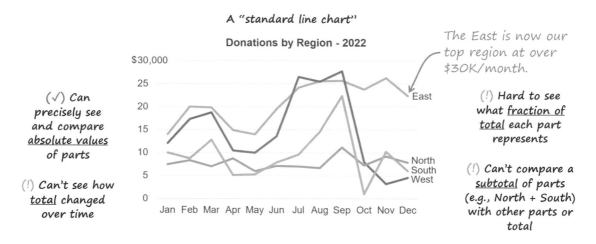

A "standard line chart"

Donations by Region - 2022

The East is now our top region at over $30K/month.

(✓) Can precisely see and compare *absolute values* of parts

(!) Can't see how *total* changed over time

(!) Hard to see what *fraction of total* each part represents

(!) Can't compare a *subtotal* of parts (e.g., North + South) with other parts or total

Standard line charts with "total" line

On the next page is the same standard line chart that we just saw, but with a "total" line added. The strengths and weaknesses are similar to those of the standard line chart above except that the total is now visible. Note that the total line is shown on its own scale because the total is typically much greater than the parts and so would crush the "parts" lines down near the bottom of the chart if the parts and the total were shown on the same scale.

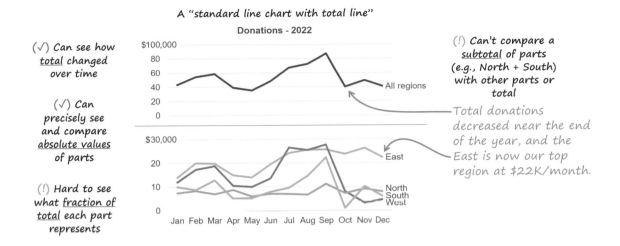

A "standard line chart with total line"

(✓) Can see how <u>total</u> changed over time

(✓) Can precisely see and compare <u>absolute values</u> of parts

(!) Hard to see what <u>fraction of total</u> each part represents

(!) Can't compare a <u>subtotal</u> of parts (e.g., North + South) with other parts or total

Total donations decreased near the end of the year, and the East is now our top region at $22K/month.

Stacked area charts

Stacked area charts are less common than standard line charts, but there's a good chance that you've seen them before:

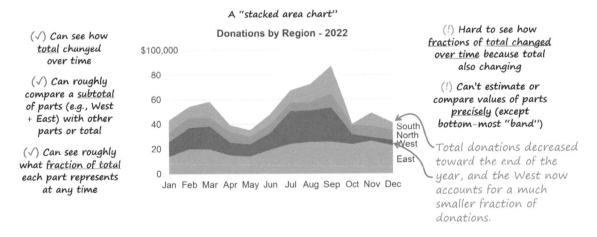

A "stacked area chart"

(✓) Can see how <u>total</u> changed over time

(✓) Can roughly compare a <u>subtotal</u> of parts (e.g., West + East) with other parts or total

(✓) Can see roughly what <u>fraction of total</u> each part represents at any time

(!) Hard to see how <u>fractions of total changed over time</u> because total also changing

(!) Can't estimate or compare values of parts <u>precisely</u> (except bottom-most "band")

Total donations decreased toward the end of the year, and the West now accounts for a much smaller fraction of donations.

Note that audiences with relatively little chart-reading experience might not grasp that the lines are "stacked" and might think that, for example, the top of the stack is the value for the South region, not the total for *all* regions. If that's a risk, we should make sure to explain to the audience how this chart type works using the "gentle reveal," "bait and switch," and/or "duh insights" tricks that we saw earlier.

Stacked bar charts

Stacked bars are basically the same as the stacked area chart that we just saw, but the lines have been switched to bars. As we saw when comparing lines and bars in the "Line charts and other ways to show data over time" chapter, bars are a better choice when we want the audience to focus on individual periods (individual months, in these examples) rather than the overall pattern of change (spikes, dips, cycles, etc.). Because it's basically the same as a stacked area chart, a stacked bar chart has pretty much the same set of strengths and weaknesses.

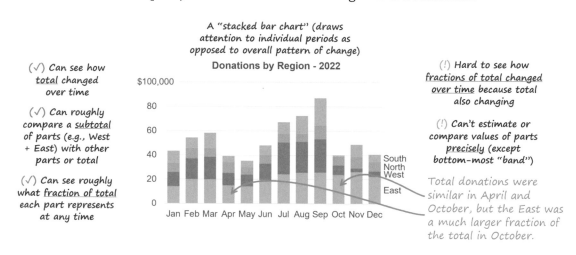

A "stacked bar chart" (draws attention to individual periods as opposed to overall pattern of change)

Donations by Region - 2022

(✓) Can see how total changed over time

(✓) Can roughly compare a subtotal of parts (e.g., West + East) with other parts or total

(✓) Can see roughly what fraction of total each part represents at any time

(!) Hard to see how fractions of total changed over time because total also changing

(!) Can't estimate or compare values of parts precisely (except bottom-most "band")

Total donations were similar in April and October, but the East was a much larger fraction of the total in October.

100% stacked area charts

100% stacked area charts are similar to the stacked area chart that we saw a moment ago, but we've switched from showing actual values (donation dollars, employee headcount, etc.) to showing the *percentage of the total* that each part represents during each period (each month, in these examples). Because of this, the total is now always the same (100%) for each period. This change substantially affects the types of insights that the chart can communicate effectively:

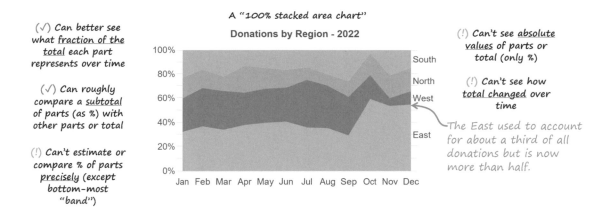

As with regular stacked area charts, less experienced audiences may not know how to read this chart type, so we might need to use the "gentle reveal," "bait-and-switch," and/or "duh insights" tricks to get our audience up to speed, if necessary.

100% stacked bar charts

100% stacked bar charts are basically the same as the 100% stacked area charts that we just saw, but the lines have been switched to bars. As we saw earlier, bars are a better choice when we want the audience to focus on individual periods rather than the overall pattern of change. Because 100% stacked bar charts are basically the same as 100% stacked area charts, they have pretty much the same set of strengths and weaknesses.

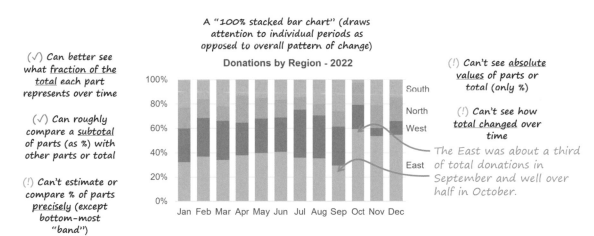

> Wow. That's a lot of information to keep in mind. How do I choose among these chart types in practice?

Happily, all of this information is summarized in a handy-dandy...

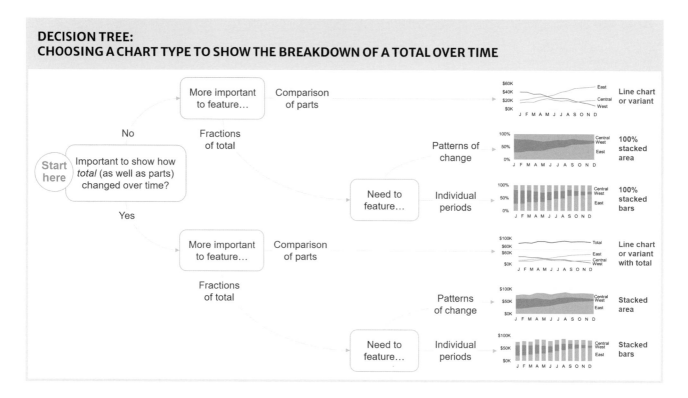

DECISION TREE:
CHOOSING A CHART TYPE TO SHOW THE BREAKDOWN OF A TOTAL OVER TIME

We've now seen all the important ways to show the breakdown of a total (or totals) that we're likely to need for everyday charts, so let's move on to...

FORMATTING PIE CHARTS

A quick reminder that all the formatting guidelines that we saw in "Part 1: General chart formatting guidelines" (choosing colors, avoiding legends, etc.) apply to all chart types, including pie charts. There are some *additional* formatting guidelines that apply only to pie charts; those are what we'll see in this section and summarize at the end in a handy cheat sheet.

To learn about formatting pie charts, let's start with one that suffers from several common formatting problems and improve it step by step. There are five formatting improvements that would make the nasty pie chart on the next page more effective; see whether you can spot them all before moving on to the list of improvements that immediately follows.

Here's the nasty pie chart:

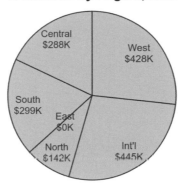

And here are the formatting improvements that I'd recommend:

1. Make the slices different colors.

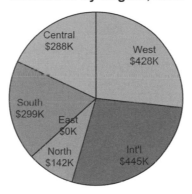

This is usually the first improvement that participants in my workshops suggest. Technically, it's not necessary because the parts are already distinct from each other, so, as we saw back in the chapter on colors, we don't need to further distinguish the categories by making them different colors. But, having said that, I actually *agree* that making the slices of a pie chart different colors is an improvement.

Why? I think it has to do with a limitation of how human vision works. To see this limitation for yourself, try focusing on the label for the West region in the pie chart above and, without shifting your gaze, try to read the labels for the other slices. Weird, right? Because our vision is surprisingly blurry outside the exact center of our field of view (called the "fovea"), when we look at one slice, the other slices tend to "blur together" into a single blob if they're all the same color.

Making the slices different colors makes them visually distinct enough that they look like separate shapes in our peripheral vision while we're focusing on one of the slices, so I think it's warranted.

2. Remove the borders, and use thin gaps to separate the slices.

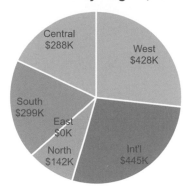

Two benefits:

1. Reduces visual clutter

2. Allows borders to be used selectively to visually highlight specific slices (we'll see an example of this shortly)

Depending on the software we're using, we might need to "fake" thin gaps between slices by applying a border to the slices that's the same color as the background behind the chart (white, in this example).

3. Move the labels from inside the slices to outside.

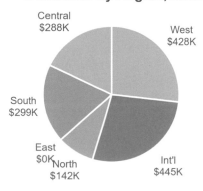

Three reasons:

1. Text labels are easier to read against a plain background than against a busy background of pie slices.

2. There's more room outside of the slices to show longer label names if necessary.

3.   As we saw earlier, we aren't very good at comparing the sizes of pie slices; overlaying visually distracting text labels on top of the slices probably doesn't help.

4. Sort the slices from largest to smallest (or smallest to largest).

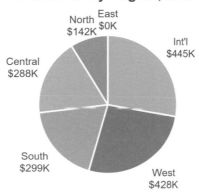

As we saw way back during our discussion of categorical scales in Part 1, whenever we have non-sequential categories, sorting them from largest to smallest (or, sometimes, smallest to largest) tends to make charts easier to read. This applies to pie charts as well. In the pie chart above, the audience is probably most interested in the regions with the largest donations, so those should be listed first. In a pie chart, "first" means "starting at the 12 o'clock position" and then moving clockwise, so the region with the highest donations starts at the 12 o'clock position, and the smaller parts appear after it in a clockwise direction.

5. Do something about "East, $0K."

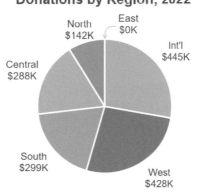

In workshops, participants sometimes suggest removing the "East, $0" label altogether because they assume that the fact that its value is zero means that it's unimportant. **The fact that a value is zero doesn't automatically mean that it's unimportant, however.** Maybe the East region was expected to have high donations, so the fact that it's zero could be the single most important piece of information in this chart.

That's why it's often necessary to visually emphasize very small or "zero-sized" slices so that they don't go unnoticed. "Leader lines" such as the light gray arrow in the previous image are a good way to do that.

> **Key takeaways: Slices of zero size**
>
> • Zero isn't the same thing as "unimportant" or "unknown." Only omit slices of zero size if they're known to be irrelevant.
> • Visually emphasize very small or zero-size slices with leader lines to ensure that they don't go unnoticed.

Before reviewing what we've just learned about formatting pie charts, I want to mention a technique that you've probably seen before for visually highlighting slices in a pie chart:

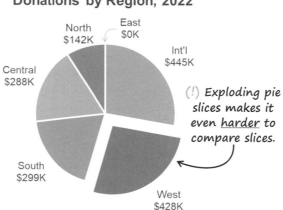

This technique is called "exploding" pie slices. I avoid it because putting distance between pie slices makes it even harder for audiences to compare the sizes of the slices with the total or one another. There are perceptually safer options for highlighting slices, such as using a color that's darker than the rest of the palette or putting a border around slice(s) that we want to highlight (we'll see even more visual highlighting options in the "Part 5: Making charts obvious" section later on in the book):

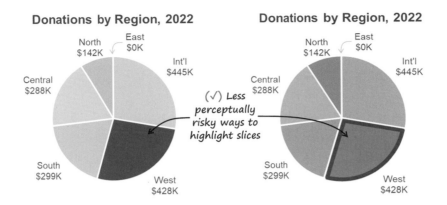

Key takeaways: Highlighting slices

- Avoid using the "exploded pie slice" technique to highlight slices in a pie chart.
- Consider other highlighting techniques instead, such as using darker colors or adding borders.

As usual, everything we saw in this section is summarized in a handy...

CHEAT SHEET:
FORMATTING PIE CHARTS

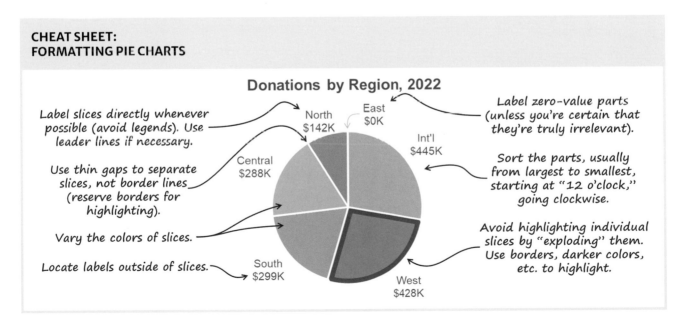

Are we done with pie charts yet? Nope. (WTH!) There are still one or two common pie chart-related questions that come up in workshops that we haven't addressed yet, so let's tackle them in a...

PIE CHART FAQ

What about donut charts?

There's a good chance that you've seen a version of a pie chart that looks something like this before:

A donut chart is basically a pie chart with the center removed. Why remove the center? As far as I can tell, there are two reasons that chart creators sometimes use donut charts rather than pie charts:

- Some audiences find donut charts slightly more aesthetically pleasing than pie charts (although others don't).

- Placing the value of the total in the center rather than above or below the chart can save a bit of space, which can be useful in certain situations, like on a dashboard where space is at a premium.

The downside of donut charts is that they offer fewer "visual clues" to help audiences estimate and compare the parts. For example, the internal angles of the slices aren't visible in a donut chart, but they are in a pie chart. This suggests that audiences might not be able to estimate or compare values in a donut chart quite as well as they can in a pie chart. This is borne out by research, which suggests that most audiences are, at best, slightly worse at estimating and comparing values in donut charts than in pie charts.

I personally don't think that donut charts are super-problematic, but I tend to use pie charts instead of donut charts because I don't think that their (minor) advantages outweigh their (minor) disadvantages.

> **Key takeaway: Donut charts**
>
> • Although I don't consider donut charts to be very problematic, I consider them to be slightly less effective than pie charts, so I recommend using pie charts instead.

Why do so many people hate pie charts?

Well, *I* don't hate pie charts, so I can only go by what I hear and read from those who feel that pie charts are never the best choice.

Pie charts have been around since at least 1801, and the controversy around them has been around since at least the 1910s. During the past 100 years or so, many research studies have been published about pie charts and the early ones tended to suggest that the weaknesses of pie charts always outweighed whatever strengths they had. Well-known experts then wrote influential articles and books that interpreted those findings to mean that pie charts should never be used. For a number of years, I was convinced by those arguments and recommended against using pie charts, as well.

However, on re-reading those books and articles in recent years, I've come to believe that they exaggerated pie charts' weaknesses and under-valued pie charts' strengths. I'm not alone in this view, and, since at least the early 2010s, I've noticed that views on "the pie chart question" seem to be shifting. As I write this in 2023, the majority of people with whom I interact in the dataviz community, from in-the-trenches practitioners to dataviz educators and researchers, now seem to also believe that pie charts can sometimes be the most effective choice. Although many people still believe that pie charts should never be used, the balance of opinion seems to be shifting. I'm not saying that more believers makes a given belief correct, only that this question is now more controversial than it once was.

Nonetheless, there are still plenty of never-pie-charters out there, and there's a chance that there will be some in your audience. If that's the case, they may assume that your use of pie charts indicates that you "don't know basic dataviz best practices," and they may even call you out on it, which can derail the conversation into talking about pie charts rather than talking about the data. If you feel that that's a risk, the benefits that pie charts offer may be outweighed by the risk of derailing the conversation, so you might be better off using another chart type even if a pie chart would do a better job in the situation at hand. Ideally, you'll have the time and opportunity to try to sell the audience on why pie charts can sometimes be the most effective choice (if that's what you believe), but I know that that's not always possible in real-world settings.

> **Key takeaways: Pie chart hate**
>
> • Although many people now consider pie charts to be the most effective choice in certain situations, many others still consider that pie charts are never a good choice and that using them is a "bad dataviz practice."

- **If you feel that using a pie chart may cause controversy or credibility issues, it may be best to use another chart type in situations when you'd normally use a pie chart.**

Now we're done with pie charts. 'bout bloody time, amiright? As it turns out, "simple" chart types aren't very simple! Let's move on to…

Chapter 8

Maps

ODDLY, THE MOST important takeaway from this chapter might just be…

WHEN *NOT* TO USE A MAP

If a data set contains location information (country names, postal codes, etc.), many chart creators automatically assume that they need to show that data as a map. A map *might* be the most effective choice, but it's not *always* the most effective choice, and there are some important downsides to be aware of if we decide to show our data as a map instead of, say, a bar chart or a line chart. What, exactly, are the downsides of maps? Let's look at an example:

Let's say we work for a charity, and we've divided our U.S. donors into six regions. The map below uses *bubbles* to show total donations for each region:

Donations by Region, 2022

Donations
- $100K
- $150K
- $200K
- $250K
- $300K

© 2020 Mapbox © OpenStreetMap

Seems like a perfectly reasonable chart until we try to actually use it to answer some basic questions about this data: Which region had the lowest donations? Hmm… Well, at least we can see which region had the highest donations, but what, exactly, is the donation total for that largest region? $250K? $300K? Uhhh…

What if a different type of map were used? Would that allow us to estimate and compare the values in the map more precisely?

None of these allows for precise comparisons of values!

Not really. With all these types of maps—and, in fact, *any* type of map—the audience will only be able make rough estimates and comparisons of the values for each region. There simply aren't any ways to show values on a map with high precision (that I'm aware of, anyway). Although the "bars on regions" map above on the right offers a *bit* more precision that the other options, the facts that the bars are offset (the bottoms of the bars aren't aligned) and that they're far apart from one another makes it hard to compare their lengths precisely.

However, many "non-map" chart types (bar charts, line charts, etc.) *do* allow the audience to estimate and compare values with high precision:

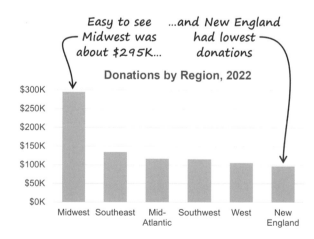

Many chart creators don't realize that, when they choose to show data as a map instead of, say, a bar chart or a line chart, the audience will only be able to make very rough estimates and comparisons of the values for each region in the map. Now, that might or might not be a problem, depending on the specific insight that needs to be communicated. In the scenario above, for example, if we only needed to show that the Midwest had much higher donations than the other regions, any of the four types of maps that I showed would work just fine. If, however, we needed to communicate that New England had the lowest donations, no map can offer enough precision to show which of the similar, smaller values was smallest, so we'd need to switch to a bar chart or other non-map, high-precision chart type to show that insight.

There's another important factor to consider when deciding whether to show data as a map or not: the importance of *geography* in the specific insight that we're communicating. In the "donations" scenario above, for example, is it important to show where each region is physically located, how big each region is, which regions border which other regions, etc.? No, when it comes to charitable donations, geographical details like those probably aren't important at all, so showing the data on a map isn't actually adding much useful information, and something like a bar chart would be fine (and more precise).

There are also plenty of situations in which geography *is* important, however. For example, remember the "shipping times" map that we saw way back in our discussion of color in Part 1?

In this scenario, geographical information such as which regions are farther from distribution centers, the fact that there are clusters of adjacent countries which are all experiencing longer shipping times, etc., is highly relevant. Showing this data as, say, a bar chart instead of a map would hide that important geographical information, so a map is a better choice in this situation. Even though the shipping times for different regions can't be estimated or compared precisely in a map like this, that isn't as important as showing the geographical locations of the values for many of the insights that we'd probably want to communicate about this data.

Therefore, when it comes to deciding whether or not to use a map, **we first need to decide what's more important: allowing values to be estimated and compared *precisely*, or showing the *locations* of the values, because we can't have both in a single chart** 🙁 If both location *and* high precision are important for the specific insight that we need to communicate, we need to show a map with a bar chart or line chart of the same data alongside it, and I find myself doing exactly that fairly often.

Key takeaways: When *not* to use a map

- Don't assume that, just because a data set contains location information, it should be shown as a map.
- It's not possible to show values with high precision on a map.
- If estimating or comparing values with high precision is more important than showing the locations of values, consider using a bar chart, line chart, or other high-precision chart type instead of a map.

For the examples in the rest of this chapter, I'm going to assume that showing the locations of values *is* more important than showing values with high precision so that we can talk more about…

ESSENTIAL MAP TYPES

A moment ago, I showed a variety of different map types (bubbles on regions, colored regions, colored dots on regions, bars on regions). These different types of maps have different strengths and weaknesses, and choosing a good map type for the situation at hand can make or break a map. Unfortunately, chart creators often don't choose a good map type for the situation at hand, which causes maps to flop with audiences distressingly often.

Like other chart type decisions that we've seen, choosing a map type can be tricky, and there are a variety of factors to take into account, so let's have a closer look at when it makes sense to use each type. As usual, we'll summarize what we've learned in a decision tree at the end of this chapter that can guide us to good map type choices in a wide variety of situations.

Let's look at the types of maps that we're likely to need for day-to-day reporting and decision making, beginning with…

Colored regions (a.k.a. "choropleth maps")

Probably the most common way to show values on a map is the "choropleth method":

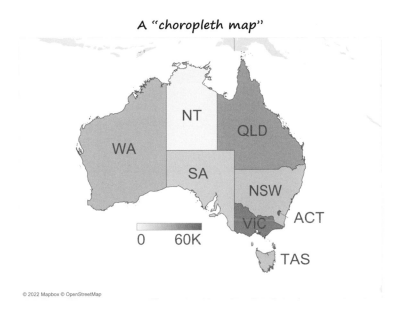

A "choropleth map"

© 2022 Mapbox © OpenStreetMap

Although it's very popular, this is the map type that I use the least often because it has two significant downsides:

1. Large regions always draw attention even when they're unimportant.

In the choropleth map above, the WA region (Western Australia) will always be very noticeable—whether it warrants attention or not—simply because it's *big*. If we were showing something like cancer rates, that region might have a very average value that doesn't warrant attention, but it will draw a lot of attention anyway because of its geographical size. In choropleth maps of South America, we have the same problem with Brazil. For U.S. states, it's Texas, California, and Alaska. For choropleth maps of the world, it's Russia and Canada.

Probably an even bigger concern with choropleth maps is that…

2. Small regions can be unnoticeable or invisible.

In the choropleth map above, the tiny ACT (Australian Capital Territory) region actually has the largest value, but it's almost unnoticeable because it's so geographically small. In choropleth maps of Europe, we always have this problem with geographically small countries like Luxemburg, Monaco, and Andorra. In choropleth maps of U.S. states, regions like Washington D.C. and Rhode Island are virtually invisible. In Asia, it's Singapore and Hong Kong. Imagine if we were showing something like "Average household income"; some of those small regions might have very large values, but those important values would be all but invisible in a choropleth map.

Other map types that we'll see next don't have those same perceptual problems, so does that mean that we should avoid using choropleth maps altogether? Pretty much, IMHO. An exception might be if we're showing an area in which all regions happen to be more or less the same size and shape, but that's very rare in practice.

> **Key takeaway: Choropleth maps**
>
> • Avoid using choropleth maps unless all regions are more or less the same geographical size and shape (which is rare).

Colored dots on regions

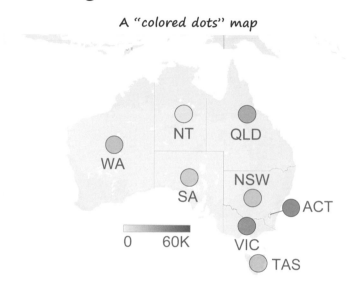

A "colored dots" map

© 2023 Mapbox © OpenStreetMap

Colored dots are safer than choropleth maps because the dots for all regions are the same size, so the geographical sizes of the regions don't affect how the audience perceives the values in the map. Values for large regions don't draw unwarranted attention, and values for small regions don't disappear.

If a region is very small, it might get completely hidden by its dot, but this can be avoided by simply moving the dot to the side and connecting it to the small region with a "leader line" as I did with the dot for the ACT region in the map above.

> **Key takeaway: Colored dots on regions**
>
> • Colored dots on regions are generally a safe option for showing values on a map.

Tile maps

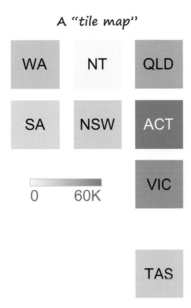

A "tile map"

Tile maps are also safer than choropleth maps because the regions have all been "normalized" to the same size and shape, so geographically large regions don't visually dominate, and small regions don't disappear.

The obvious downside of tile maps is that they seriously distort the underlying geography. The tile map above, for example, no longer looks like Australia, and it makes it look like the Australian Capital Territory (ACT) shares a border with Queensland (QLD), which it definitely doesn't. Now, this may or may not be a problem, depending on the situation. If we're showing something like election results, for example, those geographic details might not matter, and just showing very rough locations of values might be fine.

Another potential downside of tile maps is that they aren't a built-in chart type in many dataviz software products, so creating them can be a challenge.

So, when should we use a tile map? The main and possibly only advantage of tile maps is that they can look less visually busy than maps with a detailed geographical base layer (like the "colored dots" example that we saw before), but they still provide a general idea of the locations of values. If showing detailed geography is truly unnecessary in the situation at hand, then a tile map is an option.

Key takeaway: Tile maps

- If it's only necessary to show the general locations of values and it's not necessary to show detailed geography, a tile map can be considered.

Bubble maps

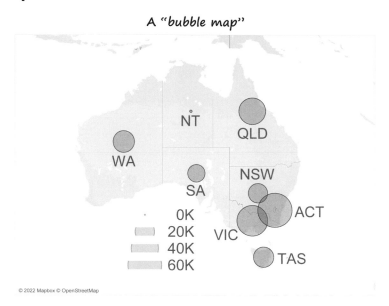

A "bubble map"

© 2022 Mapbox © OpenStreetMap

The only real risk with bubble maps (a.k.a. "proportional symbol maps") is that small values may become unnoticeable because they'll appear as tiny dots that might be easy to miss (or mistaken for town markers, small lakes, etc.). This could cause the audience to think that a region doesn't have a value when, in fact, it does (albeit a small one). For example, the bubble for Northern Territory (NT) in the map above could easily be missed, causing the audience to think that that region doesn't have a value even though it does. Therefore, **if the data contains very small values, bubble maps should be avoided.**

Some readers might suggest that another risk of bubble maps is that a large bubble could completely hide a smaller one, but that risk can be eliminated by making the bubbles semi-transparent and putting a thin outline around them as I've done in the bubble map above. This way, a small bubble underneath a large one would still be visible.

Key takeaways: Bubble maps

- Bubbles are generally a safe option for showing values on a map; however, they should be avoided if the data contains very small values that might be missed as very small bubbles.
- Always make bubbles in bubble maps semi-transparent with a dark border.

Bars on regions

A "bars on regions" map

As we saw earlier, bars on a map offer a bit more precision than other map types but still not as much precision as a regular (non-map) bar chart.

Bars on maps have the same risk as bubbles in that very small values appear as very short bars that could be easily missed on the map, causing the audience to assume that a region with a small value has no value at all.

Another consideration with bars on regions is that, on a map with many regions and values (e.g., a world map with values for 195 countries), bars can look visually busier and make it harder to spot "spatial" patterns, such as geographical clusters of high or low values, compared with bubbles or colored dots.

Yet another consideration with bars on maps is that, for some reason that I completely fail to understand, many dataviz software products don't support this kind of map as a built-in chart type. If that's the case for your software product, you might end up drawing rectangles on a map by hand, which could be tedious.

Key takeaways: Bars on maps

- Bars on maps offer slightly higher precision than other map types.
- Bars on maps should be avoided when the data includes very small values that might not be noticeable as very short bars, or when there are many values on a map and it's important to be able to spot spatial patterns among values.

So far, we've just been looking at ways of showing a static snapshot of data on a map, but what about…

SHOWING VALUES WITH LOCATIONS CHANGING OVER TIME (LINES ON REGIONS)

What if we need to show how values that are associated with locations changed over time? Although it's not a great solution, the best we'll probably be able to do is to put mini line charts on a map:

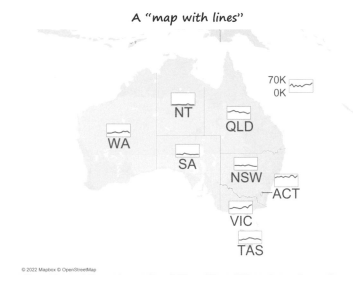

This makes it hard to compare the patterns of change for different regions because the lines aren't arranged for easy comparison, so now is probably a good time for a reminder that, as always, when it comes to using a map, we should start by asking whether showing locations of values is more important than offering high-precision comparisons. If making high-precision comparisons is more important than showing the locations of values, we should skip the map altogether and just show a standard line chart because that will make it considerably easier for the audience to precisely compare the patterns of change in different regions:

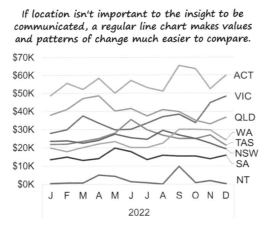

If location isn't important to the insight to be communicated, a regular line chart makes values and patterns of change much easier to compare.

Key takeaways: Lines on maps

- To show values associated with locations changing over time, consider showing line charts on maps.
- If high-precision comparison is more important than showing the locations of values, show a regular (non-map) line chart.

As usual, let's summarize what we've learned about when to use these various map types as a...

DECISION TREE: CHOOSING A MAP TYPE

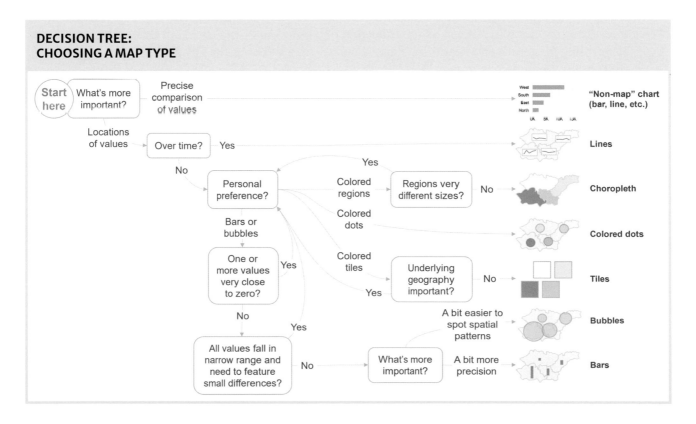

A close look at the previous decision tree will reveal that, when choosing a map type, there's a small bit of room for subjective personal preference, unlike with most other chart type decisions (note the "Personal preference?" box in the decision tree). There are some situations in which two—or possibly even three—map types would work equally well, so we won't go wrong if we pick whichever type we prefer from among the available options.

A few final thoughts before we leave maps behind:

There are a few "soft" advantages of maps compared with bar charts, line charts, etc. that I didn't mention but that can legitimately bias us toward choosing to show data on a map in certain situations:

1. Maps tend to be more visually engaging than bar charts, line charts, etc. If we're designing an infographic or other chart where the main goal is to grab attention, it might make sense to be biased toward using a map unless the higher precision of a bar or line chart is absolutely required.

2. If the audience is very familiar with the geography of an area, they may be able to associate values with the regions in that area more quickly on a map than in a bar or line chart that shows the names of the regions.

3. Compared with something like a bar chart or line chart, maps make it more immediately obvious that the audience is looking at values that are associated with locations in much the same way that pie charts make it more immediately obvious that the audience is looking at the breakdown of a total.

Also, note that I've only used geographical examples in this chapter, but a "map" can be any two-dimensional space, such as the floorplan of a building or the layout of a circuit board. Regardless of what type of two-dimensional space we're showing, the guidelines in this chapter remain the same.

Finally, I want to mention that there are many other types of maps in addition to those that we saw in this chapter. Cartography is a rich field with innumerable specialized map types for everything from finding good locations for cellular network antennas to identifying buried archeological sites. As mentioned earlier, I've limited this book to chart types that are likely to be needed for everyday reporting and decision making in most organizations.

That's it for maps, so let's move on to an obscure little chart type that you may never have heard of, that is…

Chapter 9

Bar charts

Whatthewhat??? Why have we waited this long to talk about what's probably the single most common chart type on the planet?

ODDLY ENOUGH, WE already *have* seen when it does or doesn't make sense to use a bar chart. In all the chart type decision trees that we've seen, bar charts were always an option:

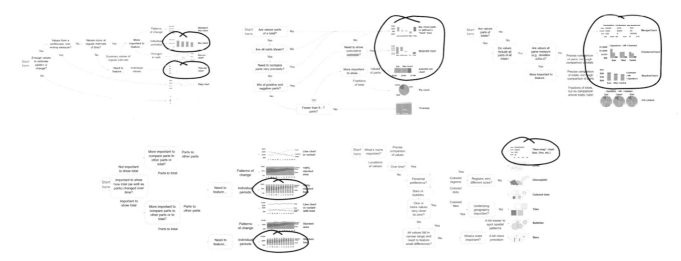

So, as it turns out, we *already* know when it makes sense to use a bar chart instead of a pie chart, a bar chart instead of a line chart, a bar chart instead of a map, etc.

Bar charts are unique among chart types because they can be used to show *any* type of quantitative data (time series, breakdown of a total, etc.); they're always an option in every situation. They're also a high-precision chart type, which is a plus.

> So why not **always** use bar charts in all situations?

Two reasons:

1. Bar charts aren't as good as other chart types at showing many types of patterns and relationships. For example, we've seen that pie charts are better at showing fractions of a total, and line charts are better at showing patterns of change. Bar charts *can* show those patterns and relationships, but other chart types often do a better job of it.

2. Because bar charts can show virtually any kind of data, the audience must *figure out* what kind of data they're looking at by reading the chart's title, axis labels, etc.:

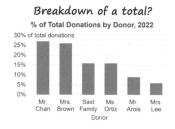

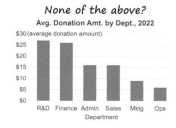

However, when the audience sees a line chart, pie chart, map, etc., they *instantly* know what kind of data they're looking at, even before reading any text in the chart. Yes, when the audience reads a bar chart's title and labels, they'll figure out what kind of data they're looking at, but other chart types skip that cognitive step altogether.

Participants in my workshops sometimes say that they also avoid bar charts because they're *boring* (bar charts, that is, not workshop participants ☺). Randomizing chart types just for the sake of variety, however, isn't a good way to make charts more interesting. If a bar chart is the truly most effective choice in a given situation, choosing another chart type to "spice things up" will just make key insights less obvious and possibly confuse—or even mislead—the audience. There are better ways to make charts more engaging (yes, even bar charts), such as adding visual highlighting, comparison values, and insights in callouts, which we'll talk more about in "Part 6: Making charts less boring."

Because we've already seen when it does and doesn't make sense to use a bar chart, we can jump straight to the bar chart decision tree. To be honest, I'm not expecting anyone to actually use this tree to choose a chart type in practice because the alternatives to bar charts are "every other chart type," which isn't that useful. This decision tree, therefore, is more of a review of all the other chart types that we've seen:

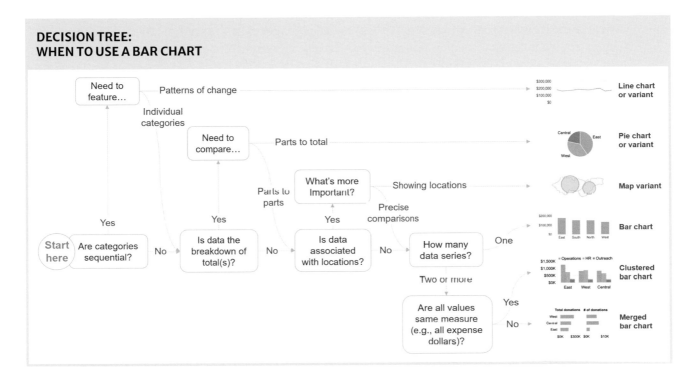

DECISION TREE: WHEN TO USE A BAR CHART

Key takeaways: Bar charts

- Bar charts are an option in every situation, but they aren't always the most effective option.
- Knowing when to use a bar chart in any given situation requires knowing when to use all other major chart types.

FORMATTING BAR CHARTS

As one might expect, formatting bar charts is pretty straightforward. There are really only two formatting guidelines that might not be obvious to most chart creators:

1. Including zero in the scale

We already talked about when the quantitative scale in a chart can be "truncated" (started at something other than zero) in our discussion of quantitative scales in Part 1, but I want to add a note that's specific to bar charts regarding this design choice. Although it can be tricky to determine when we can or can't truncate the scale of a line chart, dot plot, etc., **truncating the scale of a bar chart is *always* a bad idea** even though I see chart creators do this pretty often in practice.

Why is truncating the scale of a bar chart *always* a bad idea? Bar charts represent quantities as *bar lengths*. A bar that's twice as long as another bar should, therefore, represent twice the quantity. If the scale of a bar chart is truncated, though, that's no longer true:

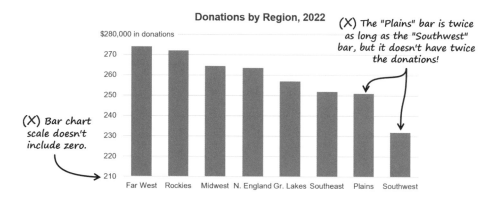

Unfortunately, some dataviz software products will happily generate a chart like the one above by default, so it's important to be aware of this guideline so that we know to correct a chart like this before it's shown to an audience.

Why would a chart creator even be tempted to truncate the scale of a bar chart? It's almost always because they need to show small differences among values that all fall in a narrow range that's far from zero:

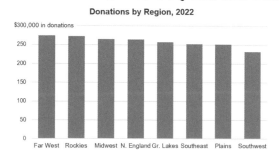

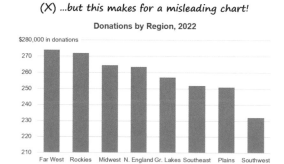

As we saw in our discussion of quantitative scales in Part 1, there's another, better solution in these situations, although it rarely occurs to chart creators:

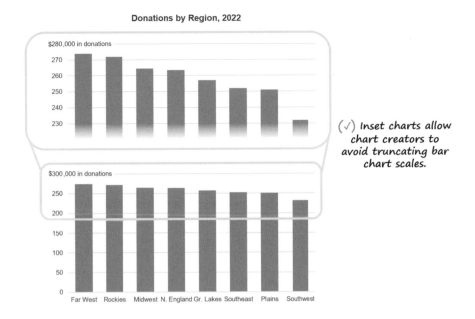

With inset charts, we can always include zero in our bar chart scales and use insets to feature small differences among values (assuming that those small differences are relevant to the insight being communicated).

2. Labeling "zero-length" bars

If our bar chart happens to contain a "zero-length" bar like the one below, it will be unclear what the zero-length bar represents unless it's explicitly noted:

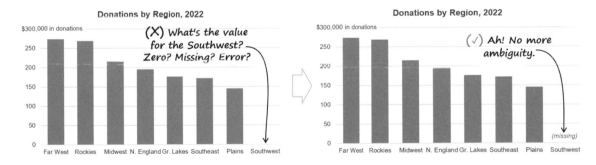

As we've seen, a value of "zero" is very different than a "missing value" or "error." "Zero" means we *know* what the value was; it was zero. When we have a zero-length bar in a bar chart, then, **we *must* note, directly in the chart, what the zero-length bar represents** ("zero," "unknown," "TBD," "error," etc.). Chart creators often fail to do this, leaving audiences guessing what the values in a bar chart actually are.

There are other guidelines for designing bar charts, but they're either very obvious, or we've talked about them already, so let's recap in a…

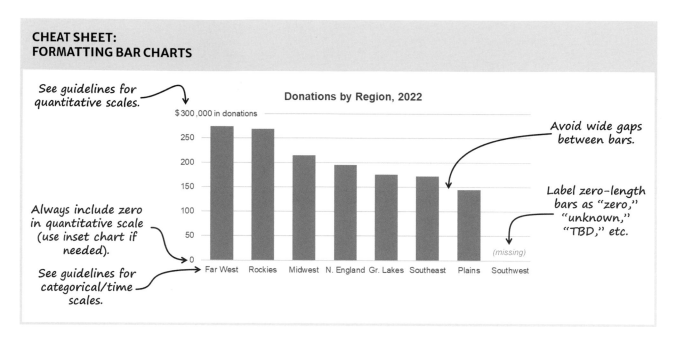

**CHEAT SHEET:
FORMATTING BAR CHARTS**

See guidelines for quantitative scales.

Donations by Region, 2022

Avoid wide gaps between bars.

Label zero-length bars as "zero," "unknown," "TBD," etc.

Always include zero in quantitative scale (use inset chart if needed).

See guidelines for categorical/time scales.

$300,000 in donations
250
200
150
100
50
0

Far West   Rockies   Midwest   N. England   Gr. Lakes   Southeast   Plains   Southwest (missing)

Hopefully, it's now clear that we have, in fact, been talking about bar charts since the beginning of this part of the book, so we actually *didn't* wait this long to talk about them ☺

On to another little-known chart type, that is…

Chapter 10

Tables

THE FIRST DESIGN choice that we usually need to make when designing a chart is whether to show the data as a table or a graph. It's probably obvious to you by this point in the book that this design choice can make a *big* difference in how the audience perceives the underlying data. Many chart creators and audiences don't seem to appreciate just how dramatic that difference can be, and some might even consider that tables and graphs are "pretty much the same." It's worth taking a moment, then, to compare…

TABLES VERSUS GRAPHS

To see for yourself just how differently we perceive tables versus graphs, try the following demonstration:

Try to spot as many patterns or insights as you can in the table below, even fairly obvious ones, such as "The East has higher revenue than the West for all months." Try spot at least three before turning to the next page.

Monthly Revenue by Region | 2022

	Jan	Feb	Mar	Apr	May	Jun	Jul	Aug	Sep	Oct	Nov	Dec
East	$53,201	$57,276	$49,452	$55,494	$59,388	$54,184	$60,384	$62,555	$50,611	$60,686	$64,514	$59,523
West	$48,271	$46,676	$47,529	$48,591	$49,109	$47,752	$48,752	$48,499	$41,249	$48,626	$50,094	$50,074

Now, turn to the next page, and try to spot potentially interesting insights in the same data shown as a graph…

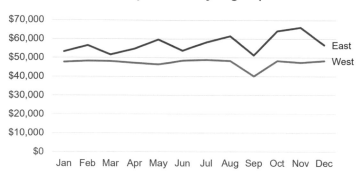

Not only is it far faster and easier to spot insights in a graph than in a table, but many insights are also far more obvious, i.e., more likely to get noticed in the first place. For example, in the table, did you notice the cyclical pattern in the East? Or the "double dip" in September? Or that the East is trending slightly upward, but the West is flat? With enough time and effort, you might have eventually spotted those insights in the table, but, realistically, how often are audiences going to spend put in that kind of time and effort?

Compared with tables, graphs generally:

- Make insights more obvious.

- Are much faster to interpret.

- Require less mental effort to interpret, so readers are less likely to skip reading them.

- Are more visually interesting than tables, which also reduces the risk that they'll get skipped.

- Make the nature of the data more obvious (breakdown of a total, time series, location-based, etc.).

- Convey "the big picture" more quickly, e.g., "five big values and two small ones," "four things increasing and one thing decreasing," etc.

> **Key takeaway: Advantages of graphs over tables**
>
> - Graphs have several significant advantages over tables, but many chart creators and audiences aren't aware of those advantages.

Does that mean that we should *always* use graphs instead of tables? Let's test that idea.

In training workshops, when I introduce the topic of tables, I start by asking participants for situations in which they'd choose to show data as a table rather than a graph. Participants always come up with a variety of situations in which they feel that they should—or even must—use a table rather than a graph. For almost all the situations that they describe, however, I'm able to show examples of graphs that would usually be more effective in those same situations. For example…

When there are many values

Chart creators sometimes assume that, if there are many values in a data set, they can't be shown as a graph and must be shown as a table. In this book, however, we've already seen many examples of graphs that not only *can* show hundreds or even thousands of values, but that are far easier to consume than if the same data were shown as a massive table of numbers:

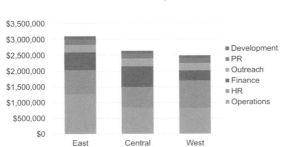

Graphs can show many values.

When the data includes both details (i.e., breakdowns) and totals

Chart creators sometimes assume that breakdowns and totals can't be shown in a graph because the totals are always much larger than the breakdown values. However, we've already seen many examples of graphs that show both breakdowns and totals effectively:

Graphs can show breakdowns (details) and totals.

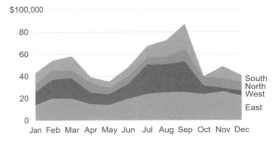

When the data contains outliers

Chart creators sometimes assume that data that contains outliers must be shown as a table because outliers tend to "crush" the smaller values in graphs. Again, we've already seen a variety of examples of graphs that contain outliers but that are very effective, usually because they use inset charts to avoid "crushing" the smaller values:

Graphs can show outliers.

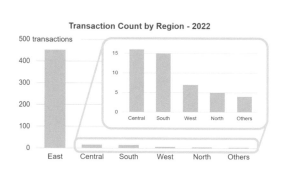

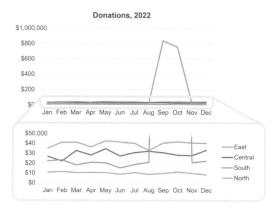

When the data contains several different measures

Chart creators sometimes assume that data that contains multiple different measures (e.g., Average Donation Amount *and* Donor Satisfaction Rating *and* Average Household Income) must be shown as a table because different measures can't be shown in the same graph. We've already seen several examples of effective graphs that show multiple different measures, usually using "merged" or "index" charts (we'll talk more about index charts later in "Part 5: Making charts obvious"):

Graphs can show multiple measures.

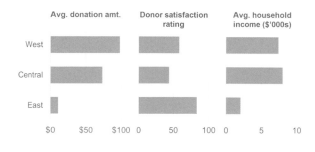

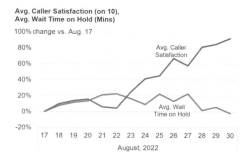

When the structure of the data is complex (i.e., multi-dimensional)

Surprisingly often, we need to show data with a mix of different measures and categories, i.e., data with a complex structure. For example, maybe we need to show some sales information that includes four measures (Sales in $, Sales in Units, Profit in $, Discount %) for three product categories (Furniture, Office Supplies, Technology) over time (12 months):

Multiple categories   *Multiple measures*   *Over time*

Monthly key results by product category, 2017

		Jan	Feb	Mar	Apr	May	Jun	Jul	Aug	Sep	Oct	Nov	Dec
Furniture	Sales ($K USD)	159	3,333	693	541	171	1,584	2,740	1,697	7,003	1,369	448	1,697
	Quantity (Units)	4	21	22	19	3	20	30	14	41	22	8	37
	Profit ($K USD)	-1	102	3	-23	-6	26	301	168	1,072	-9	41	-148
	Avg. Discount	10%	22%	7%	14%	20%	23%	13%	12%	16%	13%	4%	13%
Office Supplies	Sales ($K USD)	85	364	1,190	246	183	732	395	5,841	2,078	2,140	1,135	3,581
	Quantity (Units)	27	21	50	39	12	44	25	112	96	59	65	132
	Profit ($K USD)	21	152	118	89	69	181	149	1,614	696	705	167	299
	Avg. Discount	30%	14%	9%	11%	10%	25%	0%	10%	14%	2%	7%	14%
Technology	Sales ($K USD)	352	1,294	15,848	275	36	2,805	1,557	1,544	5,027	687	5,121	1,552
	Quantity (Units)	5	14	21	11	3	21	7	14	43	21	42	15
	Profit ($K USD)	33	82	7,278	47	-1	277	312	395	358	55	717	389
	Avg. Discount	10%	25%	5%	0%	20%	15%	0%	20%	14%	15%	13%	12%

Chart creators often assume that data with a complex structure like this can't be shown as a graph and therefore must be shown as a table. However, it's almost always possible to show data with a complex structure as a graph. This requires a relatively high level of dataviz skill, which we'll learn shortly in "Part 3: Showing data with a more complex structure (small multiples)":

Graphs can show data that has a complex structure.

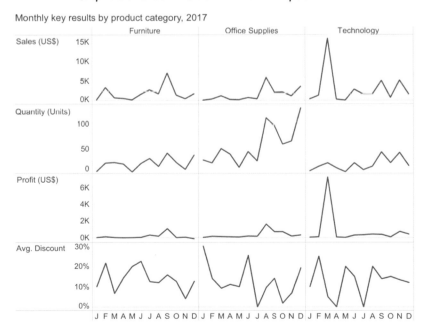

Monthly key results by product category, 2017

Yes, graphs of data with a complex structure like the one above are a little complicated to interpret, but a table of the same data is *also* complicated. When an audience sees the data as a graph, however, they can see patterns and relationships more quickly and easily (e.g., the "March spikes" in the Technology category) than when viewing the same data in a table.

When the audience needs to see exact values

As we've seen, even the most precise graph shows the data with some loss of precision. A table, however, offers perfect precision, down to the last digit. Audiences sometimes insist that they need to see exact values all the time and therefore insist on seeing data as tables instead of graphs. In my experience, however, exact values aren't needed for most decision making. In most situations, the precision that graphs provide is more than enough.

Having said that, there are times when showing exact values is genuinely necessary, for example, if a chart will be included in a financial report that needs to show exact values for legal reasons. We can provide tables in these situations, but, as I hope is now clear, tables are far slower and more cognitively effortful to read, and they make insights far less obvious. Is there a better option? Yes: show both!

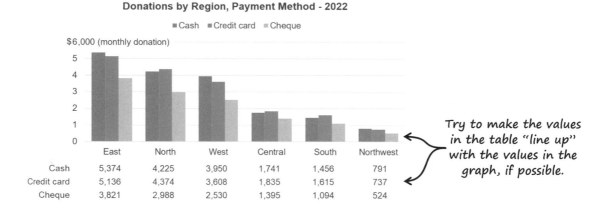

As we saw in Part 1, I show tables with graphs of the same data pretty often in practice because this offers the best of both worlds: the speed and insightfulness of a graph along with the exact precision of a table.

When the audience has accessibility challenges

Tables are generally more accessible than graphs to audience members with certain visual, cognitive, or physical challenges, so, if we know that our audience includes people with those types of challenges, it can be a good practice to ensure that our data is available as tables. That doesn't mean that we should *only* show data as tables, however. As we just saw, showing tables *and* graphs of the same data offers the best of both worlds, making things easier for those with visual, cognitive, or physical challenges, as well as for those without.

When the audience prefers tables (often, because they have a financial background)

Some chart consumers—especially those with financial backgrounds—insist on seeing data as tables instead of graphs because they're "more comfortable with tables" or are "more used to reading tables."

Remember the "try to spot insights in this table versus this graph" demonstration that we did at the beginning of this chapter? I've run that demonstration for audiences with financial backgrounds to show them just how many insights they've probably missed over the years by only looking at data as tables and not as graphs. Most of those audiences were shocked when they saw how much more informative graphs can be compared with tables and started asking for graphs along with tables thereafter.

Although some audiences may *think* they're just as a good at spotting patterns and insights in tables as in graphs, the human visual system (eye, optic nerve, and visual cortex) is a lot better at doing so in graphs—even the visual systems of accountants 😃

If your audience insists on tables, try to get them to do the "spot insights in this table versus this graph" demonstration. If they still only want tables after that, give them graphs alongside the tables. If they still only want tables with no graphs, try sneaking some graphical elements into their tables (the old "putting kale in the lasagna" trick), which can actually make tables a lot more informative and quicker to consume:

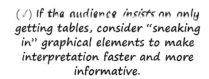

(✓) If the audience *insists* on only getting tables, consider "sneaking in" graphical elements to make interpretation faster and more informative.

Funds Raised (US$) by Event by Region

		South	West	East	Central	Total
06-Jan-2021	5K Walk	133,213	85,240	112,564	84,501	415,519
09-Feb-2021	Telethon	124,864	76,939	59,710	76,578	338,091
06-Mar-2021	Pancake Breakfast	143,532	108,022	95,531	87,011	434,096
24-Apr-2021	Country Fair	90,896	137,051	91,057	81,661	400,665
13-Jun-2021	5K Walk	124,161	140,023	80,571	73,330	418,085
17-Dec-2021	Black Tie Gala	116,269	70,750	85,637	82,340	354,997
		732,935	618,025	525,071	485,421	2,361,453

Funds Raised (US$) by Region (Jan-May 2022)

	Jan	Feb	Mar	Apr	May	Trend	Total
North	87,011	95,531	136,690	143,532	108,022		570,786
South	73,330	80,571	91,027	124,161	140,023		509,112
Central	81,661	91,057	103,358	90,896	137,051		504,023
East	84,501	112,564	73,939	133,213	85,240		489,458
West	76,578	59,710	52,355	124,864	76,939		390,447
	403,081	439,434	457,369	616,666	547,275		2,463,825

Funds Raised (US$) by Region (Jan-May 2022)

	Jan	Feb	Mar	Apr	May	Total
North	87,011	95,531	136,690	143,532	108,022	570,786
South	73,330	80,571	91,027	124,161	140,023	509,112
Central	81,661	91,057	103,358	90,896	137,051	504,023
East	84,501	112,564	73,939	133,213	85,240	489,458
West	76,578	59,710	52,355	124,864	76,939	390,447
	403,081	439,434	457,369	616,666	547,275	2,463,825

When you need to "just show the data" with none of the interpretation that a graph would introduce

Many chart creators think of tables as "just the numbers," i.e., that tables don't contain any interpretation by the chart creator. That's not quite true, however (unfortunately). As we'll see in "Part 5: Making charts obvious," both graphs and tables are laced with the chart creator's interpretations of the data and their assumptions about why the audience needed to see that data because it's unavoidable.

Don't believe me? Consider this simple table:

Expenses vs. Budget, 2021

	Expenses	Budget
Operations	$534,942	$497,496
Marketing	$377,123	$343,182
Finance & Admin	$363,122	$374,016
IT	$161,994	$158,754
R&D	$133,800	$115,068

This table *looks* like raw, interpretation-free, "just the numbers" data, but it reflects dozens of design choices on the part of the chart creator, such as:

- Showing expenses broken down by department, and not by expense type or some other type of category

- Not showing budget deviations in dollars, percentages, changes from the previous year, etc.

- Not showing the percentage of total expenses that each department represents

- Showing annual totals rather than, say, quarterly or monthly ones

- Not showing the expense total for all departments or the deviation of total expenses from total budget

- Not showing breakdowns of departmental expenses by sub-department, authorizing manager, etc.

- Showing all the digits instead of rounding values to the nearest "K"

Because of these design choices and many others, the table above will be good at featuring *some* insights about this data but not others. For example, it's clear which departments had the highest and lowest expenses, but it's not clear which departments did a better or worse job of sticking to their budget, or which departments' expenses are increasing or decreasing. Those insights—and many others—would require a different table design. Like graphs, tables must be designed based on the chart creator's interpretation of the data and the specific reasons why the audience needs to see that data in the first place. This is unavoidable; the alternative would be to make *random* design choices.

Therefore, **tables aren't the "neutral," "interpretation-free," "just the numbers" charts that many people assume them to be.** Graphs might make the chart creator's interpretation of the data and the purpose of the chart more obvious, but the chart creator's interpretations are still very much there in tables as well, even if they're less obvious.

> **Key takeaways: Showing data as a table or a graph**
>
> - In most situations, it's possible and preferable to show data as a graph rather than a table.
> - In situations when a table must be shown, consider showing a graph of the same data with the table.
> - Tables aren't the "interpretation-free" charts that many people assume them to be.

> Are there any situations in which it makes sense to only show a table with no accompanying graph?

Yes, but very few. In fact, there are only three very specific situations in which I'd show a table with no accompanying graph:

1. When the sole purpose of the chart is to look up values

In some situations, the only reason the audience needs a chart is to look up individual values. For example, maybe the chart will be used solely to answer questions during a meeting such as, "What were insurance expenses in August of last year?" If that's the *only* purpose that the chart will serve (i.e., it doesn't need to show insights, patterns, the "big picture", etc.), there's no need to show a graph along with the table.

2. When the sole purpose of the chart is to allow the audience to import the data into another application

Sometimes, the only reason the audience needs a chart is to import the data from that chart into another application, such as Microsoft Excel or a database. If that's the *only* purpose that the chart will serve, there's obviously no need for an accompanying graph.

3. When none of the values are directly comparable

Sometimes, none of the values in our data are directly comparable with one another. For example, in the list of "key metrics" values below on the left, it doesn't make sense to directly compare "Funds raised ($M)" with "Admin Overhead (%)," or to compare any of the values with any of the other values in the list:

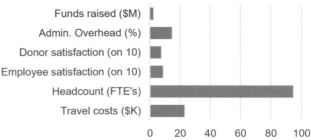

Key Metrics - November 2022

Funds raised ($M)	**2.337**
Admin. Overhead (%)	**14.6**
Donor satisfaction (on 10)	**7.43**
Employee satisfaction (on 10)	**8.66**
Headcount (FTE's)	**94.5**
Travel costs ($K)	**22.8**

(X) If values aren't directly comparable, showing them as a graph is confusing or possibly misleading!

Key Metrics - November 2022

Showing values like these as a graph invites the audience to compare these values with one another, which is confusing at best and misleading at worst. In these situations, therefore, we should avoid showing the values as a graph and only show them as a table.

Key takeaways: When to only show a table with no accompanying graph

- Only show a table with no accompanying graph if the sole purpose of the chart is to look up individual values or to import the data into another application, or if none of the values are directly comparable with one another.
- In all other situations, try to show data as graphs, or as graphs with tables.

Now that we have a good understanding of the important differences between tables and graphs and when it makes sense to use each, let's look at some guidelines for…

FORMATTING TABLES

Chart creators often assume that visual design only matters when it comes to graphs and that designing tables doesn't require much skill. As we'll see, that definitely isn't true. There are, in fact, many guidelines for formatting tables, and the fact that many chart creators aren't aware of those guidelines explains why so many tables are unnecessarily hard to read, prone to misinterpretation and, well, ugly.

To learn about table formatting guidelines, let's start with a poorly designed table and then improve it step by step. As usual, we'll summarize the key takeaways from this chapter in a cheat sheet at the end.

Spend a few unpleasant minutes looking at the table below and try to spot as many design problems and potential improvements as you can. I can spot about a dozen. I'll wait.

Funds Raised by Event by Region

Date	Event	Central	East	Northwest	South	Total
January 5, 2021	5K Walk	$84,501.28	$112,564.29	$73,938.88	$133,212.89	$404,217.34
February 9, 2021	Telethon	$76,577.54	$59,710.32	$52,355.47	$124,863.92	$313,507.25
March 6, 2021	Pancake Breakfast	$87,011.00	$95,531.00	$2,300,529.00	$143,532.00	$2,686,603.00
April 24, 2021	Country Fair	$81,661.00	$91,057.00	$103,358.00	$90,896.00	$366,972.00
June 13, 2021	5K Walk	$73,330.11	$80,571.40	$91,026.58	$124,160.98	$369,089.07
July 21, 2021	10K Run	$113,658.46	$51,457.53	$63,347.24	$2,152,220.60	$2,380,683.83
September 1, 2021	TV Raffle	$1,978,422.42	$122,914.67	$126,824.20	$100,277.92	$2,328,439.21
October 23, 2021	Teddy Bear Drive	$94,848.42	$81,772.13	$136,689.78	$144,215.17	$457,525.50
December 17, 2021	Black Tie Gala	$82,340.27	$85,637.17	$84,841.05	$116,269.49	$369,087.98
	Total:	$2,672,350.50	$781,215.51	$3,092,910.20	$3,129,648.97	$9,676,125.18

Okey-dokey then. Let's improve the design of this nasty table in steps. To begin, let's…

Minimize digits

Do we really need to show these values down to the cents? Maybe, depending on what this table will be used for, but let's assume that we consult with the audience for this table and determine that they don't need the cents, so we can get rid of those. They do need the dollars for legal reasons, however, so we can't, for example, round all the values to the nearest "$K" in this case.

Funds Raised by Event by Region

(✓) Only show as many digits as the purpose of the chart requires.

Date	Event	Central	East	Northwest	South	Total
January 5, 2021	5K Walk	$84,501	$112,564	$73,939	$133,213	$404,217
February 9, 2021	Telethon	$76,578	$59,710	$52,355	$124,864	$313,507
March 6, 2021	Pancake Breakfast	$87,011	$95,531	$2,360,529	$143,532	$2,686,603
April 24, 2021	Country Fair	$81,661	$91,057	$103,358	$90,896	$366,972
June 13, 2021	5K Walk	$73,330	$80,571	$91,027	$124,161	$369,089
July 21, 2021	10K Run	$113,658	$51,458	$63,347	$2,152,221	$2,380,684
September 1, 2021	TV Raffle	$1,978,422	$122,915	$126,824	$100,278	$2,328,439
October 23, 2021	Teddy Bear Drive	$94,848	$81,772	$136,690	$144,215	$457,526
December 17, 2021	Black Tie Gala	$82,340	$85,637	$84,841	$116,269	$369,088
	Total:	$2,672,351	$781,216	$3,092,910	$3,129,649	$9,676,125

Remove or tone down borders

As we saw in "Part 1: General chart formatting guidelines," when it comes to borders, tick marks, and other "non-data" elements, it's best to get rid of what we can and minimize (i.e., thin or lighten) the rest:

Funds Raised by Event by Region

(✓) Remove non-essential borders.

(✓) Tone down ones that remain.

Date	Event	Central	East	Northwest	South	Total
January 5, 2021	5K Walk	$84,501	$112,564	$73,939	$133,213	$404,217
February 9, 2021	Telethon	$76,578	$59,710	$52,355	$124,864	$313,507
March 6, 2021	Pancake Breakfast	$87,011	$95,531	$2,360,529	$143,532	$2,686,603
April 24, 2021	Country Fair	$81,661	$91,057	$103,358	$90,896	$366,972
June 13, 2021	5K Walk	$73,330	$80,571	$91,027	$124,161	$369,089
July 21, 2021	10K Run	$113,658	$51,458	$63,347	$2,152,221	$2,380,684
September 1, 2021	TV Raffle	$1,978,422	$122,915	$126,824	$100,278	$2,328,439
October 23, 2021	Teddy Bear Drive	$94,848	$81,772	$136,690	$144,215	$457,526
December 17, 2021	Black Tie Gala	$82,340	$85,637	$84,841	$116,269	$369,088
	Total:	$2,672,351	$781,216	$3,092,910	$3,129,649	$9,676,125

Adjust row and column spacing

With most of the borders removed, our table now looks cleaner, but it might be trickier for readers to visually scan across a row, and there's a risk that they might accidentally "skip a row" when doing so, which would be bad. By playing around with spacing, we can significantly reduce those risks:

(✓) Reduce the gaps between columns to reduce the distance that the eye needs to travel from one value to the next.

Funds Raised by Event by Region

Date	Event	Central	East	Northwest	South	Total
January 5, 2021	5K Walk	$84,501	$112,564	$73,939	$133,213	$404,217
February 9, 2021	Telethon	$76,578	$59,710	$52,355	$124,864	$313,507
March 6, 2021	Pancake Breakfast	$87,011	$95,531	$2,360,529	$143,532	$2,686,603
April 24, 2021	Country Fair	$81,661	$91,057	$103,358	$90,896	$366,972
June 13, 2021	5K Walk	$73,330	$80,571	$91,027	$124,161	$369,089
July 21, 2021	10K Run	$113,658	$51,458	$63,347	$2,152,221	$2,380,684
September 1, 2021	TV Raffle	$1,978,422	$122,915	$126,824	$100,278	$2,328,439
October 23, 2021	Teddy Bear Drive	$94,848	$81,772	$136,690	$144,215	$457,526
December 17, 2021	Black Tie Gala	$82,340	$85,637	$84,841	$116,269	$369,088
	Total:	$2,672,351	$781,216	$3,092,910	$3,129,649	$9,676,125

(✓) Add some extra spacing to visually separate the "Total" column from the other columns.

(✓) Increase the spacing between rows to reduce the risk of visually "skipping a row."

Workshop participants sometimes suggest adding "zebra striping" (shading every other row in a table) to help readers visually scan across rows. There are several problems with zebra striping, however, and, as we just saw, playing with spacing can address potential "visual scanning" concerns, which is why I almost never use zebra striping:

Funds Raised (US$) by Event by Region

		South	Northwest	Central
2021-01-05	5K Walk	133,213	73,939	84,501
2021-02-09	Telethon	124,864	52,355	76,578
2021-09-01	TV Raffle	100,278	126,824	1,978,422
2021-10-23	Teddy Bear Drive	144,215	136,690	94,848
2021-12-17	Black Tie Gala	116,269	84,841	82,340
		618,839	474,649	2,316,690

(!) Zebra striping adds a lot of visual clutter and "non-data" elements.

(!) Stripes can look like highlighting (which they definitely aren't).

Adjust alignment/justification within cells

You probably noticed that the alignment (a.k.a. "justification") within cells could be improved in a few spots:

(✓) Make the alignment of column headings the same as that of the column below.

Funds Raised by Event by Region

Date	Event	Central	East	Northwest	South	Total
January 5, 2021	5K Walk	$84,501	$112,564	$73,939	$133,213	$404,217
February 9, 2021	Telethon	$76,578	$59,710	$52,355	$124,864	$313,507
March 6, 2021	Pancake Breakfast	$87,011	$95,531	$2,360,529	$143,532	$2,686,603
April 24, 2021	Country Fair	$81,661	$91,057	$103,358	$90,896	$366,972
June 13, 2021	5K Walk	$73,330	$80,571	$91,027	$124,161	$369,089
July 21, 2021	10K Run	$113,658	$51,458	$63,347	$2,152,221	$2,380,684
September 1, 2021	TV Raffle	$1,978,422	$122,915	$126,824	$100,278	$2,328,439
October 23, 2021	Teddy Bear Drive	$94,848	$81,772	$136,690	$144,215	$457,526
December 17, 2021	Black Tie Gala	$82,340	$85,637	$84,841	$116,269	$369,088
	Total:	$2,672,351	$781,216	$3,092,910	$3,129,649	$9,676,125

(✓) Right-align numbers so that the "ten" digits line up vertically, as do the hundreds, thousands, etc. (makes numbers easier to compare).

Note that, if we have a column of values in a table that we *don't* want the audience to compare directly, a handy convention is to *left*-align those numbers, which provides a visual clue to the audience that the numbers in that column shouldn't be compared directly:

Key Metrics - November 2022

Funds raised	$2.337M
Admin. overhead	14.60%
Donor satisfaction (on 10)	7.43
Employee satisfaction (on 10)	8.66
Headcount (FTE's)	945.5
Travel costs	$22,847

(✓) Left-align columns of numbers that the audience should NOT compare directly.

Un-highlight unimportant elements, highlight important ones

With the heavy borders in our table removed, what's visually "popping out" now? Anything that's bolded, and that big, nasty red title. Should those be the most noticeable elements (i.e., are they the most important elements) in this table? Probably not. Those three crazy outlier values should probably be highlighted though…

(✓) No need to make the title huge/red/etc. Its location above the table is enough to identify it as the title.

Funds Raised by Event by Region

Date	Event	Central	East	Northwest	South	Total
January 5, 2021	5K Walk	$84,501	$112,564	$73,939	$133,213	$404,217
February 9, 2021	Telethon	$76,578	$59,710	$52,355	$124,864	$313,507
March 6, 2021	Pancake Breakfast	$87,011	$95,531	$2,360,529	$143,532	$2,686,603
April 24, 2021	Country Fair	$81,661	$91,057	$103,358	$90,896	$366,972
June 13, 2021	5K Walk	$73,330	$80,571	$91,027	$124,161	$369,089
July 21, 2021	10K Run	$113,658	$51,458	$63,347	$2,152,221	$2,380,684
September 1, 2021	TV Raffle	$1,978,422	$122,915	$126,824	$100,278	$2,328,439
October 23, 2021	Teddy Bear Drive	$94,848	$81,772	$136,690	$144,215	$457,526
December 17, 2021	Black Tie Gala	$82,340	$85,637	$84,841	$116,269	$369,088
	Total:	$2,672,351	$781,216	$3,092,910	$3,129,649	$9,676,125

(✓) The heading row, "Total" row and "Total" column are already visually distinct from the rest of the table, so there's no need to bold and draw attention to them.

(✓) With all other table elements "calmed down," even subtle highlighting is very noticeable.

Choose better date and number formats

The "Date" column is a little tough to read because the days of the month and the years don't line up vertically, so they "jump around" as the reader is scanning down the column (as we saw back in Part 1 in our discussion of date formats). We also probably don't need to tell the audience that these values are in dollars ($) 50 times. We can address both of these concerns by choosing better date and number formats:

(✓) Using a date format in which days, months and years always have the same number of characters makes columns of dates easier to read.

Funds Raised (US$) by Event by Region

(✓) Avoid repeating the unit of measurement in table values.

Date	Event	Central	East	Northwest	South	Total
05-Jan-2021	5K Walk	84,501	112,564	73,939	133,213	404,217
09-Feb-2021	Telethon	76,578	59,710	52,355	124,864	313,507
06-Mar-2021	Pancake Breakfast	87,011	95,531	2,360,529	143,532	2,686,603
24-Apr-2021	Country Fair	81,661	91,057	103,358	90,896	366,972
13-Jun-2021	5K Walk	73,330	80,571	91,027	124,161	369,089
21-Jun-2021	10K Run	113,658	51,458	63,347	2,152,221	2,380,684
01-Oct-2021	TV Raffle	1,978,422	122,915	126,824	100,278	2,328,439
23-Oct-2021	Teddy Bear Drive	94,848	81,772	136,690	144,215	457,526
17-Dec-2021	Black Tie Gala	82,340	85,637	84,841	116,269	369,088
	Total:	2,672,351	781,216	3,092,910	3,129,649	9,676,125

I think this table is in much better shape now. Although the table that we started with was usable, this better-formatted version would be considerably easier and faster for the audience read, and it looks more credible and professional to boot. Let's recap what we've learned about designing tables in a...

CHEAT SHEET:
FORMATTING TABLES

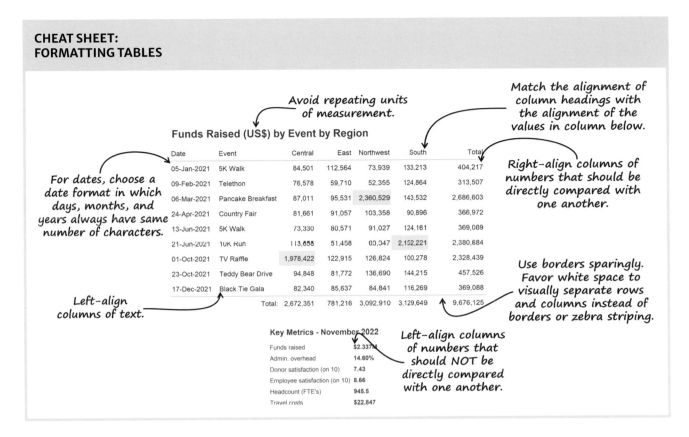

That caps off our discussion of tables.

The next chart type that we'll see isn't really a "chart type" *per se*, it's…

Chapter 11

Combo charts

PARTICIPANTS IN MY training workshops often ask about "combo charts," i.e., single charts that combine two or more chart types. There are many different chart type combinations, but probably the most common one is a bar chart combined with a line chart:

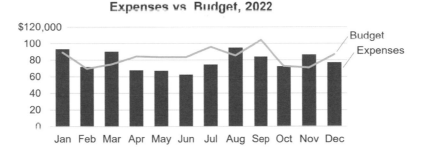

A "combo chart" (bar chart + line chart)

Note that in this situation, it wasn't necessary to use a combo chart, and a single chart type could have been used. For example, the chart above could have used only lines or only bars:

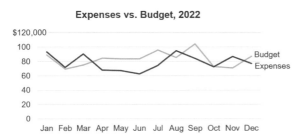

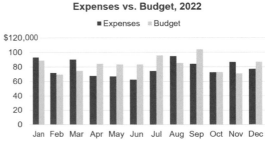

Is the combo chart a more effective choice than the "only lines" chart or the "only bars" chart in this situation? As we've seen many times in this book, different chart types cause audiences to perceive the underlying data differently. For example, lines make patterns of change more obvious than bars, and bars draw attention to individual periods (e.g., individual months) rather than the overall pattern of change. Therefore, the question in the above scenario is whether the designer of this chart wants to make patterns of change more obvious (i.e., use lines) or draw attention to individual periods (i.e., use bars). As usual, that depends on the specific insight that the chart is intended to communicate.

The combo chart would only be the most effective choice if the chart creator wanted to make patterns of change more obvious in the budget (i.e., show it as a line) but draw attention to individual periods in the expenses (i.e., show them as bars). There's nothing in the chart title and there are no callouts to suggest that that's what this chart is intended to communicate, however. Why would the designer of the original chart have used a combo chart? It was probably an attempt to make the chart more *visually interesting* than a "bars only" or "lines only" chart; in other words, this was a random choice. Obviously, randomly assigning chart types is *not* a good way to make charts more interesting. We'll see in "Part 6: Making charts less boring" that there are better ways to make charts more interesting.

Does that mean that we should *never* use combo charts? No, in rare situations, there are good reasons to use different chart types in a single chart. For example, let's say that we wanted to draw attention to expenses for individual months (i.e., not feature patterns of change) and just include the budget numbers as secondary, contextual information:

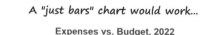

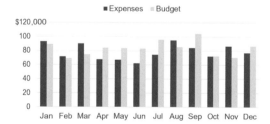

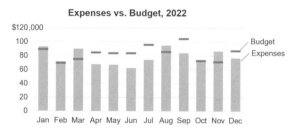

What I want you to notice is that different chart types in the combo chart above on the right were chosen for *specific reasons*, not randomly, and those reasons didn't include "to identify different data series." As we saw in earlier chapters, a better way to identify different data series is to use different colors (e.g., dark blue for expenses and light blue for budget) or, sometimes, different marker symbols (triangles, X's, circles, etc.) because neither of those affect how audiences perceive the underlying data in the same way that changing the chart type does.

> ### Key takeaways: Combo charts
>
> - Avoid combining different chart types in a single chart solely to make that chart visually interesting.
> - Avoid using different chart types in a single chart to identify different data series in the chart; instead, consider using different colors or marker symbols to identify different data series.
> - Only use combo charts when different chart types are needed to communicate the specific insight or answer that the chart is intended to communicate.

Now that we've seen the 30 chart types that I recommend for everyday charts, how about a few that, IMHO, are...

Chapter 12

Chart types to use cautiously or avoid

As we've seen in various parts of this book so far, there are a number of chart types that I recommend avoiding when it comes to everyday charts for reports and presentations:

- **Dual-axis charts** (consider merged charts or index charts instead)

- **Smoothed line charts** (consider standard line charts instead)

- **Donut charts** (consider pie charts instead)

- **Slope charts** (consider arrow charts instead)

- **Choropleth maps** (consider bubbles, bars, or colored dots on maps instead)

In addition to those chart types, there are a few others that I don't recommend for everyday charts:

- Word clouds

- Packed bubble charts

- Bullet graphs

- Funnel charts

- Radar graphs

- Three-dimensional (3D) charts

Some of these chart types might (or might not) be good choices if we're creating data art, infographics, advertisements, or other charts for which communicating information as clearly and quickly as possible might not be a high priority, but I don't recommend these types for *everyday* charts where clear, quick communication is always a high priority. Why, exactly, do I avoid these chart types when creating everyday charts? Let's start with…

Word clouds

A word cloud shows how often words occur in a text by showing the most commonly occurring words in a larger font size within a "cloud" of words. For example, the word cloud below on the left represents the text of U.S. President John F. Kennedy's speech during the early 1960s in which he committed to landing a man on the moon before the end of the decade:

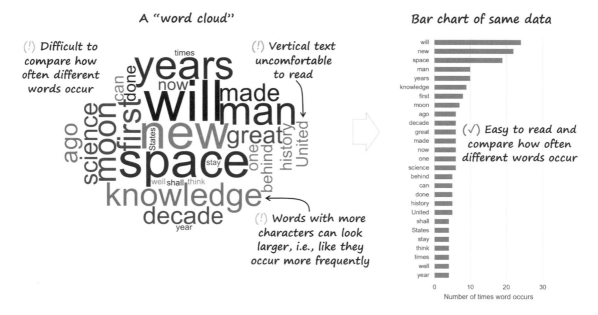

As we can see from my purple callouts, word clouds make it difficult to compare how often words occur because comparing different font sizes with any kind of precision is quite tricky, and the fact that many word clouds contain vertical (and sometimes diagonal) text doesn't make those comparisons any easier. Word clouds may be OK for an ad on the side of a bus, but a bar chart is a better (albeit less sexy) choice if it's important to communicate the information as clearly and quickly as possible.

Packed bubble charts

In a packed bubble chart, values are shown as bubbles of different sizes. The packed bubble chart below on the left, for example, represents donation amounts for 15 donors as bubbles of different sizes:

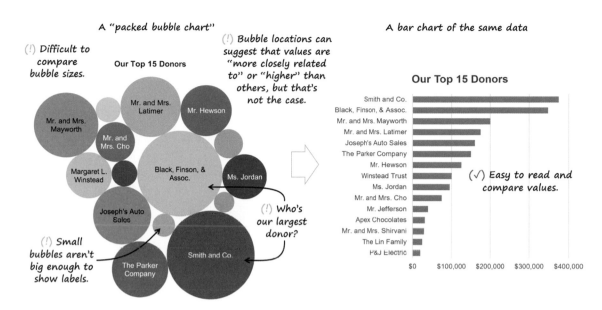

The purple callouts in the packed bubble chart above point out several perceptual problems with this chart type. A bar chart of the same data, however, doesn't have any of those problems. Less sexy, sure, but more informative and quicker and easier to read than the packed bubble chart.

Bullet graphs

Bullet graphs are sometimes used on information dashboards to help users determine how to *feel* about the current value of a metric (Is it good or bad? Does it require action?):

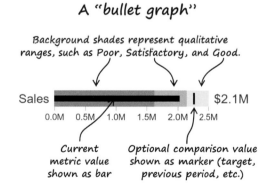

Although the context that bullet graphs provide can be very useful, it can be hard to spot metrics that require attention on a dashboard with many bullet graphs on it. They can also make dashboards very visually busy, they don't work well with certain types of metrics, and have several other important downsides. A few years ago, I designed an alternative called "action dots," which, I believe, don't have any of the downsides of bullet graphs:

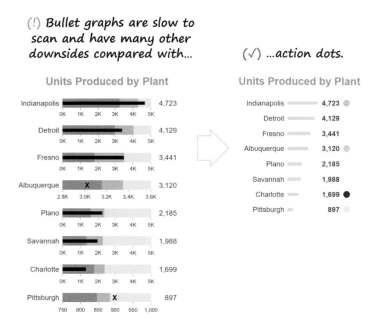

For more information about the downsides of bullet graphs and why I now recommend action dots instead, visit practicalreporting.com/pc-resources, and click "Bullet graphs."

Funnel charts

Funnel charts are sometimes used to represent processes in which a set of items go through a series of stages, with some items being lost or eliminated at each stage. For example, funnel charts are often used to show the number of sales prospects declining at each stage of a sales process, which is what the funnel chart below on the left depicts:

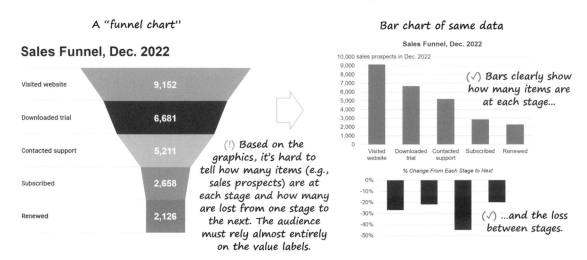

As you can see from my purple callouts, I don't think funnel charts are a good chart type because the graphics (i.e., the "layers" in the funnel shape) only allow for extremely rough comparisons of the number of items at each stage. Yes, the funnel shape makes it a bit more obvious that the chart is showing a decreasing number of items, but this shape does very little to actually communicate the values in the chart. The fact that the graphical elements in funnel charts are almost useless explains why they almost always have value labels in them. If a graph is almost useless without labeling all the values in it, well…

Radar graphs

Radar graphs (also called "spiderweb graphs" or "spider charts") are a less common chart type that's sometimes used to compare several items based on multiple characteristics of those items. For example, the radar graph below on the left is designed to allow four car models (Exodus, T-300, Varga, Elora) to be compared based on five attributes (value, safety, performance, comfort, reliability). The scores for each attribute of a car model are represented as a line that forms a different shape for each vehicle. This allows the audience to compare the items (e.g., the cars) by comparing their corresponding shapes.

Well, that's the theory, anyway…

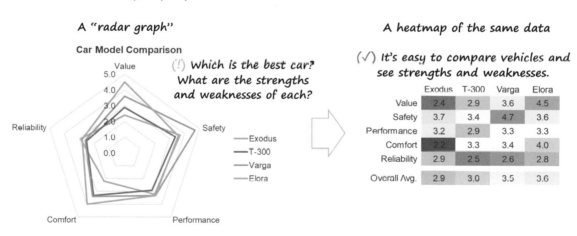

Why would a chart creator decide to show something like car model data as, basically, a line chart wrapped in a circle? To be honest, I'm not sure, and just about every radar graph that I've ever seen would be more informative and easier to read as something like a heatmap, such as the one above on the right.

There *is* one very specific situation that I'm aware of in which it might make sense to use a radar graph, which is when the audience thinks of the data itself as being "circular" or "polar." For example, if we're showing data about wind directions, the audience probably thinks of that kind of data as being "circular" in the sense that the wind can come from any direction, i.e., the 360° of a circle. That's probably why radar graphs of wind direction are common in aviation and marine navigation. This type of chart even has a specific name in those domains: a "wind rose."

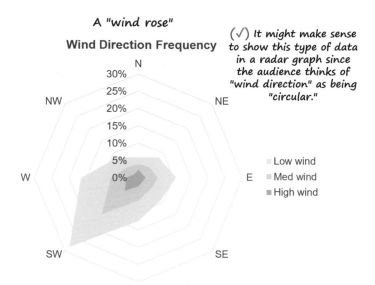

A "wind rose"

Wind Direction Frequency

(√) It might make sense to show this type of data in a radar graph since the audience thinks of "wind direction" as being "circular."

Audiences don't think of most types of data as being "circular," however, so it's unintuitive to show something like car model attributes in a circular graph such as a radar graph.

3D charts

3D isn't really a chart type but a technique that can be applied to almost any chart type. There are two ways to use 3D in charts, neither of which I recommend for everyday charts.

The first way is to apply a 3D effect to a 2D chart:

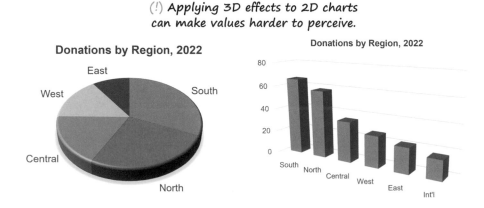

(!) Applying 3D effects to 2D charts can make values harder to perceive.

Donations by Region, 2022

Donations by Region, 2022

Thankfully, this technique fell out of fashion in the early 2010s because most chart creators realized that adding 3D effects didn't make their charts more engaging or impressive looking, and because these effects often make it harder to perceive values in the chart accurately as a result of distortions that occur when viewing 3D objects from different angles (a.k.a. "parallax effects").

The second way to use 3D goes a step further by adding an additional variable along a "z" axis, i.e., depth, in addition to width (x) and height (y):

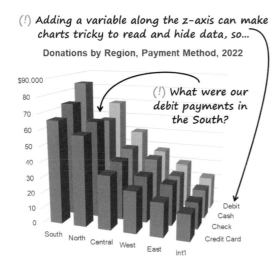

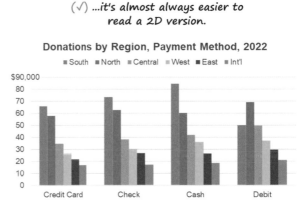

Charts with a variable along the z-axis also suffer from parallax effects and make it trickier to estimate and compare values with one another than in a 2D chart, such as the version above on the right. As an added bonus, some of our data might get hidden behind other data in a 3D chart, as in the example above on the left. For these reasons, it's generally best to avoid 3D altogether in everyday charts. 3D charts can be useful for doing advanced mathematical or scientific analysis, but they require special training and software to interpret correctly.

> So why do chart creators sometimes use these "avoid or use cautiously" chart types and techniques in everyday charts?

In my experience, it's usually because the chart creator is trying to make their chart more "visually interesting." We've already seen a variety of more reliable ways to get audiences interested in our charts than using eye-candy chart types, however, and we'll see more in "Part 6: Making charts less boring."

Key takeaway: Chart types to use cautiously or avoid

- When it comes to everyday charts, there are almost always more effective chart types than dual-axis charts, donut charts, slope charts, choropleth maps, word clouds, packed bubble charts, bullet graphs, funnel charts, radar graphs or 3D charts.

A FINAL WORD ABOUT CHOOSING CHART TYPES

We've just learned when to use 30 chart types, along with about 10 others that I suggest avoiding.

I know. That's a lot.

As I mentioned earlier in the book, chart types are the "vocabulary" of dataviz and having a large vocabulary of chart types allows us to create clear, easy-to-understand charts in a wide variety of situations, and it substantially reduces the risk that we'll accidentally mislead our audience by using a chart type that, although familiar, can't represent the data accurately. Now that you know what all these chart types are and when to use each, I suspect that you'll find yourself needing to use most or all of them regularly.

The remaining parts of the book deal with challenges that arise all the time in practice, but that aren't specific to any particular chart type, such as…

PART

3

Showing data with a more complex structure ("small multiples")

In this part of the book, we'll look at challenging but common situations in which the data that we need to show has a more complex structure, with multiple categorical and/or quantitative variables. While these situations are challenging, they come up all the time and learning how to show this kind of data effectively can deliver huge benefits for audiences (and for chart creators).

What does data with a more complex structure look like?

In most of the scenarios that we've seen in this book so far, the underlying data had just two or three variables, such as "Region," "Donation Amount," or "Month":

Data with two variables

Region	Donations
Central	$1,515K
West	$996K
North	$612K
East	$498K
Int'l	$189K

Data with three variables

Region	Jan.	Feb.	Mar.	Apr.	May	Jun.	Jul.	Aug.	Sep.	Oct.	Nov.	Dec.
Central	$128K	$117K	$128K	$126K	$129K	$120K	$133K	$130K	$123K	$130K	$121K	$130K
West	$82K	$78K	$84K	$83K	$89K	$85K	$89K	$81K	$80K	$84K	$77K	$84K
North	$50K	$45K	$52K	$49K	$54K	$48K	$52K	$54K	$51K	$53K	$50K	$53K
East	$43K	$39K	$44K	$40K	$39K	$40K	$42K	$43K	$43K	$40K	$42K	$43K
Int'l	$16K	$14K	$15K	$17K	$16K	$15K	$18K	$16K	$16K	$15K	$15K	$16K

However, we often need to show data that has more than three variables. For example, the data below has four:

Data with more than three variables

Donations ($K) by Payment Method, Region, Month, 2022

Payment Method	Region	Jan.	Feb.	Mar.	Apr.	May	Jun.	Jul.	Aug.	Sep.	Oct.	Nov.	Dec.
Credit Card	Central	49.8	50.5	50.8	49.6	52.7	49.2	54.7	52.2	50.2	51.4	49.1	52.5
	East	17.1	15.8	19.2	16.3	16.2	16.8	17.7	17.5	18.9	16.0	16.8	16.7
	HQ	6.3	6.0	6.1	6.9	6.4	5.7	7.0	6.1	6.5	6.6	6.2	6.6
	North	20.7	18.9	21.8	18.0	22.2	20.4	19.1	22.0	21.7	21.5	19.7	23.2
	West	33.7	30.6	35.7	32.9	34.5	34.6	35.9	34.2	33.9	34.6	31.2	35.0
Check	Central	49.3	40.0	48.1	47.1	45.6	42.7	50.3	48.3	43.2	48.8	43.9	46.7
	East	16.3	14.8	14.9	14.2	12.8	13.7	13.9	15.8	14.0	14.9	15.6	17.2
	HQ	6.3	4.3	4.9	6.9	5.3	5.6	7.3	5.9	6.0	4.4	5.4	6.0
	North	17.6	15.6	17.5	18.9	20.3	16.0	20.9	19.3	18.4	18.4	18.7	19.1
	West	29.7	29.1	28.7	31.2	35.0	31.9	32.6	28.1	28.2	30.2	26.7	30.4
Cash	Central	28.9	26.7	28.8	29.0	30.8	27.9	28.3	30.0	29.4	30.0	27.6	30.3
	East	10.0	8.9	9.7	9.3	9.8	9.9	10.4	9.7	9.7	9.3	9.4	9.4
	HQ	3.8	3.6	3.8	3.2	4.0	3.9	3.7	4.0	3.7	3.7	3.8	3.1
	North	12.2	10.1	12.5	11.8	11.7	12.0	12.3	12.3	10.8	12.8	12.0	11.0
	West	19.0	17.8	19.5	19.2	19.2	18.3	20.5	19.0	17.7	19.5	19.0	18.2

When the data has a larger number of variables like this, many chart creators immediately assume that they must show the data as a table because it would be difficult or impossible to show it as a graph. But what will audiences typically do if we give them a big table of numbers like the one above? That's right: They'll skip it altogether unless they have absolutely no choice but to slog through it.

As we saw when we were contrasting tables and graphs in the "Tables" chapter, tables are slow and cognitively effortful to read, and it's harder to notice patterns, outliers, etc., in tables than in graphs. If we can figure out how to show data with a more complex structure as a graph, then, our audience will be much more likely to actually *read* it and get meaningful insights from it. How, exactly, could we show complex data like this in a graph? Remember, way back in "Why read this book? What will you learn?" I said that there was one topic in this book that was wasn't very straightforward? Well, *bienvenidos…*

While it's not very straightforward, it's important to learn how to visualize data with a larger number of variables because this situation often arises in practice. Unfortunately, though, it's hard to formulate specific guidelines for designing graphs of data with a more complex structure. Trial and error, practice, and experience play significant roles in this kind of situation. I can offer some *general principles* that may be helpful, however.

Ironically, the main challenge when trying to figure out how to visualize data with more than three variables is that there are always *many* ways to show this kind of data as a graph. For example, one way to show the "donations" data in the table on the previous page would be like this:

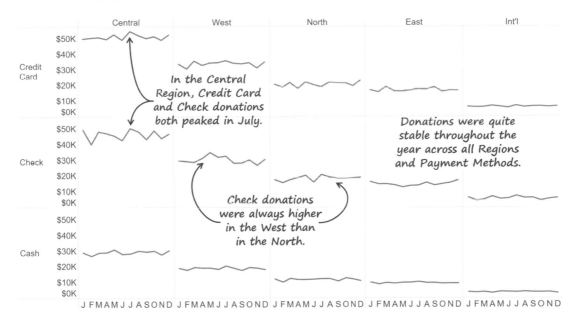

The jargony name for multiple, related charts in a table-like arrangement like this is a "small multiples" arrangement. Yes, the example above is relatively complex as far as charts go, and it might take 10 or 15 seconds for the audience to figure out how to read it, but it's far quicker and easier to digest than the "wall of numbers" table that we started with. Not only that, this chart is also much more *informative*; insights like those in the blue callouts are far more obvious than they were in the original "wall of numbers" table.

Although the small multiples chart above shows many different insights about this data, the arrangement of the information makes it hard for the audience to make some types of comparisons:

This small multiples arrangement is very informative, but there are some types of comparisons that are harder to make:

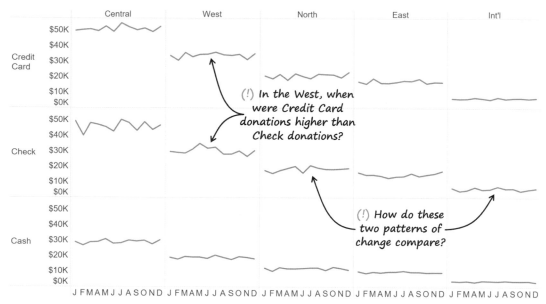

As I mentioned, though, there are plenty of other ways that we could use to show this data. For example, we could also show it like this:

(!) This version is busier and more complex...   *(✓) ...but it does allow for a wider variety of comparisons.*

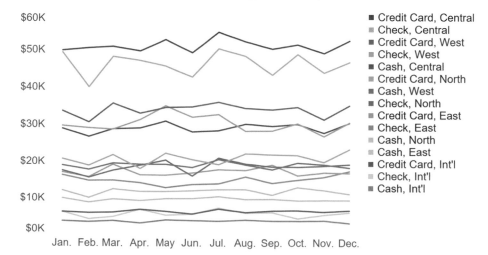

Yikes! Obviously, this is a pretty spaghetti-y chart, and I wouldn't show it to most audiences because it might, well, scare them. The thing is, this version is more *flexible* than the simpler arrangement that we saw just before it; the audience can compare the pattern of change of any line with any other line and compare the height of any line with the height of any other line because everything is in the same chart. It's just kind of visually overwhelming.

Therefore, when choosing how to show data with more than two categorical variables, there's always a simpler arrangement that's less flexible (i.e., more graphs with less data in each graph) and a more complex arrangement that's more flexible (i.e., a single graph or small number of graphs, each of which contains a lot of data).

There are also always arrangements that fall somewhere in between those two extremes, with an intermediate number of graphs, each of which contains an intermediate amount of data:

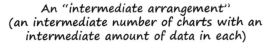

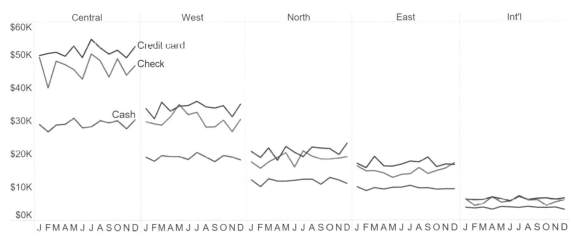

So, when showing data with a more complex structure, there's always a *range* of arrangements to choose from, ranging from simple-but-less-flexible arrangements to complex-but-more-flexible arrangements:

When showing data with a more complex structure,
there's always a *range* of arrangements to choose from:

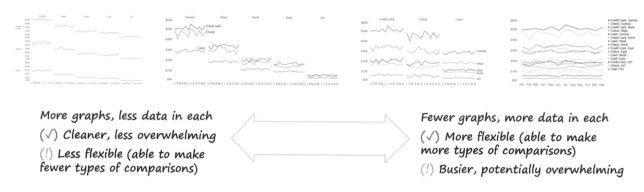

More graphs, less data in each
(✓) Cleaner, less overwhelming
(!) Less flexible (able to make fewer types of comparisons)

Fewer graphs, more data in each
(✓) More flexible (able to make more types of comparisons)
(!) Busier, potentially overwhelming

So, which arrangement should we choose? As with so many design decisions, it depends entirely on the specific insight that we need to communicate about the data:

Which arrangement to choose depends entirely on
the specific insight to be communicated.

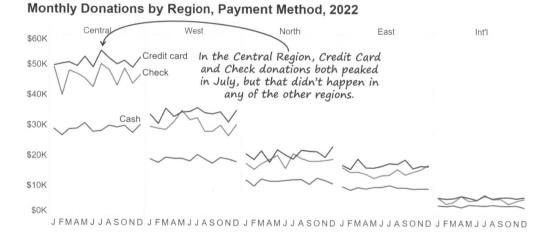

Monthly Donations by Region, Payment Method, 2022

In the Central Region, Credit Card and Check donations both peaked in July, but that didn't happen in any of the other regions.

In my experience, the most effective choice usually ends up being one of the "intermediate" arrangements, but not always.

As I mentioned, it's hard to provide specific guidelines for these situations beyond these general principles because each situation is quite unique. Really, the best advice I can offer is to try a variety of different arrangements and see which one seems to best communicate the specific insight at hand. Using a dataviz software product that allows us to generate different arrangements quickly and easily is helpful here because it makes the trial-and-error process quicker.

Now, it's very important to keep in mind that, just because the underlying data has more variables, that doesn't mean that we always need to show the data broken down by *all* of those variables. **In many situations, the insight to be communicated only requires the data to be broken down by one or two of the variables:**

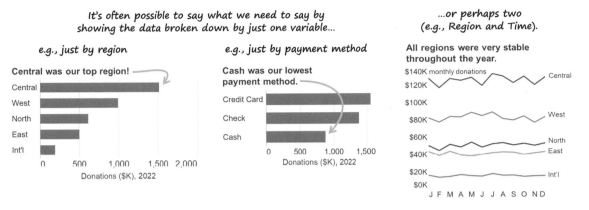

Reducing the number of variables makes for charts that are much simpler for us to design and for audiences to read. We're happier. The audience is happier. Everyone's happier. Chart creators often automatically assume, however, that they must show the data broken down by *all* the variables and end up making complex small multiples arrangements when simpler charts would have done the trick. Therefore, we need to get into the habit of asking ourselves whether we need to show the data broken down by *all of* the variables in order to communicate the specific insight at hand, or whether we can get away with just showing a breakdown by one or two variables instead.

There will be plenty of situations in which we're not so lucky, and the insight that we need to communicate requires showing a breakdown by more than two variables. However, that should be our last option, not our first.

Also, note that almost any chart type can be used in a small multiples arrangement, not just line charts:

Almost any chart type can be used in a small multiples arrangement.

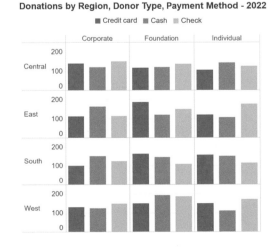

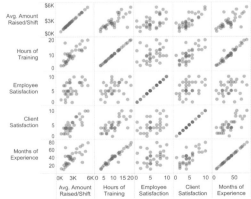

I know. It isn't easy to figure out how to show data with a more complex structure as a graph, but, as we've seen, the results can be quite powerful and far more useful than a big table of numbers that probably won't get read. If we practice and get good at this skill, though, we can expect "oohs" and "ahs" from our audiences.

Key takeaways: Showing data with a more complex structure

- Whenever possible, show the data broken down by just one or two variables, even if there are more variables than that in the underlying data.
- When the data needs to be shown broken down by more than three variables, avoid the temptation to use a table, and consider using a small multiples arrangement.
- When designing small multiples arrangements, try a variety of arrangements, and then choose the one that best communicates the insight at hand.

Phew! Like I said, this is the one dataviz skill that I consider to be hard to learn. Everything before and after this section is considerably more forehead-slappy, for example…

PART

4

Interactive filters and chart animations

Participants in my workshops sometimes ask about adding interactive filters to charts, and many dataviz vendors have been touting chart animation features in their recent product releases as I write this in early 2023. How useful are these features when it comes to everyday charts?

Although these features look super-useful and impressive at first, I'm not particularly sold on their usefulness, at least not in their current forms. As usual, you can make up your own mind, but this is my take on these features, beginning with…

Chapter 13

Interactive filters in charts

WHEN WORKSHOP PARTICIPANTS see the spaghetti chart below on the left, during our discussion of small multiples arrangements, they sometimes suggest adding an interactive filter to make the chart less visually overwhelming:

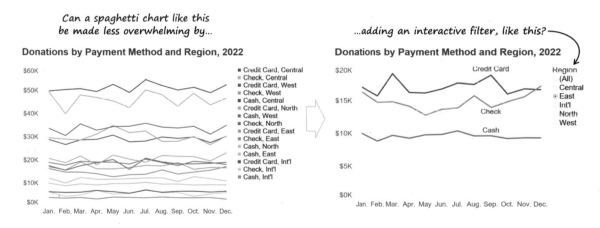

The filtered view on the right *does* look at lot cleaner and simpler, but let's try to actually use that chart to answer some basic, common questions that we might want to answer for our audience, such as:

- "Which region had the highest credit card donations?"
- "Did any regions have check payments that were decreasing?"
- "What was the most popular payment method in each region?"

Hmm. In order to answer any of these basic questions, the audience needs to compare all of the regions, which means that the audience would need to click through every filter option (i.e., every region), try to remember what the data looks like for each region, and then mentally compare them. Needless to say, that would be extremely cognitively demanding, and the audience might not even be able to do it. Well, not very accurately, anyway.

So, as it turns out, adding an interactive filter only made this chart *seem* simpler. In reality, the filter actually made it much more complicated for the audience to use this chart. That's the problem with filters: If the audience can only see one or a few "slices" of the data at a time, it's difficult or impossible to compare all the slices (e.g., compare all the regions), which many insights require. Really, the only time that the audience doesn't need to compare all the slices of data is when they just need to look up individual values, such as what credit card donations were in the East in September.

That's why, when it comes to everyday charts for communicating to an audience, I only use filters when the sole purpose of a chart is to allow the audience to look up values, and comparing all the values isn't necessary. Of course, comparing all the values often *is* necessary to say what we need to say about the data, so I generally recommend avoiding interactive filters in everyday charts and instead trying to make all the data visible at the same time.

Does that mean that we should show our audience a spaghetti chart like the one above on the left? No, as we saw in the preceding part of this book, with a bit of practice, it's often possible to come up with small multiples arrangements that show all the data but that aren't too overwhelming:

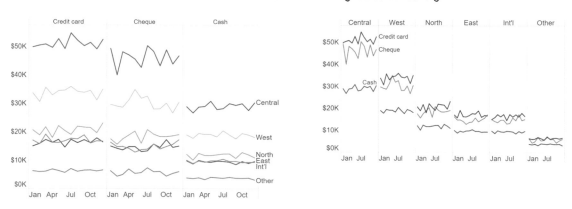

At first glance, these charts may *look* more complex than a chart with an interactive filter, but they're actually much easier for audiences to use than a chart that only shows one slice of data at a time.

Now, having said that, I'll add that there are situations in which the data contains a lot of categories (imagine 100 regions instead of the 6 in the charts above), and any small multiples arrangement that we could possibly come up with would be visually overwhelming. In those situations, we might have no choice but to use an interactive filter to manage the amount of data being shown. Just be aware of the cognitive work that the filter will impose on the audience and of the kinds of insights and comparisons that the filter will make difficult or impossible for the audience to see.

> **Key takeaways: Adding interactive filters to charts**
>
> - Generally, avoid adding interactive filters to charts.
> - Only add interactive filters if the main purpose of the chart is for lookup and not to compare values with one another (which is rare), or if there's too much data to show all of it at the same time.

Chapter 14

Animated charts

SOME DATAVIZ SOFTWARE vendors have started to introduce chart animation features into their products in recent years. This usually involves "morphing" one view of the data into another:

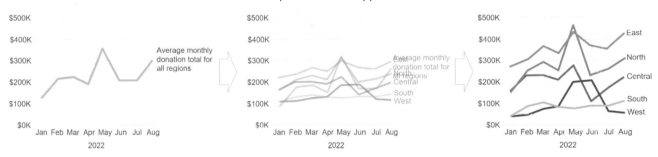

Some dataviz software products now support animated charts.

Animated charts tend to have a high "wow" factor and can be great ways to grab attention (and to sell dataviz software), but they make many types of insights harder to see. Like charts with filters, animated charts usually only show *some* of the data at any one time, so they force the audience to try to remember values that disappear as the animation plays. For example, in the animation sequence above, the audience will probably want to compare the "average" line with the individual "region" lines, but that's hard to do because they can't see the region lines and the average line at the same time; they can only see one or the other. This is why users will often play and rewind chart animations multiple times when viewing them; it's difficult if not impossible to remember in detail what each stage of the animation looked like.

For most animated chart demos that I've seen, I can imagine a static (non-animated) version that, I suspect, would make most insights clearer by allowing all the data to be seen at the same time:

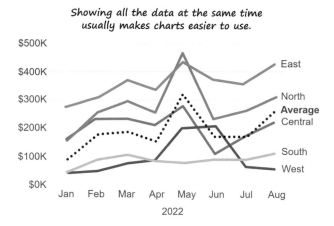

Yes, a static version will have more data in it and so won't look as simple as an animated version, but, as we saw with filters, simpler-looking doesn't necessarily mean simpler to use.

This isn't to say that animation is *always* problematic; it's just important to understand the problems that animation can introduce. If we're just showing small changes (e.g., two points in a line chart moving to new positions), animation can be effective. But if the whole chart morphs into a completely different chart, that's generally harder for audiences to interpret.

Key takeaways: Animated charts

- Generally, avoid using animated charts unless the main purpose of the chart is to grab attention rather than to communicate insights clearly and quickly.
- Animated charts can work well if only small changes occur in the chart during the animation.

We just saw two ways to make charts *un*obvious, so now's probably a good time to talk about…

PART

5

Making charts obvious

A major reason that charts flop with audiences is that they're not obvious enough, that is, the audience has to work too hard to figure out what the point of the chart is. Are they supposed to notice an unexpected pattern? An interesting outlier? A problem that should be acted on? An opportunity?

"Screw it! I don't have time to figure out what this chart should mean to me."

In this part of the book, we'll see six ways to make our charts more obvious. Let's start with the most obvious one, which is...

ADDING INSIGHTS IN CHART TITLES AND CALLOUTS

The most obvious way to make our charts more obvious is to directly tell the audience what key insights and takeaways they should get from the chart, in the title of the chart, callouts, or both:

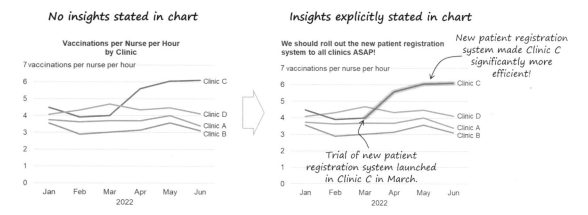

OK, at this point, I want to directly address the disapproving frown that just appeared on many readers' faces because they have…

CONCERNS ABOUT ADDING OUR OWN INTERPRETATION OF THE DATA TO CHARTS

In training workshops, when I talk about adding insights and takeaways as callouts in charts, participants sometimes raise objections like…

- "A chart should just show the data and leave the interpretation of that data to the audience. It's unethical for chart creators to add their own interpretations to charts because that would bias how the audience interprets the data."

- "A well-designed chart should make the point of a chart obvious without having to explicitly state it in the chart. If you have to explicitly tell the audience what the point of a chart is, then the chart is poorly designed and should be redesigned so that the chart itself makes key insights and takeaways obvious."

That all *sounds* reasonable, but there are several problems with these objections.

In many cases, the audience lacks the necessary background knowledge to figure out what the data in a chart should mean to them. In those situations, a chart that doesn't explicitly state key insights and takeaways has zero chance of being useful to the audience, no matter how much the audience wants to understand the chart, and no matter how well designed it is.

Even when the target audience does have enough background knowledge to figure out what the data in a chart should mean to them, I still recommend stating insights explicitly. Why would I recommend that? Why not just show an "interpretation-free" chart such as the one that we saw earlier and leave any interpretation up to the audience?

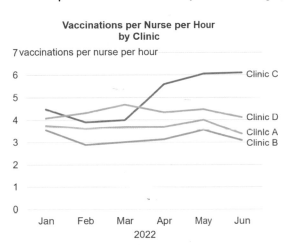

An "interpretation-free" chart (but not really...)

There are three reasons to avoid giving audiences charts like this, with no insights explicitly stated:

1. **The audience may or may not have the background knowledge that we thought they had,** or even that they claim to have. Adding explicit insights ensures that the audience will still get key insights and takeaways in those situations.

2. Explicitly stating key insights and takeaways **saves the audience the time and effort of figuring out why we decided to show them that data in the first place.** The audience may figure it out on their own eventually, but why force them to spend the time and effort to figure out why we thought they should see that data?

3. (And this is the big one...) **There's no such thing as an "interpretation-free" chart.** *All* charts are laced with the chart creator's interpretation of the data and their assumptions about why the audience should see that data, whether the chart creator wants to include those interpretations in their charts or not. Don't believe me? Hear me out...

Have another look at the "interpretation-free" chart above. Now, ask yourself what made the chart creator decide to show...

*   A line chart rather than a bar chart?

*   "Vaccinations per hour per nurse by month" rather than "Total vaccinations per month," "Average minutes per vaccination by week," or some other measure?

*   Those particular four clinics, rather than another set of clinics?

*   6 months of history rather than 12 or 18?

What caused the chart creator to make those particular design choices, rather than the innumerable others that they *could* have made? The answer is that those design choices, and most others, were made based on the specific insight that the chart creator had in mind when they designed the chart, i.e., that the new patient registration system had improved the efficiency of Clinic C and should be rolled out to the other clinics. If the chart creator had had some *other* insight in mind, their design choices would have been different, even though the underlying data would have been the same:

Different design choices for featuring different insights about the same data

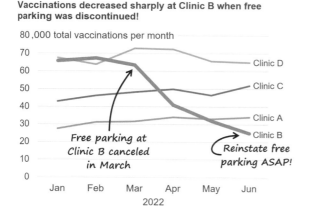
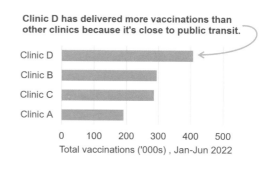

As it turns out, then, the "interpretation-free" version of this chart that we saw initially isn't interpretation-free at all. Every design choice that went into it was based on a specific insight that the chart creator needed to communicate, and that's the case for *all* charts that are designed to communicate data to an audience. The chart creator *must* have an insight in mind in order to make most design choices (choosing a chart type, choosing a color palette, choosing what to filter, etc.). If a chart creator tries to create a chart without a specific insight in mind or tries to "just show the data," the result won't be a "neutral," "objective," "unbiased," or "interpretation-free" chart, it will be a chart that *communicates random insights*, which is unlikely to be useful to the audience.

This is a hard truth about dataviz that many chart creators don't seem to realize: **It's impossible to create charts that "just show the data" without featuring specific insights *about* that data.** All charts make certain insights about the data more noticeable, less noticeable, or not visible at all. Therefore, all charts have the chart creator's interpretation of the data "baked in"—whether the chart creator wants it to be there or not.

Because our interpretation of the data is baked into every chart that we create, we might as well just tell the audience what that interpretation is, in callouts or in the chart's title. Forcing the audience to guess what led us to make the design choices that we made wastes their time, and they may not bother to try to figure it out.

Now, I'm not suggesting that we should create charts that just say whatever we want them to say. We should choose which insights to feature based on our best, most honest interpretation of the data and with the best interests of the audience in mind. Designing a chart that, for example, deliberately de-emphasizes or hides a problem that we know the audience would want to know about is no different than writing a report or email that does the same thing. It's just another form of lying.

I should also mention that, sometimes, the audience *does* have a lot of background knowledge about the data in a chart, and, in those situations, their interpretation of the data may be different than ours. For example, maybe a member of the management team attributes the increase in vaccinations at Clinic C to the fact that that clinic hired a new manager in March who's doing a great job, not to the new patient registration system. That's fine! In fact, those types of discussions can be very useful because they uncover the fact that different people have different understandings of what's going on and should probably discuss it to try to get on the same page. The solution isn't to (futilely) try to create "interpretation-free" charts that "just show the data."

> **Key takeaways: Including the chart creator's interpretation of the data in callouts and chart titles**
>
> - It's impossible to create "interpretation-free" charts that don't communicate any specific insights about the data. All charts make certain insights more noticeable, less noticeable, or not visible at all; therefore, the chart creator's interpretation of the data is reflected in every chart, whether the chart creator wanted it to be or not.
> - Explicitly stating the specific insights that the chart creator intended to communicate substantially improves the odds that a chart will be useful to the audience and reduces the risk that they won't bother to interpret the chart.

What if, try as we might, we *can't* figure out which specific insights to feature in a chart? For example, maybe the CEO has asked for a chart of the organization's expenses and budget for each department but doesn't have time to explain *why* they need that information. Does the CEO need to know which departments have the highest expenses? The highest budgets? Which departments are doing a better or worse job of sticking to their budget? Which departments are contributing most to the overall budget overage?

"I'm busy. Just make me a chart."

Ugh. These are challenging situations, but, unfortunately, they happen fairly often in practice. Is the solution to try to create a "general-purpose" chart that answers all possible questions that the CEO might have about that data? It would be awesome if we could do that, but, as we just saw, I don't think that that's even theoretically possible. What to do, then? Well, in these unpleasant situations, I (reluctantly) design…

SPRAY-AND-PRAY CHART ARRANGEMENTS

In military circles, "spray and pray" is used as an insult to refer to soldiers firing large numbers of projectiles in the general direction of the enemy in the hopes that something will hit by sheer luck.

Although this is a wasteful strategy in a war zone, it's really useful in "I don't know why I'm creating this chart" situations. When creating a spray-and-pray arrangement of charts, the idea is that, instead of trying to come up with a single chart that we hope will be useful to the audience, we hedge our bets and come up with *several* views of the data, hoping that one of them will "hit," i.e., that it will be useful to the audience:

A spray-and-pray arrangement (several views of the same data)

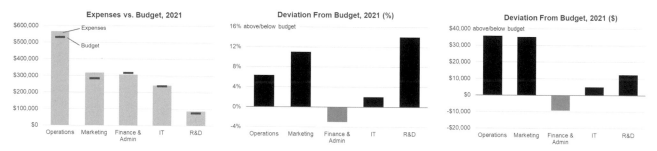

Because we're usually showing several views of the same data in a spray-and-pray arrangement, it's often a good idea to "merge" the charts:

(✓) Merging spray-and-pray charts (when possible) makes it clearer that several views of the same data are being shown.

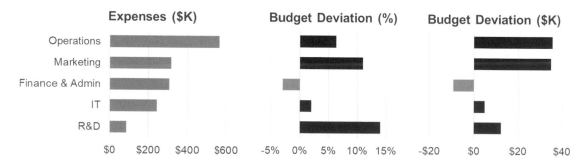

Merging the charts in a spray-and-pray arrangement makes it a bit clearer to the audience that they're looking at three views of the same data, and not three charts of completely different data. We can make the nature of the different views even clearer by titling each one with the question that it answers:

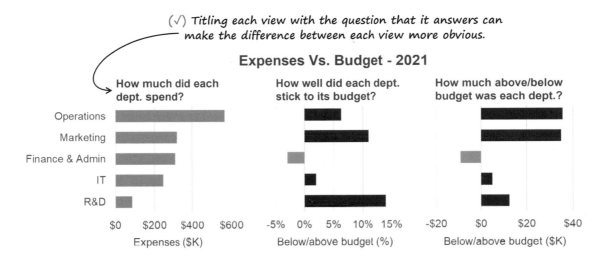

(✓) *Titling each view with the question that it answers can make the difference between each view more obvious.*

Expenses Vs. Budget - 2021

If we were to pick just one of these three views to show to the audience, the odds of that chart being useful to them are pretty low, but, when we show all three views, the odds are much higher—not 100%, but much higher.

To create a spray-and-pray arrangement, we start by brainstorming a few specific questions or insights (usually, two to four) that would probably be useful to the target audience. Yes, we'll be making guesses, but we gotta start somewhere. The more we know about the audience, of course, the better our guesses will be.

The next step is to design one view for each of our "guess" questions or insights and present those views to the audience. If we're lucky, one of the views will be a "direct hit" and be directly useful to the audience. Even if the audience doesn't find any of the views to be useful, we might get enough feedback from them to create a second round of spray-and-pray views that have a better chance of including a direct hit.

> ### Key takeaway: Spray-and-pray arrangements
>
> - When you're unable to determine specifically why the audience needs to see a given data set, consider creating a spray-and-pray arrangement instead of showing them a single view of the data.

Being in a spray-and-pray situation is no fun, but, unfortunately, it happens fairly often, and I hope that you now feel better equipped to handle those situations. For the rest of this part of the book, however, I'm going to assume that we do know what specific insights or answers our chart needs to communicate.

Now that I've (hopefully) sold you on the fact that including your interpretation of the data in charts is both useful and unavoidable, let's look at specifically how to do that with…

Chapter 15

Six ways to make charts more obvious

THERE ARE A variety of ways that we can make our charts more obvious to audiences:

1. Explicitly stating insights in chart callouts and titles
2. Making design choices that feature the specific insight(s) to be communicated
3. Visually highlighting the most important part(s) of a chart
4. Adding comparison values
5. Adding red/green (or orange/blue)
6. Showing calculated values instead of raw values

Let's have a closer look at each of these in turn, starting with the most obvious one, which is…

Explicitly stating insights in chart callouts and titles

Now that I've argued that it's not only *OK* to state insights directly in charts, but often *essential*, what, exactly, should we include in those insights? I generally try to answer as many of the following questions as possible in chart callouts and titles:

1. What are the most *important* part(s) of the chart? What should the audience notice first?
2. Why should the audience *care* about the information in the chart?
3. What *explains* the pattern/anomaly/relationship/etc. that's being featured in the chart?
4. What could/should the audience *do* in response to the information in the chart (if anything)?

For example:

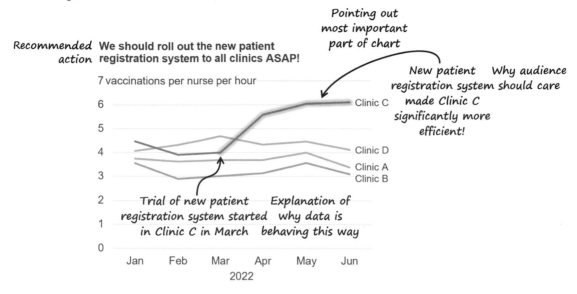

Now, I'm not suggesting that we must always answer all of these questions in all of our charts. In many cases, we either won't be able to answer them all, or we won't need to. For example, we might genuinely have no idea why something that we've observed in the data is happening, or we might not have any suggestions regarding what the audience should do in response to it. However, because we're the ones handling the data, we often *do* have knowledge or insights that the audience might not be aware of or might not have thought of. Sure, the audience might not agree with our explanations of the data or our recommendations about what they should do about it; that's OK, they don't have to accept them. In my experience, though, audiences almost always appreciate the insights and often *do* end up accepting them. This benefits us (data heroes!), our audience (brilliant decision makers!), and the organization as a whole.

By the way, sometimes, the insight to be communicated will be something like "Everything's normal" or "These are all expected values." Even in those cases, we should still state those insights in callouts or in the chart title so that the audience doesn't waste time by, for example, trying to spot problems when there are no problems to spot.

Key takeaways: Stating insights in callouts and chart titles

- Make charts obvious for audiences by stating specific insights or key takeaways in callouts or titles.
- Whenever possible, try to explicitly state what's most important in the chart, why the audience should care about it, what might explain the values in the chart, and what the audience could/should do about it.

Another powerful way to make our charts more obvious is to ensure that we're…

Making design choices that feature the specific insight(s) to be communicated

Throughout this book, we've seen many examples of choosing chart types, color palettes, scales, etc., that make insights more obvious:

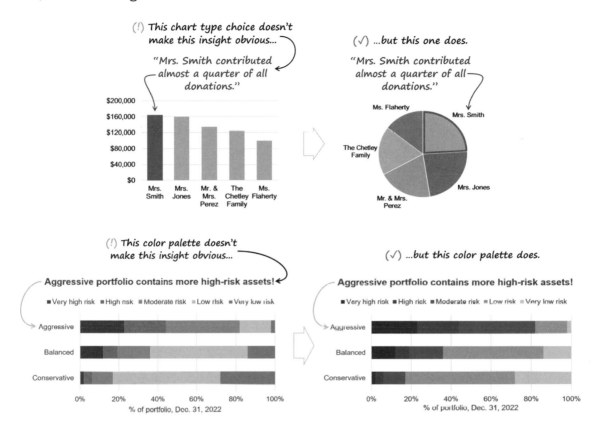

This is just a reminder, then, that a major benefit of learning and applying good dataviz "spelling and vocabulary" is that doing so makes the charts that we create much more obvious.

> **Key takeaways: Following general dataviz guidelines to make charts more obvious**
>
> • Choosing chart types, color palettes, scale formatting, etc., based on the specific insights or answers to be communicated helps to make charts obvious.

Another effective way to make charts more obvious is...

Visually highlighting the most important part(s) of a chart

In most charts, specific chart elements (specific bars, specific lines, etc.) are especially relevant to the insight(s) being communicated. Visually highlighting those elements is an effective way to make the point of a chart more obvious. There are many ways to visually highlight specific elements in a chart; any of the ones below will work well in most situations, so, in most cases, we can just pick one that we think works well for the situation at hand:

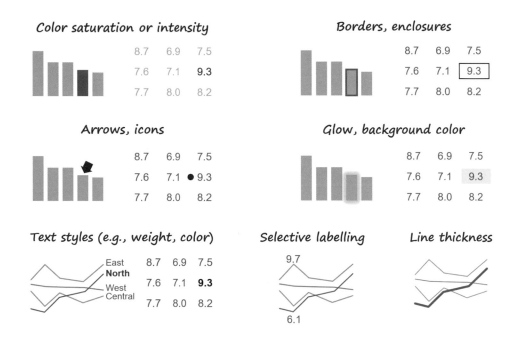

There also are a few highlighting methods that should be avoided, however:

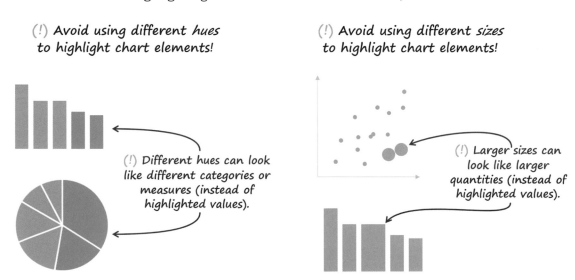

> ### Key takeaways: Highlighting the most important elements in a chart
>
> - Consider visually highlighting the most important element(s) in a chart to make the chart more obvious.
> - There are a variety of effective ways to visually highlight elements in a chart, most of which can be used in most situations.

Adding comparison values

Imagine that we've been recently hired as a manager at a charitable organization, and we've asked the data team for a chart of total donations by region for the most recent year. They come back with the chart below on the left:

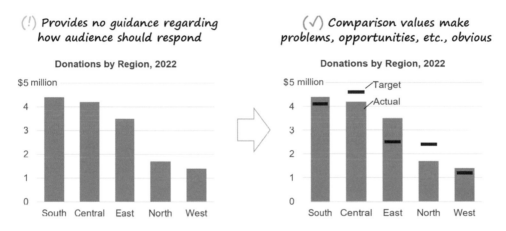

As a new hire, however, we have no background knowledge about these numbers, so we don't know how to feel about them or what—if anything—we should do in response to them. Should we be happy with what we're seeing or concerned? Are any of these numbers higher or lower than expected? Are there are any problems here that need to be addressed?

Adding comparison values such as those in the chart above on the right (donation targets, in this case), puts the numbers into context. Comparison values allow the audience to see not just what the numbers are, but how they should feel about them. Without those comparison values, there's a big risk that the audience won't know what to make of the numbers they're seeing and, therefore, won't know when or how to act on them, i.e., won't ever act on them, even when they definitely should.

There are many different kinds of potentially useful comparison values. Generally, the best kind are those that represent what was hoped for or expected, such as targets, budgets, tolerances, or forecasts. Unfortunately, those ideal comparison values often don't exist for the values that we need to show in a chart. In that case, we might need to get a bit creative and look for other types of comparison values, such as…

- Averages (e.g., compare donations for each region to the average donation amount for all regions).

- Previous periods (e.g., compare this month's value to the previous month, the same month last year, or a trailing average of the past 12 months); however, this technique has some significant limitations. To learn about those limitations, visit practicalreporting.com/pc-resources and click "Problems with 'change versus previous period' values."

- Values for comparables or peers (e.g., industry averages, values for organizations that are similar to ours, etc.).

It's often worth putting in the effort to come up with useful comparison values because, in many cases, the audience won't know what to make of the values in a chart unless comparison values are shown alongside those values, and the chart will, therefore, have zero impact on them.

Having said that, it's not *always* necessary to include comparison values in a chart. For example, if the main insight that needs to be communicated in the scenario above is that the South region had the highest donations of all the regions, no additional comparison values are needed (the other regions act as comparison values in that case).

It's also important to be aware that, sometimes, none of the potential comparison values that we're able to come up with will be truly valid comparators for the values in the chart. For example, the best that we're able to dig up might be averages from a very different industry or comparison values from several years ago. If the only comparison values that are available are questionable, don't include them in the chart. As you probably know, when comparison values are added to a chart, audiences tend to latch onto them, which can—and usually does—dramatically impact how they perceive the data in the chart. Therefore, it's essential to only include comparison values if they're truly valid. An absence of comparison values is better than questionable comparison values.

I should also mention that choosing comparison values can sometimes be controversial. For example, comparing a manufacturing plant's unit production numbers to last year's numbers might make that plant look good, but comparing them to the average for the other plants might make them look bad, so people might argue about which comparison values are "more valid."

Does this potential for controversy mean that comparison values shouldn't be included? I don't think so. To me, this kind of debate is a red flag that suggests that people in an organization don't share the same definitions of success and might not even be on the same page when it comes to the organization's overall goals. The solution in these situations isn't to avoid including comparison values in charts, it's to try to get everyone on the same page regarding what the organization is trying to accomplish and what to consider "good" or "bad."

Key takeaways: Comparison values

- It's often useful to add comparison values to charts. If the audience lacks background information about the values in a chart, they may ignore a chart that doesn't have comparison values because they don't know what to make of the numbers in the chart.

> - Comparison values that represent hopes or expectations, such as budgets, targets, forecasts, etc., are generally preferable to averages, comparables, or other forms of comparison values.
> - If no truly valid comparison values are available, don't show questionable ones in charts.

Adding red/green (or orange/blue)

As we saw in our discussion of color back in Part 1, audiences in many cultures associate red with "bad" and green with "good" (a notable exception is some Asian cultures). We can use this built-in association to make insights and key takeaways (especially problems) in charts more obvious:

Using red and green in charts can make them more obvious and engaging.

	Avg. wait time on hold (mins)	Avg. caller satisfaction rating (on 10)
West Call Center	0.55	7.8
South Call Center	0.79	● 6.6
North Call Center	1.64	7.3
Central Call Center	● 2.27	7.9
East Call Center	● 2.89	● 6.2
	(Target = 2 mins)	*(Target = 7/10)*

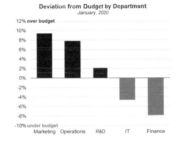

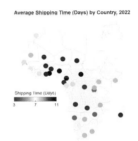

When the audience should be happy about some values in a chart and concerned about others, using red and green in the chart almost always improves it in several ways:

- The audience immediately understands that they're **looking at a "good news/bad news" situation,** which helps them grasp the chart more quickly.

- **Problems are immediately obvious,** even before the audience has read any of the chart labels.

- **Red and green (but especially red) get attention,** so charts that use red to indicate problems are less likely to be ignored.

Although not all charts show values about which the audience should feel good or bad, the majority of charts do, so we should probably be using red and green in our charts often. I use red and green in many of the charts that I create.

Although it's usually pretty obvious what to show as "good" (i.e., green) or "bad" (i.e., red) values in a chart, it can sometimes be controversial. As we just saw in our discussion of comparison values, people can disagree on what to consider good or bad numbers in a chart and might argue about where the dividing point between red and green should be. Does that mean that we should avoid using red and green in our charts? No, as with comparison values, the solution is to try to get everyone on the same page regarding what to consider as good or bad values.

A quick reminder from Part 1 that, if members of the target audience for a chart might have colorblindness, we should switch from a red-green palette to a colorblind-friendly palette, such as orange-blue. Or, better yet, we can make our charts available in both default (red-green) and colorblind-safe (e.g., orange-blue) palettes.

> **Key takeaway: Using red and green in charts**
>
> • When the audience should consider the values in a chart to be good or bad, consider using red and green (or orange and blue) in the chart to make it more obvious.

The final way that we'll discuss to make charts more obvious is…

Showing calculated values instead of raw values

Have a look at the chart below:

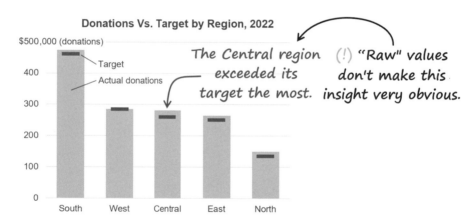

Although adding comparison values (targets, in this case) does improve this chart, showing the raw "Actual Donation" and "Target" values doesn't make the insight to be communicated very visually obvious. What if we did some quick math and, instead of showing the raw values, we showed the *differences* (a.k.a. *deviations*) between the target and actual values?

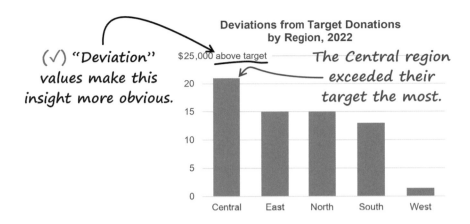

Ah! It's now much more obvious that the Central region exceeded its target more than the other regions; i.e., the insight that the chart needed to communicate is more visually obvious. In this case, then, showing *calculated* values makes the insight that we're trying to communicate more obvious than it would be if we were to show raw values. In this example, "deviation" values were used, but there are many different types of calculated values. Three types that tend to be particularly useful in everyday charts are:

- Deviation values
- Ratio values
- Indexed values

We've already seen deviation values in action, so let's look at examples of the other two types, starting with…

Ratio values

Have a look at the chart below, which is a response to a question from the management team about which of our four factories is the most dangerous:

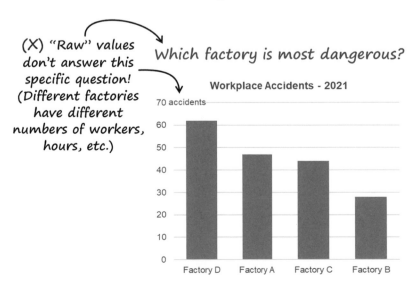

Although this chart may look like it provides a straightforward answer to the question, we can see from my callout that it doesn't! The fact that Factory D has the highest number of accidents could simply mean that it has more workers; a factory with more workers will tend to have more accidents simply because there are more workers who can have accidents, not necessarily because it's more dangerous. Therefore, the raw number of accidents isn't just less obvious in this case; it gives a *wrong answer* to the question that this chart was supposed to answer.

To answer the management team's question accurately, we'd need to account for the fact that different factories have different numbers of workers and hours worked, perhaps by showing the *ratio* of the number of accidents to the number of hours worked for each factory:

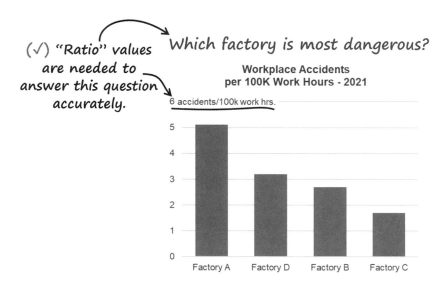

Switching to these ratio values shows that the most dangerous factory *isn't* Factory D, it's Factory A! In this case, then, ratio values didn't just make the chart more obvious, they also made it more accurate! Unfortunately, I see charts all the time that are unobvious or that misrepresent reality because they show raw values when ratio values are needed.

The third and final type of calculated values that tend to be useful in everyday charts are...

Indexed values

Have a look at the following chart, which compares the performance of three stocks over a 20-day period:

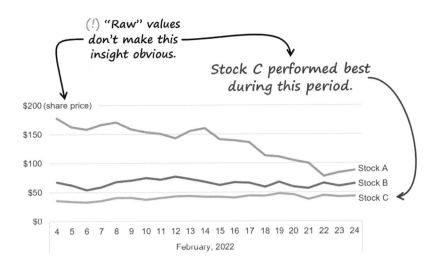

Hmm. Even though the blue callout says that Stock C was the best performer, it certainly doesn't *look* like it was the best performer. The issue here is that stock prices for different companies aren't directly comparable with one another, so it's hard to directly compare the patterns of change in prices over time to see which one actually performed best.

One way to make the insight in this chart more obvious would be to show "indexed" values instead of raw stock prices. For example, the chart below shows the value of $10,000 if it were invested in each of the three stocks on the first day shown in the chart, i.e., the stock prices are "indexed" to $10,000 on the first day:

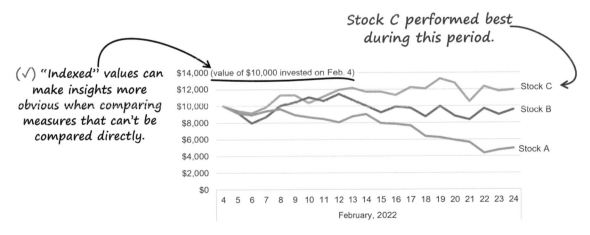

Ah! Now, it's much more visually obvious that Stock C was, indeed, the best performer during this time.

Indexed values can be very useful when we need to compare values that can't be directly compared with one another, like stock prices of different companies or advertising spending and sales revenue. By indexing different measures to a common index value ($10,000, 0%, 1, etc.), we can often compare them directly.

> **Key takeaways: Showing calculated values instead of raw values**
>
> - When designing any chart, ask yourself whether showing raw values makes the specific insight(s) to be communicated obvious, or whether showing calculated values rather than raw values would make it more obvious.
> - The most common types of calculated values used in everyday charts are deviation, ratio, and indexed values, but there are many other types.

Note that there are times when the insight to be communicated might require showing both raw *and* calculated values. For example, maybe we need to say something about which factories had the most accidents *and* which ones had the highest accident rate. Which type of values should we show? Both!

As we've now seen, there are quite a few ways to make charts obvious, beyond just explicitly stating insights in callouts and chart titles. As usual, let's summarize what we've learned in a…

CHEAT SHEET:
MAKING CHARTS OBVIOUS

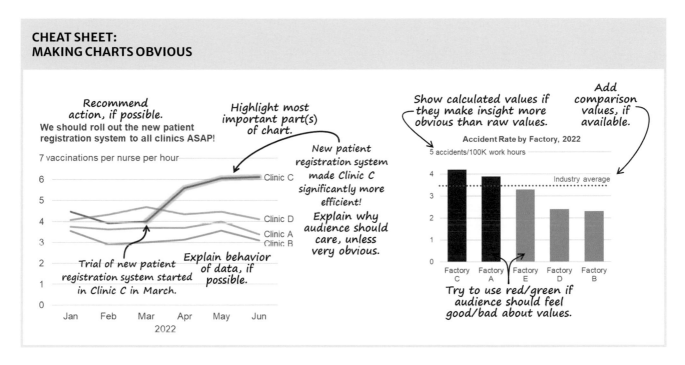

Making charts more obvious is also an extremely effective way to make charts more *engaging* and increase the odds that the audience will pay attention to our charts. There are also other ways to make charts more interesting, so let's talk about those next in…

PART

6

Making charts less boring

In this part of the book, we'll see a variety of strategies that chart makers often use to try to make their charts more visually interesting, but that actually make charts confusing, hard to read, or prone to misinterpretation. We'll then (obviously) review a variety of effective ways to make charts more engaging, many of which we've already seen in other parts of the book.

MAKING CHARTS LESS BORING

Now, I know this will come as a shock to everyone who reads this book, but sometimes, audiences don't pay attention to charts. *I KNOW!* I'll even venture to guess that, on occasion, *your* audience's eyes have glazed over when you've shown charts during presentations, or it's become obvious after the fact that readers skipped reading the charts in your reports. In these situations, the audience seems to be *bored* by our charts even though we feel that the information in those charts is genuinely valuable to them.

It's not a pleasant feeling to communicate to an audience that's clearly not interested in charts that might have taken days of work to put together and that we feel contain insights that would really benefit the audience. When that happens, it's tempting to start scrambling for ideas—any ideas—to make our charts more engaging. Unfortunately, the ideas that chart creators often come up with include:

- Randomly varying chart types in a report or presentation just for the sake of variety, i.e., *not* choosing chart types based on the insights to be communicated or the nature of the data to be shown

- Using more unusual, less common chart types when simpler, more familiar chart types are viable options

- Using "eye candy" chart types, such as packed bubble charts, word clouds, or funnel charts

- Applying visual effects such as drop shadows, gradients, 3D, or dark backgrounds

- Using bright colors, or using multiple colors when a single color would be clearer

- Adding chart animations or interactive filters that don't make the chart any more informative (and, as we saw a few chapters ago, probably makes it less so)

I hope that, by this point in the book, it's clear that all of these are bad ideas that force extra cognitive work on the audience, increase the risk of misrepresenting the data, and make insights less obvious. That's why using these techniques actually makes it *more* likely that the audience will zone out, not less.

Fundamentally, those techniques don't address the real reasons that audiences get bored by charts, which are:

1. The point of the chart isn't obvious enough, and the audience isn't willing to take the time to figure out what the chart should mean to them.

2. The chart is too complicated-looking, unfamiliar, or confusing, and the audience isn't willing to put in the effort to figure out how to interpret it.

Having read most of this book at this point, we're now equipped with many tricks and strategies to avoid those problems:

- Showing data as graphs rather than tables
- Choosing chart types, color palettes, scale ranges, etc., that make the insights to be communicated obvious, and that minimize the audience's cognitive effort
- Visually highlighting the most important part(s) of a chart
- Adding insights, key takeaways, and recommended actions in callouts and chart titles
- Using red and green to indicate "bad" and "good" values
- Adding comparison values
- Splitting up complicated charts into several simpler charts
- Etc., etc., etc.

These are far more reliable ways to get our audiences to pay attention to our charts than using the cheesy "eye candy" techniques that I mentioned earlier.

Now, I live in the real world too, and I know that some audiences want and expect "eye candy" charts and consider that a "good chart" is "a chart with fancy graphic design." How can we sell an audience like that on charts that are less fancy-looking but more useful? When designing our next chart, if time permits, we can create two versions of the same chart—a fancy version and a useful version:

Fancy version:

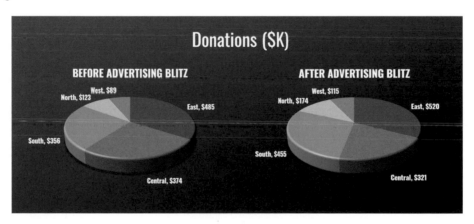

Useful version:

Then, we can show both versions to the audience *without asking them which one they prefer* (they'll probably pick the one with the pretty colors). Instead, we can try *using* the chart with them to answer basic questions like:

- Which regions improved? Which ones got worse?
- Which region improved its performance the most?
- What was our biggest region before and after the ad blitz?

Usually, after three or four rounds of questions like this, the lightbulb will go off, the link between "fancy-looking" and "useful" will be broken in the mind of the audience, and they'll start to want and expect useful charts instead of fancy ones. In a small number of cases, however, I've seen audiences that still prefer fancy charts after this exercise. In those cases, there might not be anything we can do to convince them otherwise. We should still try, however.

There's one more major cause of audience boredom that I didn't mention before because it's a problem that I can't really teach you how to avoid: creating charts that contain information that the audience doesn't need.

I have to mention this, because, fairly often, when I hear chart creators complain that their audiences ignore their charts, it's because those chart creators don't have a good understanding of what kind of information the audience needs in the first place. Obviously, when audiences are presented with information that they don't need, they get very bored, very fast. If that's what's causing our audience's eyes to glaze over, even world-class dataviz skillz™ won't make a lick of difference. The solution in those situations isn't to try to improve our charts, it's to sit in on more meetings, ask to be cc'd on more emails, and generally ~~spy on~~ study our audience to "get inside their heads" and better understand their specific challenges, concerns, goals, decisions they need to make, etc.

Another common reason that audiences get subjected to charts of information that they don't need is that those charts are in reports or presentations that are designed for a broad audience whose individual members have very different data needs. For example, a "management update" presentation for the entire management team might contain a lot of charts about marketing that the head of human resources (HR) doesn't care about, so the head of HR spends half the meeting being very bored. If that's the reason that an audience is ignoring charts, the solution is to try to make more targeted presentations and reports for specific members or segments within the audience instead of a single report or presentation for everyone. Yes, that requires more work, but it reduces the risk that the audience will get bored.

Key takeaways: Making charts less boring

- "Eye candy" chart types and techniques aren't reliable ways to increase interest in charts and can make charts harder to read, less obvious, or more prone to misinterpretation.

- Applying the design guidelines in this book produces charts that are interesting to audiences because the charts are easy to read, make insights and takeaways obvious, and aren't confusing.
- Showing charts that contain information that the audience doesn't need can be avoided by becoming very familiar with the audience's specific challenges, goals, decisions they need to make, etc., and by making charts for specific members or segments of a target audience.

Ta-daa!!! That's the final set of guidelines in this book. Congratulations! You now have considerably more dataviz chops than most of the workforce.

So...

PART

What now?

In this, the final part of the book, we'll see some tips on how to continue to improve our dataviz skills, as well as my take on emerging technologies that may (or may not) change dataviz in the future.

TIPS FOR CONTINUING TO IMPROVE

Unless you already had a substantial amount of dataviz expertise before picking up this book, all of the new knowledge acquired through these pages might feel like a nebulous mass of information swirling around in your brain. This is normal until you start *applying* what you've learned. When you start using these skills in practice, your new knowledge will start to "settle down" and "get organized" in your mind as it gets consolidated into long-term memory.

A few suggestions for accelerating that consolidation process and getting to a point where these skills feel intuitive as quickly as possible:

Practice!

At first, you might need to refer frequently to the cheat sheets in this book. With practice, these chart-making skills will become "muscle memory" and you'll find yourself referring less and less often to the cheat sheets. **Dataviz is definitely a skill that improves with practice.**

If you don't have regular opportunities to practice as part of your work, consider participating in dataviz challenges and competitions, of which there are many. Visit practicalreporting.com/pc-resources and click "Dataviz challenges and competitions" for suggestions. Be aware that judges in dataviz competitions might have different ideas about what constitutes a "good chart" than the ideas presented in this book, however. Some judges might favor charts that are creative or artistically impressive over charts that "do their job as quickly, comfortably, and safely as possible." There's nothing wrong with evaluating charts through different lenses; you just need to be aware of the lens used by those who might be judging your charts.

Experiment!

It's important to not fall into the trap of trying to come up with the perfect chart design on the first try. When I design charts, I often try several design iterations. If you're not sure about a particular design change, it's best to actually try it—or at least to mock up it or sketch it out—rather than trying to *imagine* how well that change might work. When you see the actual results of a particular design choice, you'll often notice things that weren't apparent when you only imagined what it would look like.

Critique!

Evaluating someone else's chart is a fantastic way to improve your own skills, in addition to generating potentially useful suggestions for the other chart creator.

If you're looking for charts to critique, it's depressingly easy to find charts from major news media outlets and other high-profile sources that are very worthy of critiquing, so you might consider posting (polite, constructive) critiques or redesigns on social media for others to comment on and learn from.

If there are others within your organization who've read good dataviz books or taken good dataviz courses, consider instituting a peer review process that requires any chart that will be included in a major publication (board presentation, press release, etc.) to be reviewed by at least one other trained person. Both the chart reviewer and the chart creator improve their skills by doing this, and you'll end up with better charts in your organization's important publications.

Participate in the dataviz online community!

Consider following hashtags like #dataviz and #datavisualization on social media and use those to discover and follow dataviz thought leaders. Kick off or join online discussion threads. Join organizations like the Data Visualization Society and dataviz interest groups on social media. There's a vibrant dataviz online community, and, if you've read this book, you're plenty knowledgeable enough to participate constructively in that community.

Another great way to learn is to post original charts that you've designed and ask the community for feedback. Although you might be unlucky and get a troll who delights in trashing other peoples' work, the odds are much higher that you'll get useful, constructive feedback.

Keep learning!

Although you now have enough skills to handle most of the dataviz challenges that are likely to come up in your day-to-day work, there's always more to learn. No one knows everything there is to know about dataviz (I learn new things all the time).

Visit practicalreporting.com/pc-resources and click "Recommended books and courses" for resources to continue learning or to go deep on specialized areas of dataviz such as data art, information dashboards, scientific visualizations, and infographics. As I write this, my next book, *More Practical Charts: Additional chart types for data-savvy audiences,* is scheduled to be published in 2024. As its subtitle suggests, that book covers more "advanced" chart types that can be used with more sophisticated audiences, such as histograms, scatter plots, and cycle plots.

As in most other fields, Googling dataviz-related topics to learn more will return many blog posts, videos, articles, and other sources of tips and guidelines. There's some great info out there, and also some real garbage (just like any other topic). I hope that the information in this book will help you critically assess whatever you come across.

FUTURE DATAVIZ TECHNOLOGIES

Occasionally, workshop participants ask about technologies that could change dataviz in the future. As I write this in early 2023, two technologies are getting attention: virtual/augmented reality and artificial intelligence. I have no idea how these technologies will evolve, but here's my take on them as they stand at the moment, starting with…

Viewing charts in virtual reality or augmented reality

Every so often, a new startup or research project emerges that claims that data visualizations can be better presented or interpreted as 3D objects displayed in virtual environments (i.e., virtual reality, a.k.a. VR) or superimposed over the real world (i.e., augmented reality, a.k.a. AR) usually through a headset worn by audience members. I'm interested in the possibilities of these technologies and try demos whenever I can, but the ones I've seen so far don't seem very compelling. As far as I can tell, none of them make any insights, patterns, exceptions, etc., clearer or more obvious than they'd be on a 2D monitor.

VR and AR have real advantages when showing 3D spatial information (computer-aided design applications, flight simulators, etc.), but the advantages aren't as clear to me when showing the kind of non-spatial data that most readers of this book tend to work with (expenses, student test scores, etc.). It's entirely possible that new use cases will emerge in which viewing non-spatial data in virtual environments will offer a real advantage, so I'll keep trying the demos.

At the moment, however, the main benefit of VR and AR seems to be the novelty factor, so the main reason to use these technologies would be to get audiences more interested in a particular data set and that could work in certain situations. The barriers to actually interpreting data in this way are significant, however, and include having to wear a clunky, expensive headset, having less precise control than when using a mouse or touchscreen, and needing to create special 3D versions of charts beforehand.

Chart-creating artificial intelligence (AI)

As I write this in March 2023, there are jaw-dropping breakthroughs happening in artificial intelligence (AI) on an almost daily basis. This begs the obvious question: Will AIs be able to create expert-level charts without any human assistance, and, if so, when might that happen?

That's hard to say at this point, of course, but what seems almost certain at the moment is that the process of creating a chart is going to change dramatically in the very near future. Already, AI users can describe a chart using simple, plain-language prompts, and get an image of that chart in seconds without having to use the graphical user interface (GUI) of data visualization products like Tableau Desktop or Microsoft Excel. How good are the resulting charts? Well, in my opinion, they're currently pretty hit-or-miss and often require corrections or enhancements by a human with data visualization expertise before being shown to an audience. Given how quickly AI is advancing, though, how long might that remain the case?

I think writing computer code provides a potentially informative model here since current AIs are much more advanced when it comes to generating code compared with generating charts. The GPT-4 AI was released about a week ago as I write this, and it can produce astonishingly good code based on plain-language prompts. Does this mean that people no longer need to know how to code? Well, that doesn't seem to be the case, at this point anyway. For now, people with coding expertise are still needed for a few reasons:

1. A human coder still needs to decide *what* code is needed in a given situation, and what that code should *do*. AIs can decide what code is needed for common applications with similar examples in their training data, such as simple games or content management systems, but they have trouble with more complex, novel, or unique applications, such as custom enterprise software applications. As far as I can tell, someone without any

coding expertise would struggle to formulate prompts that would result in usable code for anything but simple, common applications.

2. AIs often make mistakes that must be identified and corrected by expert coders before the code can run without throwing errors or introducing problems like security vulnerabilities or unintended application behaviors.

This means that, for now anyway, humans with coding expertise are still needed to *guide and supervise* coding AIs. Those coders will be a lot more productive (and so potentially less numerous), but still necessary. A similar consensus seems to have emerged in recent months around car-driving AIs: For most of the last decade or so, many people assumed that humans would no longer need to know how to drive because car-driving AIs would exceed human driving abilities in all situations. In recent months, however, it's started to look more like humans will still need to know how to drive, since car-driving AIs are unlikely to perform reliably in a wide variety of situations for the foreseeable future. Yes, drivers will be more productive since they can rely on the car's AI for simpler tasks like highway driving in good conditions, but they'll still need to know how to drive so that they can correct or take over for the AI in more unusual or complex situations.

Data visualization might follow a similar path. It seems almost certain at this point that human chart-makers will become a lot more productive, because they'll be able to simply describe a chart in plain language and get that chart within seconds. In many cases (but not all), this will be faster than using the GUI of a data visualization software product to create a chart, and learning how to use an AI to create charts will be a lot quicker and easier than learning how to use data visualization software.

Even if they're using AI, however, chart makers still need data visualization expertise to decide what charts are needed in a given situation, and to supervise the AI by correcting any data visualization, reasoning, or perceptual mistakes that it might make. A human with data visualization expertise might also need to prompt the AI to make design choices that the AI might have trouble making on its own, such as deciding to visually highlight part of a chart, adding callouts with key insights, or bringing in comparison/reference values from an external source.

If this is how things play out, it would mean that people will still need data visualization skills, but the way in which they'll *use* those skills will change drastically. Instead of using those skills to make charts "by hand" using the GUI of a data visualization software application, they'll use those skills to guide and supervise chart-making AIs, just as human coders use their coding skills to guide and supervise coding AIs.

Now, a chart-making AI might not offer enough control or flexibility for some users, particularly those who create highly customized charts such as scientific charts, data art, specialized business dashboards, or novel chart types. Those users will likely still need to use data visualization GUIs or code libraries such as ggplot or D3.js, but they represent only a small minority of chart creators. I suspect that a good chart-making AI will meet the needs of most people who create charts.

I'm probably overestimating its importance, but this book might accelerate the transition from using GUIs to using AIs to make charts. As you've seen, this book contains chart design guidelines that are more concrete and specific than other books, which is exactly the kind of training data that would help a chart-making AI become more competent. On the one hand, it's frustrating to think that I might have spent the last several years writing training data for AIs. On the other hand, I recognize that AIs that include this book in their training data may allow millions of people to make better charts. This is already happening with AI-generated computer code, which often contains expert-level techniques and practices that were distilled from code in the AI's training data that was written by expert coders, and that many coders who use the AI wouldn't think of on their own. It's also happening with car-driving AIs, which can allow human drivers to perform better by, for example, slamming on the brakes to avoid a frontal collision faster than a human ever could.

Now, this situation could change, of course. Between the late 90s and early 2010s, for example, the best chess players in the world were "centaur" or "hybrid" teams consisting of a human grandmaster using a chess-playing AI to assist them. Such teams could easily beat the best AI-only players. That changed, however, when chess engines like AlphaZero came out a few years ago, which were so good that pairing a human grandmaster with them made them *worse*, not better. The question, then, is whether data visualization is more like chess, or more like car-driving? Only time will tell, but it feels more like car-driving to me at the moment, i.e., like something that will require expert human supervision for the foreseeable future.

Take all of this with a boulder of salt, of course, since this is pure speculation based on the information that's available as I write this. Some of the challenges that I've described could turn out to be much easier or much harder than expected for AIs to overcome, and things could be very different a few years from now. Or next Tuesday.

A FINAL WORD

As with any language, it takes some time and effort to learn the spelling and vocabulary of dataviz, and we've covered a lot of territory in this book:

- 40+ chart types (including the 10 or so that I recommend avoiding)
- 9 cheat sheets
- 8 decision trees
- 180+ key takeaways

I hope I've made a good case for why it's essential to learn these basic skills if you create everyday charts. Poor dataviz spelling and vocabulary isn't the only reason that charts fail, but it's probably the *main* reason, and it's difficult or impossible to reliably produce good charts if you haven't learned good dataviz spelling and vocabulary first.

Finally, if anything in this book didn't resonate, or you have any comments or suggestions, please let me know! I'm easy to find on social media (not a lot of "Nick Desbarats" floating around out there…) or visit practicalreporting.com/contact.

Bonne chance, mon ami,

Nick

Index